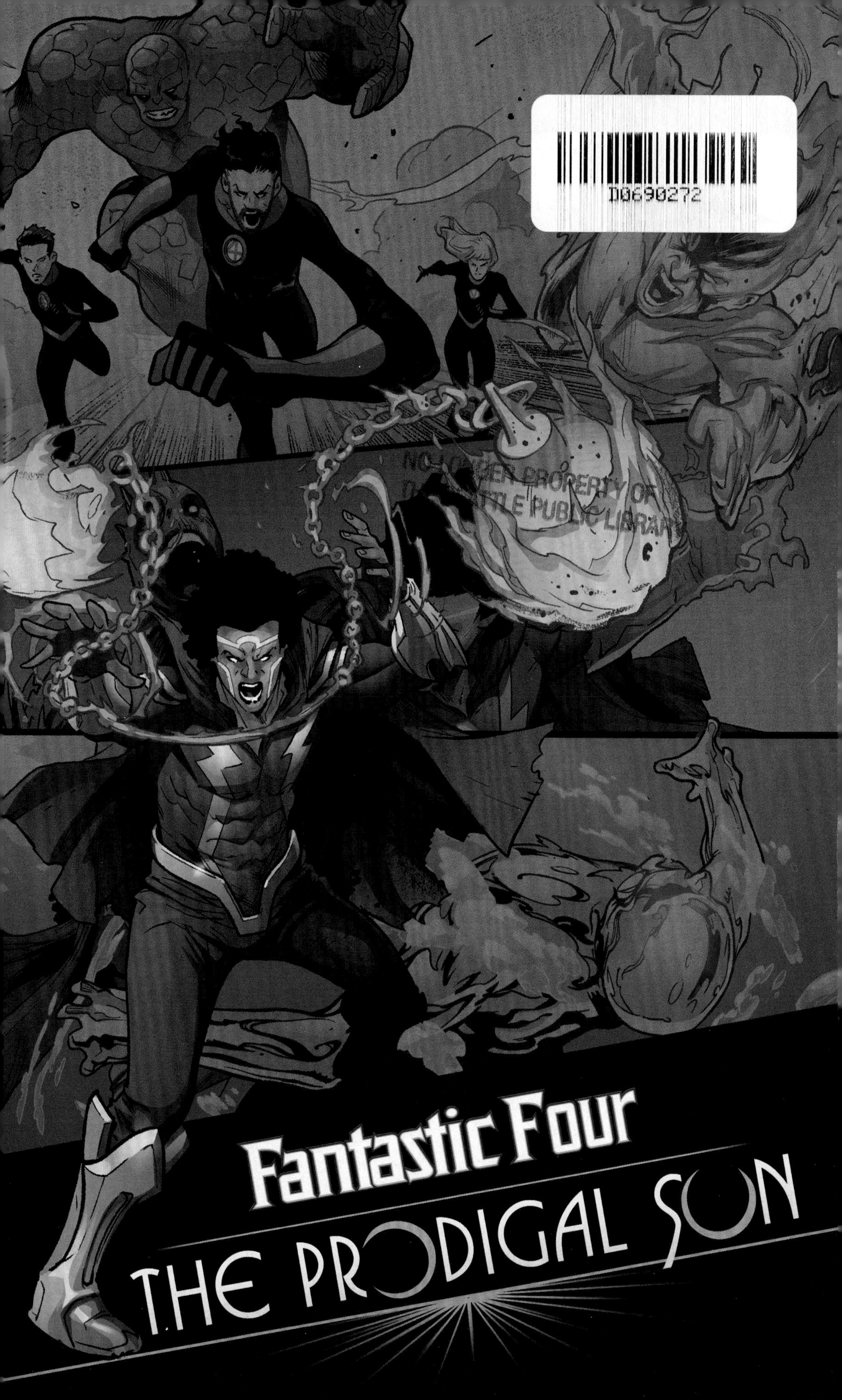
Fantastic Four
THE PRODIGAL SUN

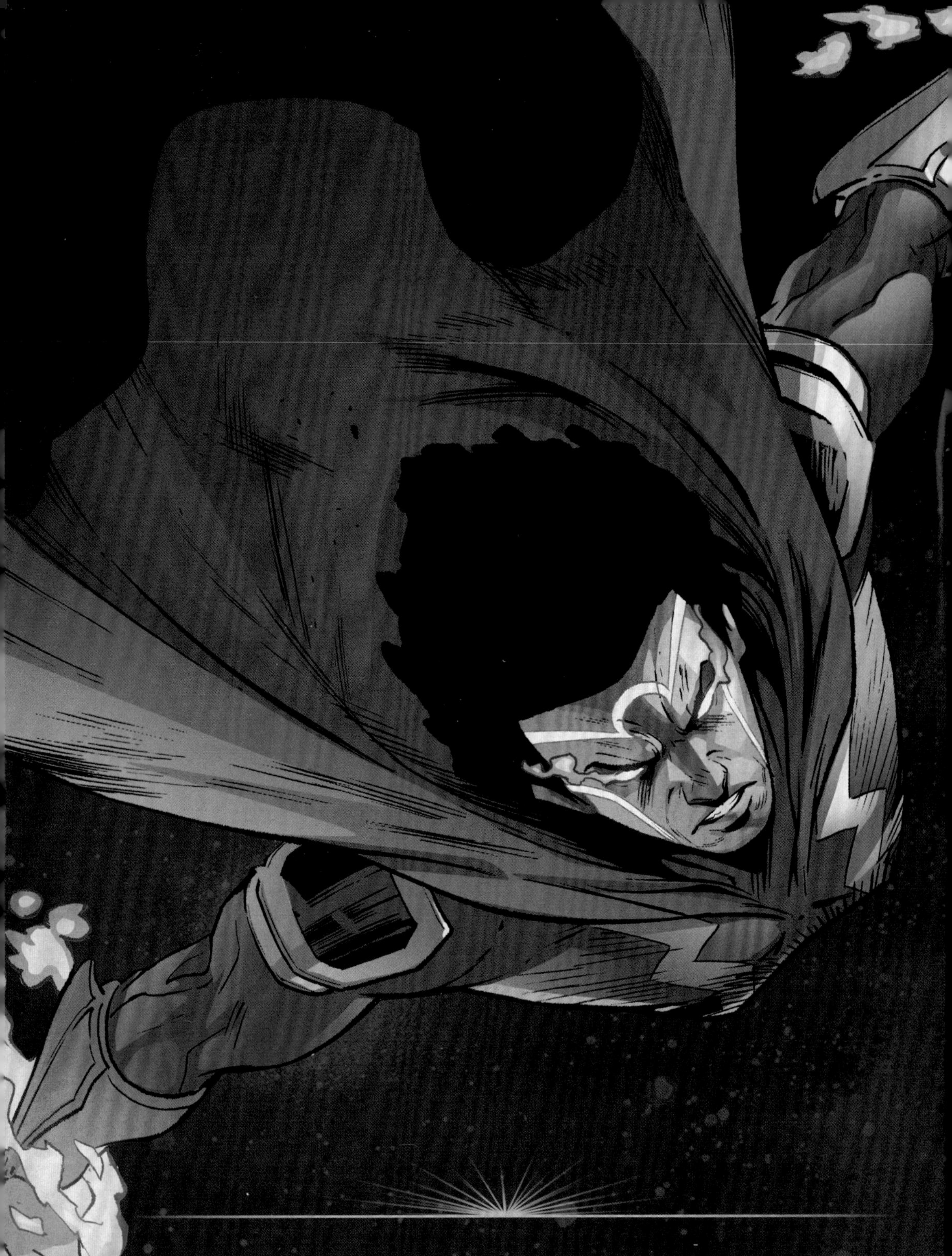


COLLECTION EDITOR **MARK D. BEAZLEY**
ASSISTANT EDITOR **CAITLIN O'CONNELL**
ASSOCIATE MANAGING EDITOR **KATERI WOODY**
SENIOR EDITOR, SPECIAL PROJECTS **JENNIFER GRÜNWALD**
VP PRODUCTION & SPECIAL PROJECTS **JEFF YOUNGQUIST**
BOOK DESIGNER **SALENA MAHINA** WITH **NICK RUSSELL**

SVP PRINT, SALES & MARKETING **DAVID GABRIEL**
DIRECTOR, LICENSED PUBLISHING **SVEN LARSEN**
EDITOR IN CHIEF **C.B. CEBULSKI**
CHIEF CREATIVE OFFICER **JOE QUESADA**
PRESIDENT **DAN BUCKLEY**
EXECUTIVE PRODUCER **ALAN FINE**

**FANTASTIC FOUR: THE PRODIGAL SUN.** Contains material originally published in magazine form as FANTASTIC FOUR: PRODIGAL SUN #1, GUARDIANS OF THE GALAXY: PRODIGAL SUN #1 and SILVER SURFER: PRODIGAL SUN #1. First printing 2019. ISBN 978-1-302-91980-1. Published by MARVEL WORLDWIDE, INC., a subsidiary of MARVEL ENTERTAINMENT, LLC. OFFICE OF PUBLICATION: 135 West 50th Street, New York, NY 10020.



**Printed in Canada.** DAN BUCKLEY, President, Marvel Entertainment; JOHN NEE, Publisher; JOE QUESADA, Chief Creative Officer; TOM BREVOORT, SVP of Publishing; DAVID BOGART, Associate Publisher & SVP of Talent Affairs; DAVID GABRIEL, SVP of Sales & Marketing, Publishing; JEFF YOUNGQUIST, VP of Production & Special Projects; DAN CARR, Executive Director of Publishing Technology; ALEX MORALES, Director of Publishing Operations; DAN EDINGTON, Managing Editor; SUSAN CRESPI, Production Manager; STAN LEE, Chairman Emeritus. For information regarding advertising in Marvel Comics or on Marvel.com, please contact Vit DeBellis, Custom Solutions & Integrated Advertising Manager, at vdebellis@marvel.com. For Marvel subscription inquiries, please call 888-511-5480. **Manufactured between 9/13/2019 and 10/15/2019 by SOLISCO PRINTERS, SCOTT, QC, CANADA.**

10 9 8 7 6 5 4 3 2 1

# Fantastic Four

# THE PRODIGAL SUN

WRITER
## PETER DAVID

ARTIST
## FRANCESCO MANNA

COLOR ARTIST
## ESPEN GRUNDETJERN

LETTERER
## VC's CORY PETIT

COVER ARTISTS
## MICO SUAYAN & RAIN BEREDO

ASSISTANT EDITORS
**SHANNON ANDREWS BALLESTEROS
& LAUREN AMARO**

ASSOCIATE EDITOR
**ALANNA SMITH**

EDITORS
**TOM BREVOORT & DARREN SHAN**

FANTASTIC FOUR CREATED BY **STAN LEE & JACK KIRBY**

Hidden within the cold stretch of Antarctica lies the Savage Land, an area unknown to and untouched by the vast majority of the Earth's inhabitants. Here, prehistoric beasts and creatures walk among man, each fighting to be the strongest and fiercest in their remote world. But a new contender has just arrived...

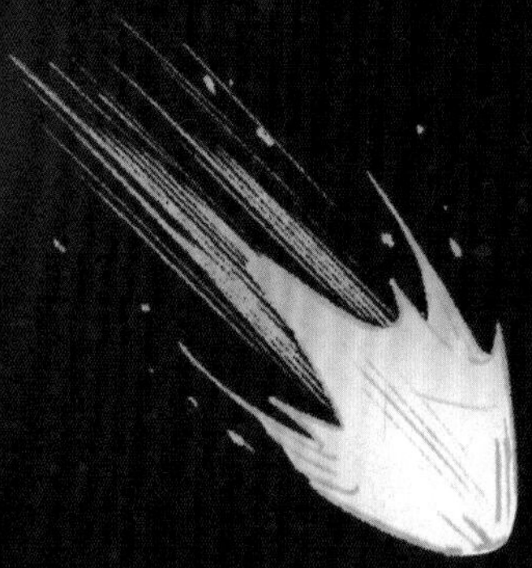

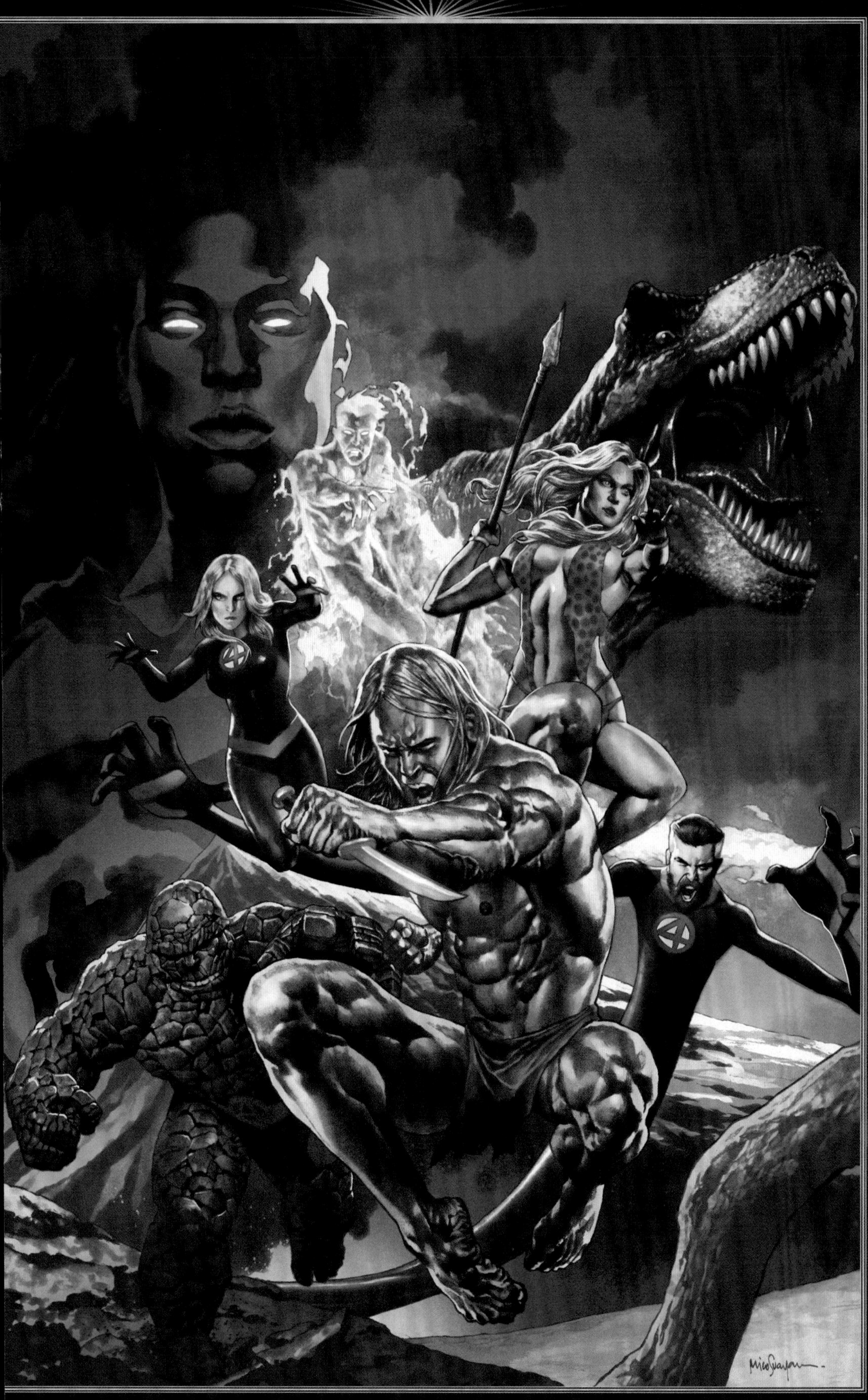

FANTASTIC FOUR: THE PRODIGAL SUN #1

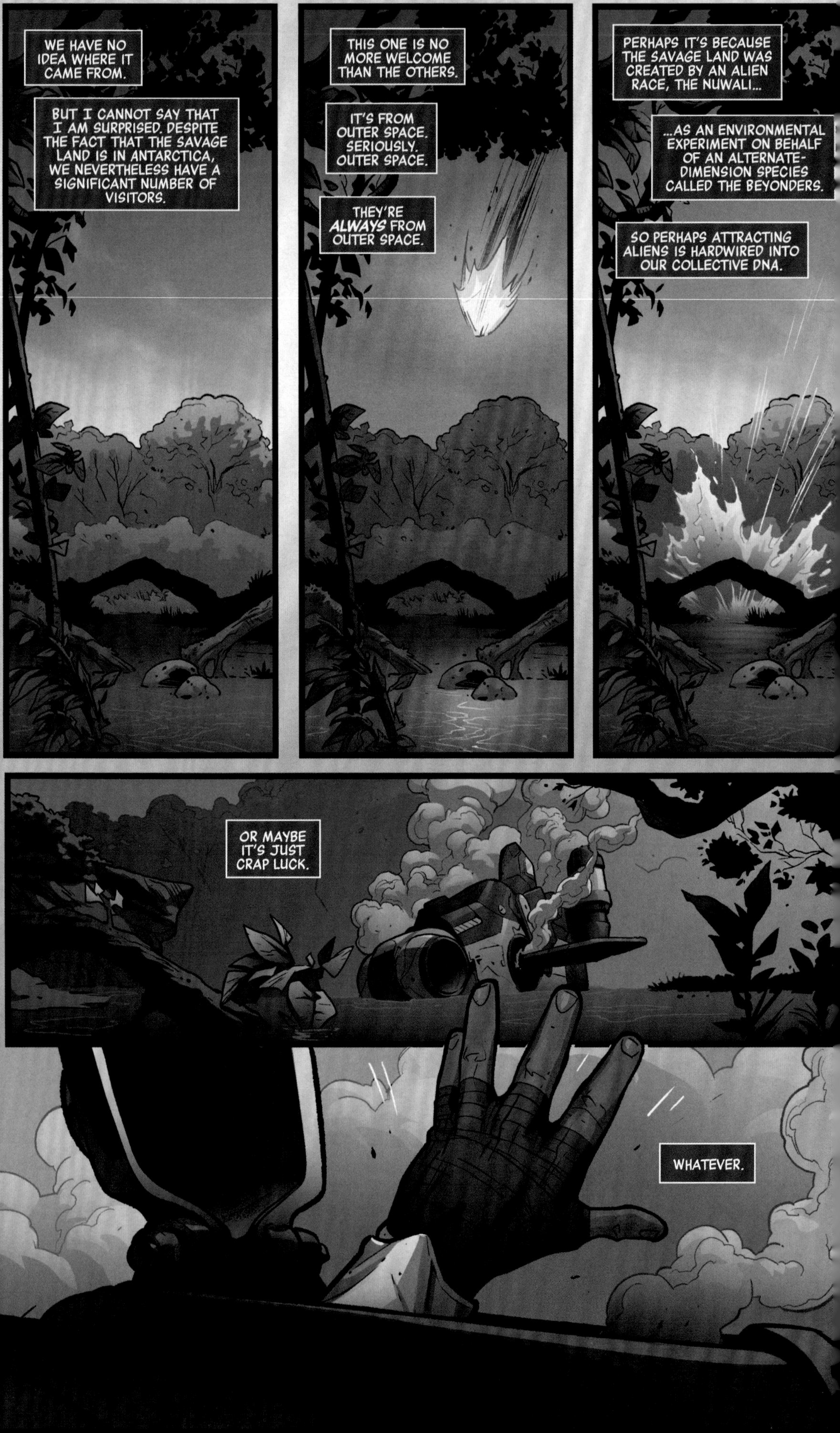
WE HAVE NO IDEA WHERE IT CAME FROM.
BUT I CANNOT SAY THAT I AM SURPRISED. DESPITE THE FACT THAT THE SAVAGE LAND IS IN ANTARCTICA, WE NEVERTHELESS HAVE A SIGNIFICANT NUMBER OF VISITORS.
THIS ONE IS NO MORE WELCOME THAN THE OTHERS.
IT'S FROM OUTER SPACE. SERIOUSLY. OUTER SPACE.
THEY'RE *ALWAYS* FROM OUTER SPACE.
PERHAPS IT'S BECAUSE THE SAVAGE LAND WAS CREATED BY AN ALIEN RACE, THE NUWALI...
...AS AN ENVIRONMENTAL EXPERIMENT ON BEHALF OF AN ALTERNATE-DIMENSION SPECIES CALLED THE BEYONDERS.
SO PERHAPS ATTRACTING ALIENS IS HARDWIRED INTO OUR COLLECTIVE DNA.
OR MAYBE IT'S JUST CRAP LUCK.
WHATEVER.

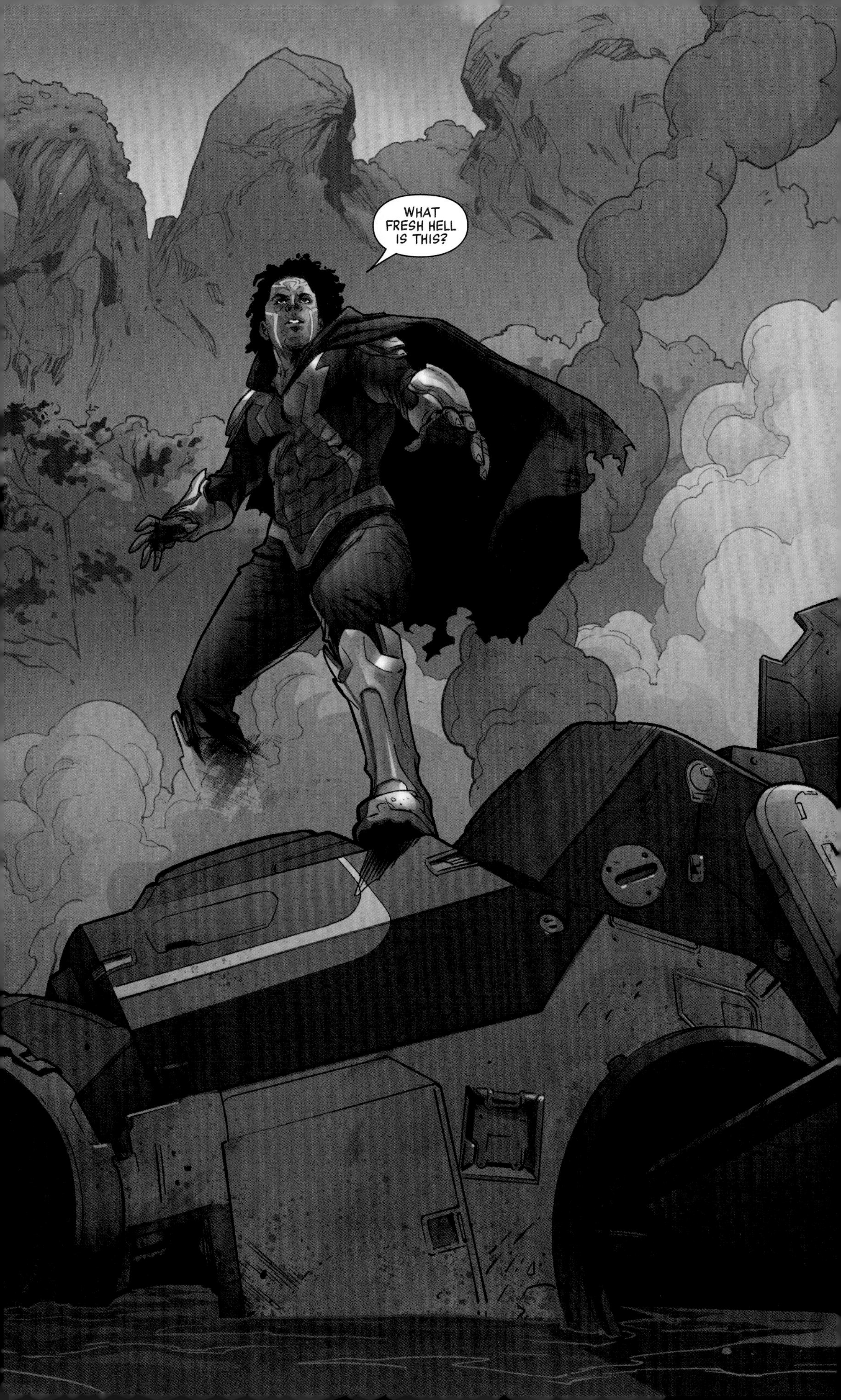
WHAT FRESH HELL IS THIS?

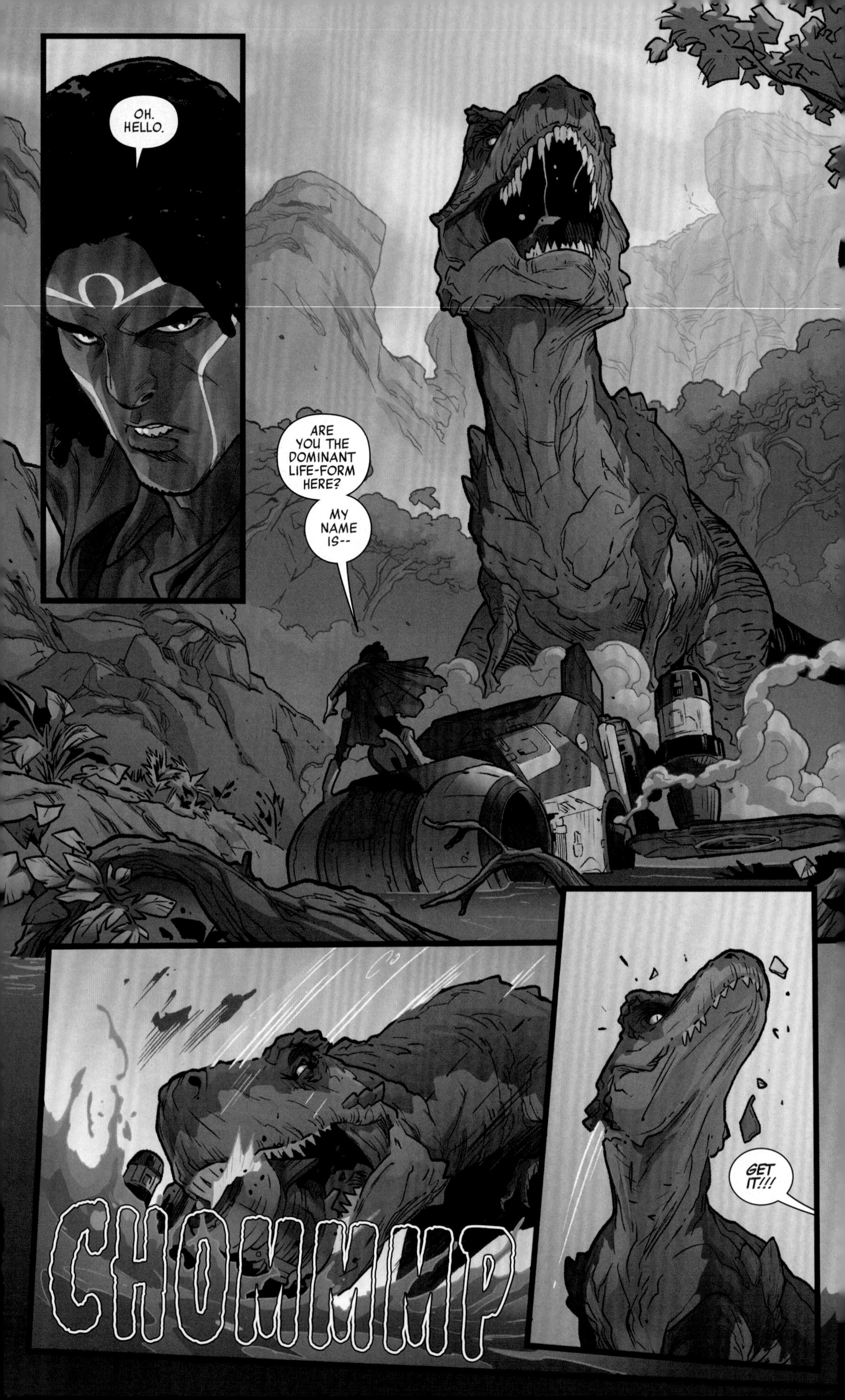

OH. HELLO.
ARE YOU THE DOMINANT LIFE-FORM HERE?
MY NAME IS--
CHOMMMP
GET IT!!!

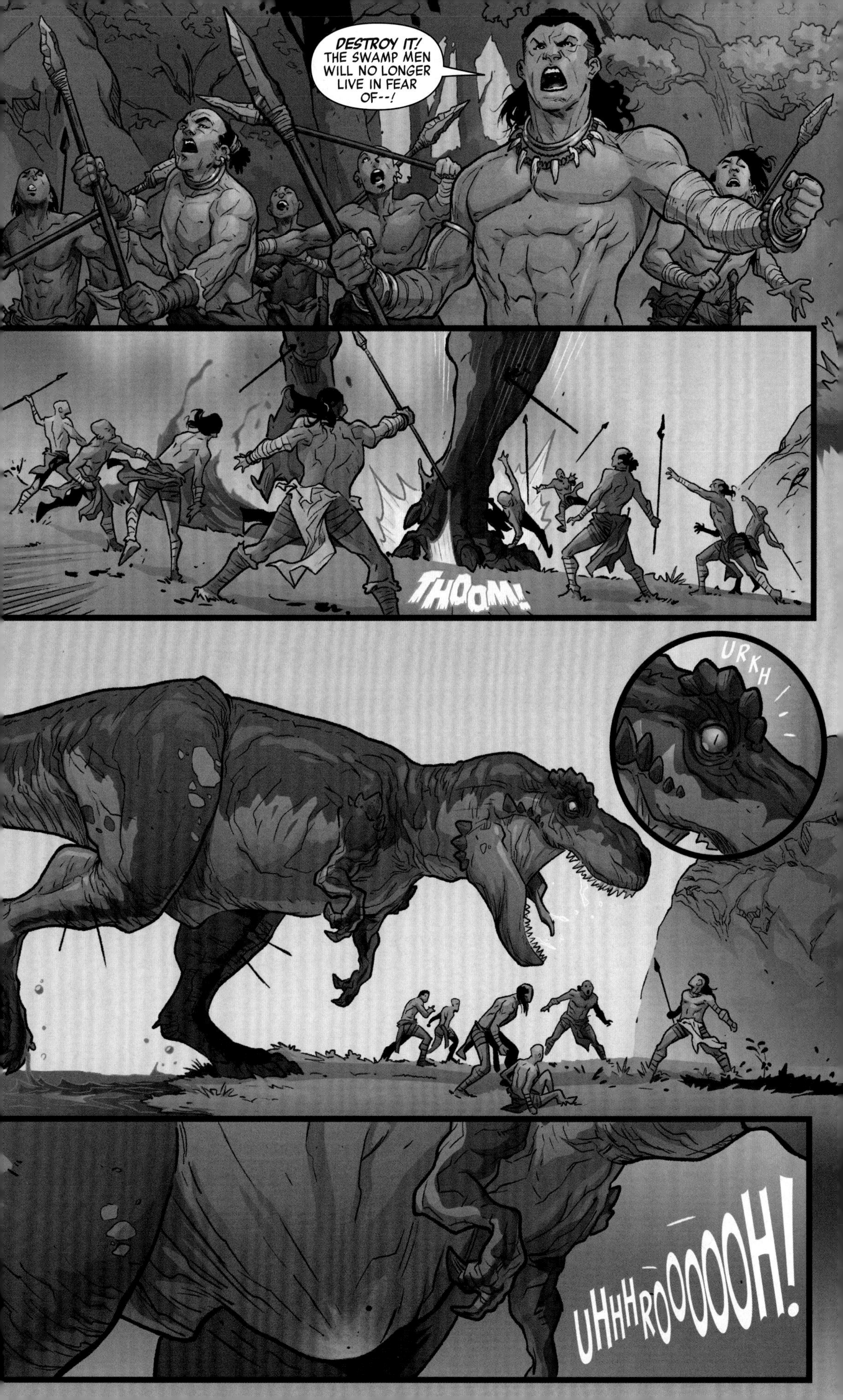

DESTROY IT! THE SWAMP MEN WILL NO LONGER LIVE IN FEAR OF--!
THOOM!
URKH
UHHHROOOOOH!

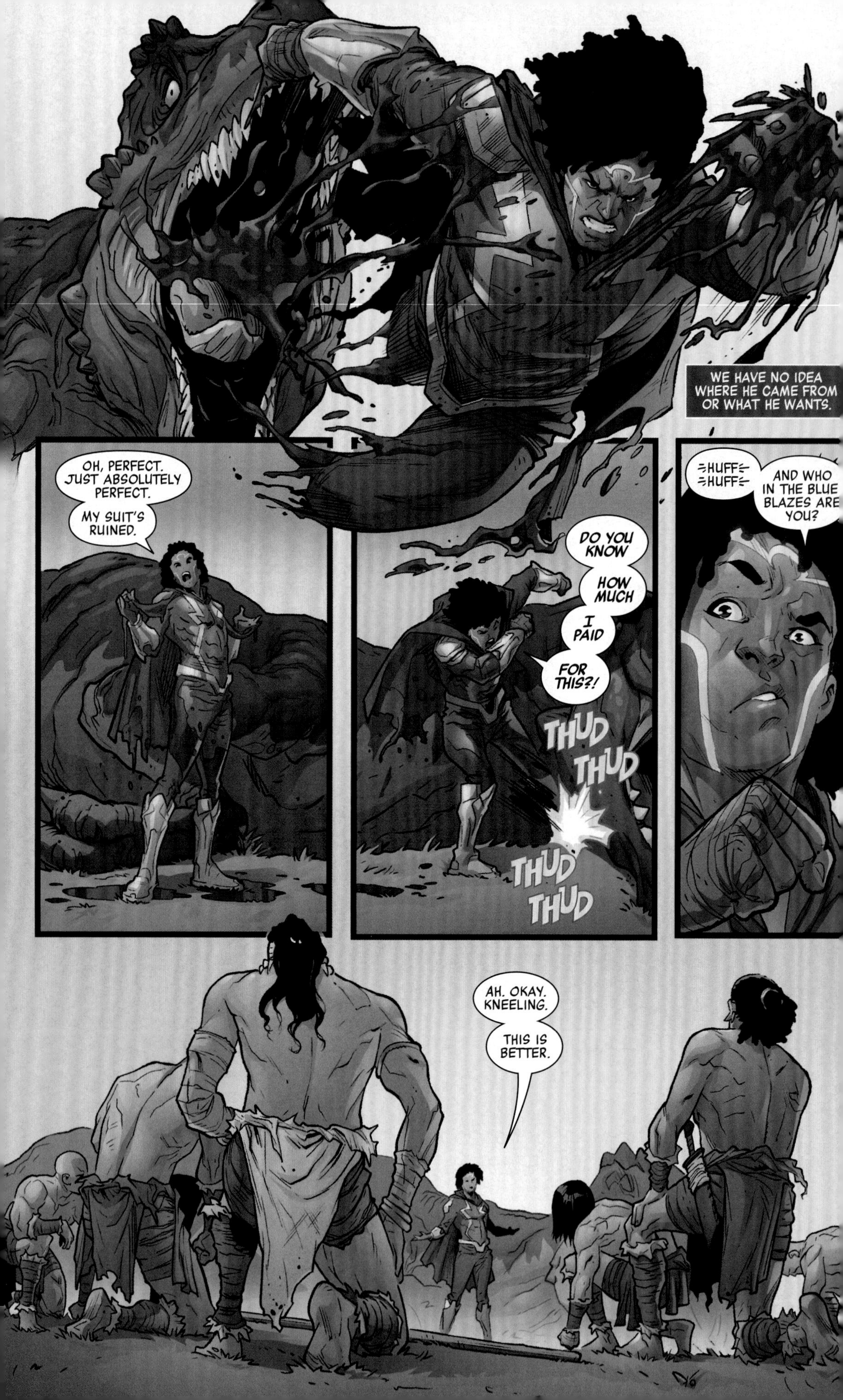
WE HAVE NO IDEA WHERE HE CAME FROM OR WHAT HE WANTS.
OH, PERFECT. JUST ABSOLUTELY PERFECT.
MY SUIT'S RUINED.
DO YOU KNOW
HOW MUCH
I PAID
FOR THIS?!
THUD THUD
THUD THUD
HUFF HUFF
AND WHO IN THE BLUE BLAZES ARE YOU?
AH. OKAY. KNEELING.
THIS IS BETTER.

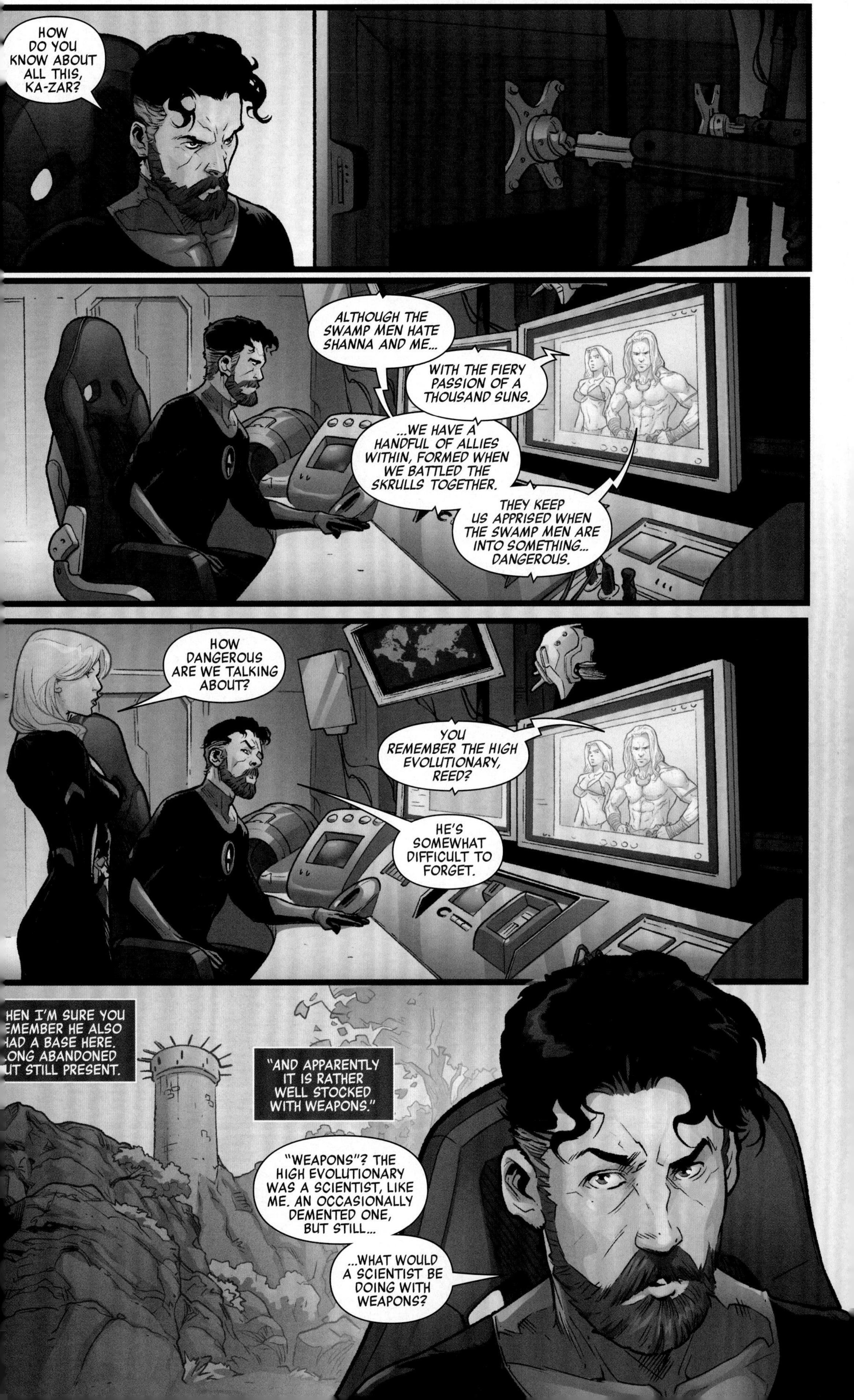
HOW DO YOU KNOW ABOUT ALL THIS, KA-ZAR?
ALTHOUGH THE SWAMP MEN HATE SHANNA AND ME...
WITH THE FIERY PASSION OF A THOUSAND SUNS.
...WE HAVE A HANDFUL OF ALLIES WITHIN, FORMED WHEN WE BATTLED THE SKRULLS TOGETHER.
THEY KEEP US APPRISED WHEN THE SWAMP MEN ARE INTO SOMETHING... DANGEROUS.
HOW DANGEROUS ARE WE TALKING ABOUT?
YOU REMEMBER THE HIGH EVOLUTIONARY, REED?
HE'S SOMEWHAT DIFFICULT TO FORGET.
HEN I'M SURE YOU EMEMBER HE ALSO HAD A BASE HERE. ONG ABANDONED UT STILL PRESENT.
"AND APPARENTLY IT IS RATHER WELL STOCKED WITH WEAPONS."
"WEAPONS"? THE HIGH EVOLUTIONARY WAS A SCIENTIST, LIKE ME. AN OCCASIONALLY DEMENTED ONE, BUT STILL...
...WHAT WOULD A SCIENTIST BE DOING WITH WEAPONS?

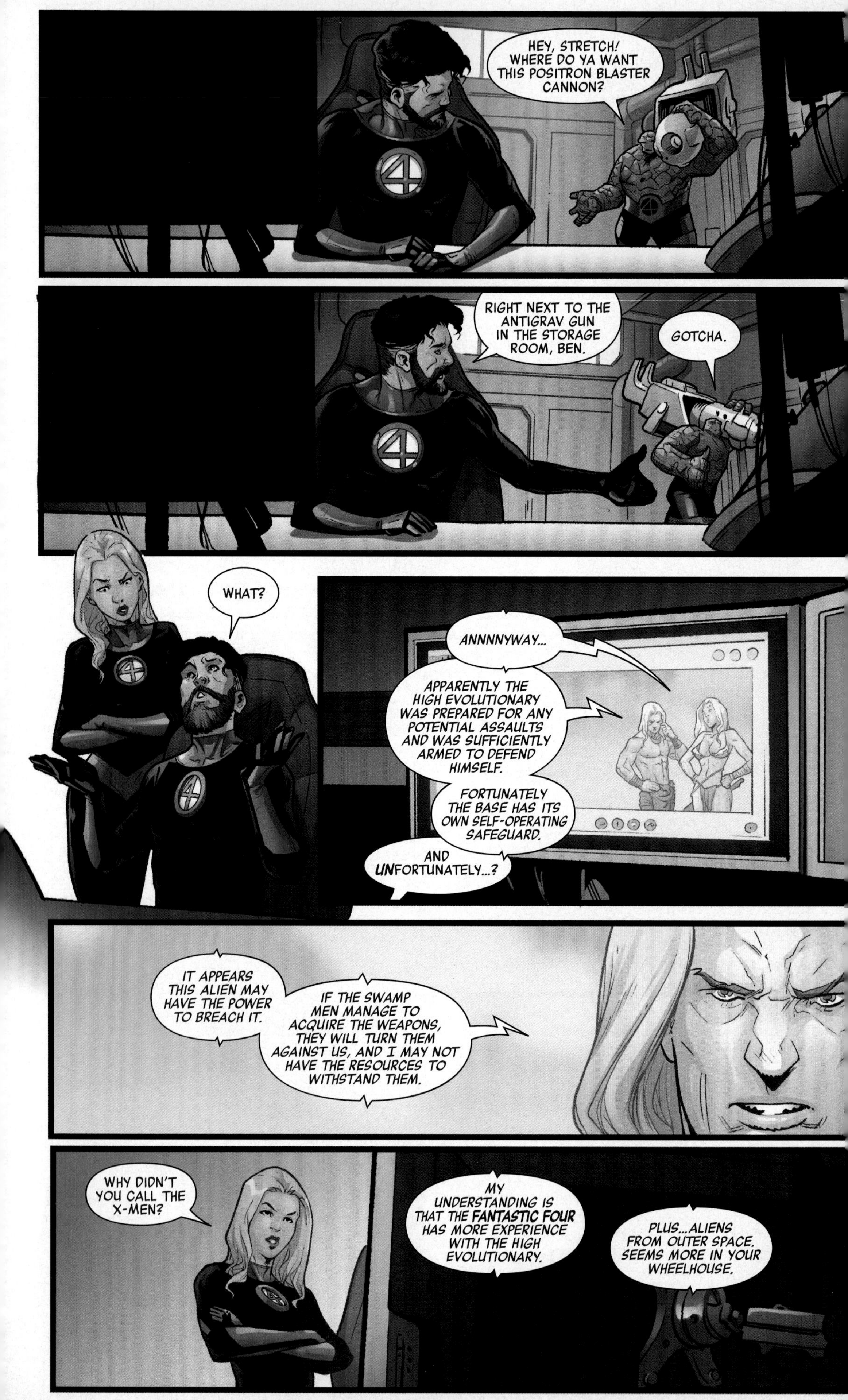

HEY, STRETCH! WHERE DO YA WANT THIS POSITRON BLASTER CANNON?
RIGHT NEXT TO THE ANTIGRAV GUN IN THE STORAGE ROOM, BEN.
GOTCHA.
WHAT?
ANNNNYWAY...
APPARENTLY THE HIGH EVOLUTIONARY WAS PREPARED FOR ANY POTENTIAL ASSAULTS AND WAS SUFFICIENTLY ARMED TO DEFEND HIMSELF.
FORTUNATELY THE BASE HAS ITS OWN SELF-OPERATING SAFEGUARD.
AND UNFORTUNATELY...?
IT APPEARS THIS ALIEN MAY HAVE THE POWER TO BREACH IT.
IF THE SWAMP MEN MANAGE TO ACQUIRE THE WEAPONS, THEY WILL TURN THEM AGAINST US, AND I MAY NOT HAVE THE RESOURCES TO WITHSTAND THEM.
WHY DIDN'T YOU CALL THE X-MEN?
MY UNDERSTANDING IS THAT THE FANTASTIC FOUR HAS MORE EXPERIENCE WITH THE HIGH EVOLUTIONARY.
PLUS...ALIENS FROM OUTER SPACE. SEEMS MORE IN YOUR WHEELHOUSE.

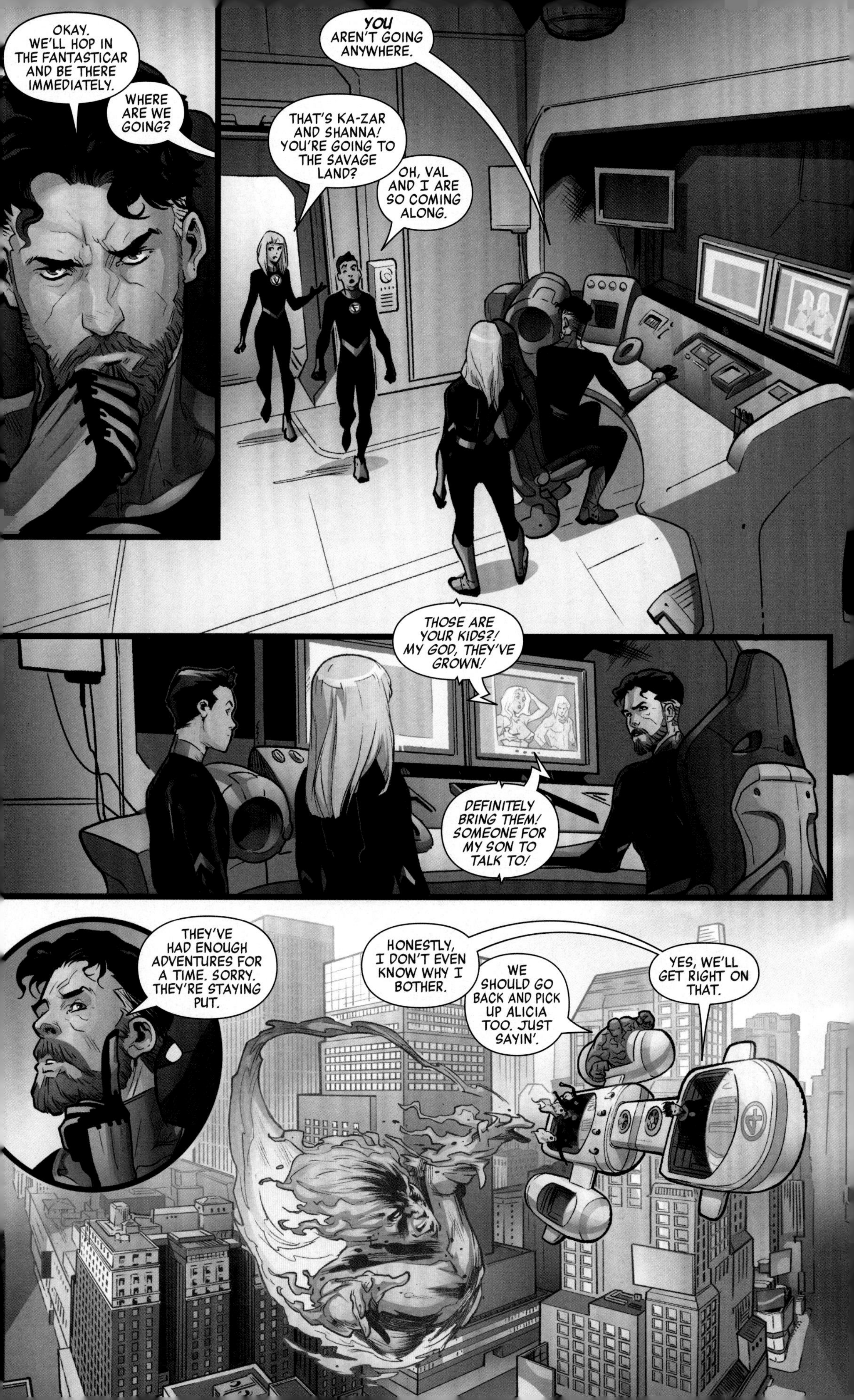
OKAY. WE'LL HOP IN THE FANTASTICAR AND BE THERE IMMEDIATELY.
WHERE ARE WE GOING?
THAT'S KA-ZAR AND SHANNA! YOU'RE GOING TO THE SAVAGE LAND?
OH, VAL AND I ARE SO COMING ALONG.
YOU AREN'T GOING ANYWHERE.
THOSE ARE YOUR KIDS?! MY GOD, THEY'VE GROWN!
DEFINITELY BRING THEM! SOMEONE FOR MY SON TO TALK TO!
THEY'VE HAD ENOUGH ADVENTURES FOR A TIME. SORRY. THEY'RE STAYING PUT.
HONESTLY, I DON'T EVEN KNOW WHY I BOTHER.
WE SHOULD GO BACK AND PICK UP ALICIA TOO. JUST SAYIN'.
YES, WE'LL GET RIGHT ON THAT.

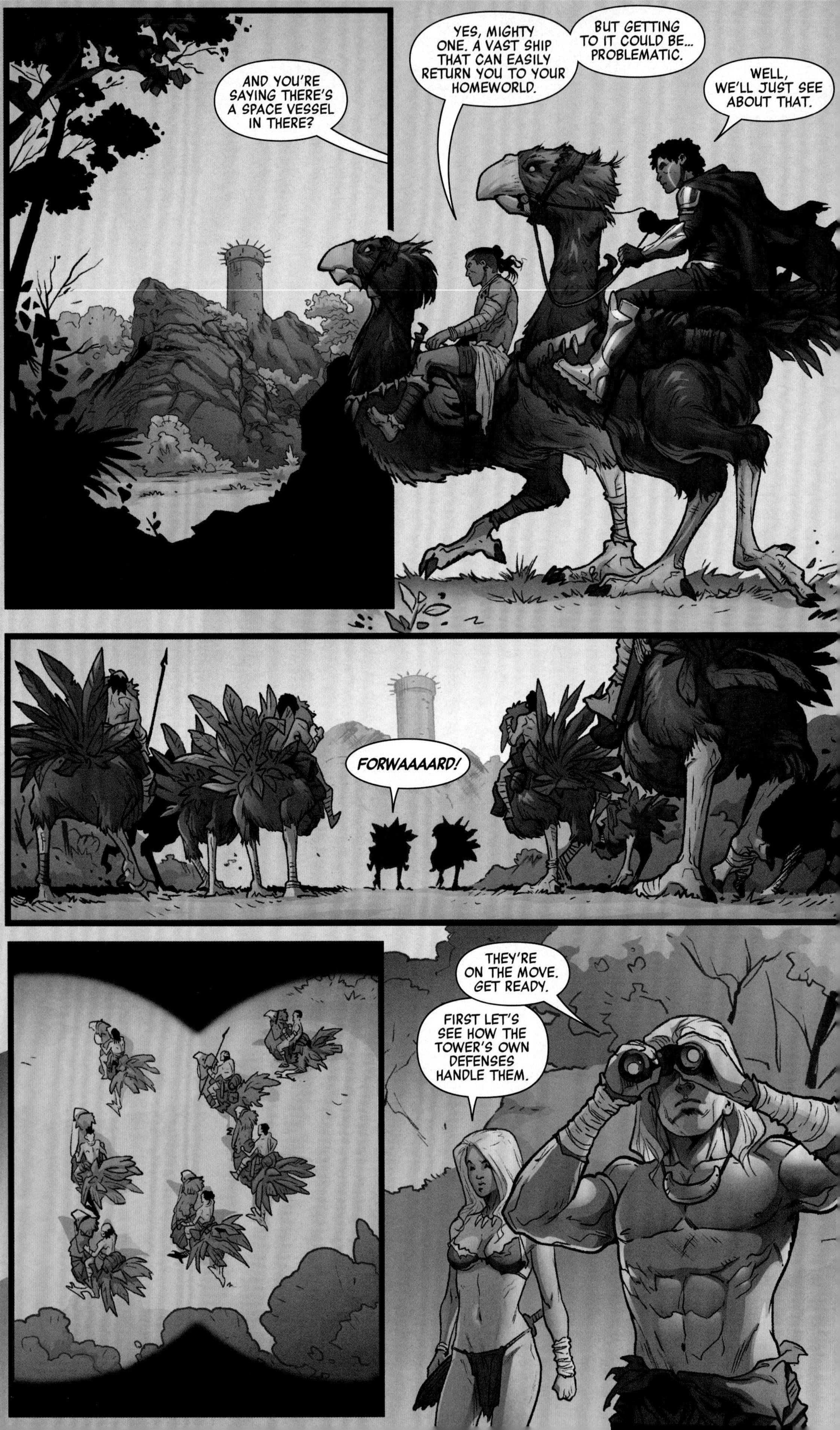

AND YOU'RE SAYING THERE'S A SPACE VESSEL IN THERE?
YES, MIGHTY ONE. A VAST SHIP THAT CAN EASILY RETURN YOU TO YOUR HOMEWORLD.
BUT GETTING TO IT COULD BE... PROBLEMATIC.
WELL, WE'LL JUST SEE ABOUT THAT.
FORWAAAARD!
THEY'RE ON THE MOVE. GET READY.
FIRST LET'S SEE HOW THE TOWER'S OWN DEFENSES HANDLE THEM.

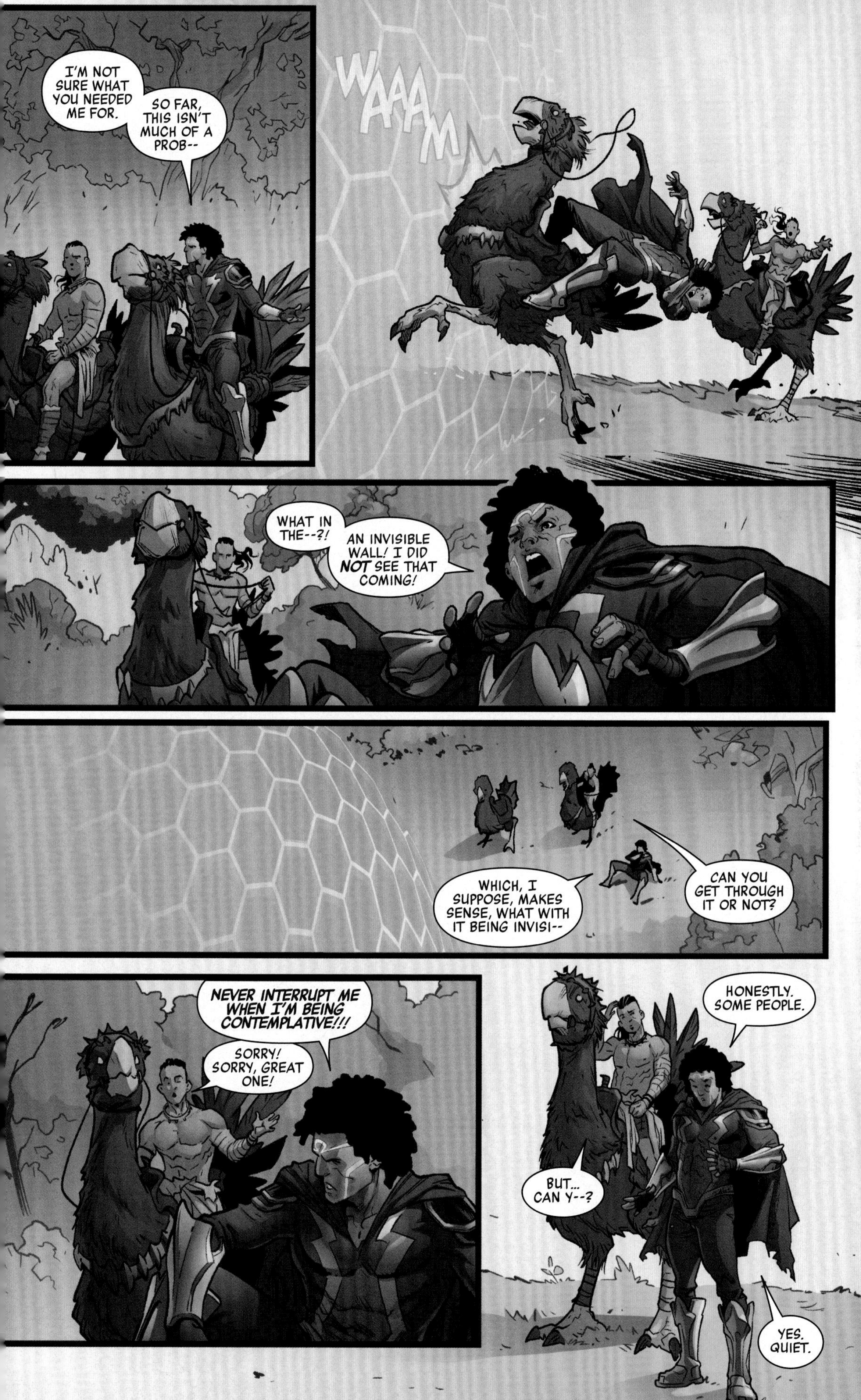
I'M NOT SURE WHAT YOU NEEDED ME FOR.
SO FAR, THIS ISN'T MUCH OF A PROB--
WAAAM
WHAT IN THE--?!
AN INVISIBLE WALL! I DID NOT SEE THAT COMING!
WHICH, I SUPPOSE, MAKES SENSE, WHAT WITH IT BEING INVISI--
CAN YOU GET THROUGH IT OR NOT?
NEVER INTERRUPT ME WHEN I'M BEING CONTEMPLATIVE!!!
SORRY! SORRY, GREAT ONE!
HONESTLY. SOME PEOPLE.
BUT... CAN Y--?
YES. QUIET.

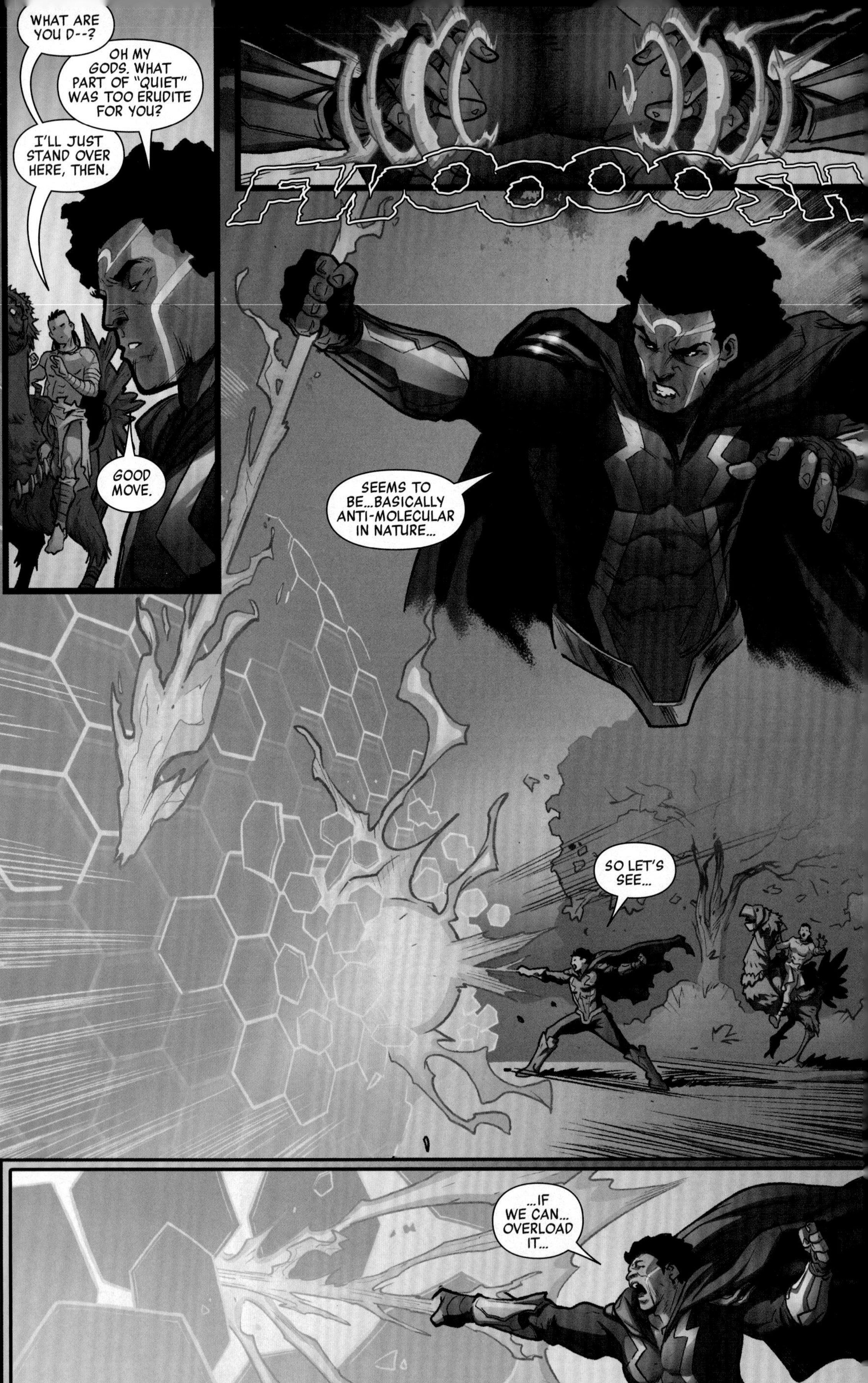
WHAT ARE YOU D--?
OH MY GODS. WHAT PART OF "QUIET" WAS TOO ERUDITE FOR YOU?
I'LL JUST STAND OVER HERE, THEN.
GOOD MOVE.
FWOOOOSH
SEEMS TO BE...BASICALLY ANTI-MOLECULAR IN NATURE...
SO LET'S SEE...
...IF WE CAN... OVERLOAD IT...

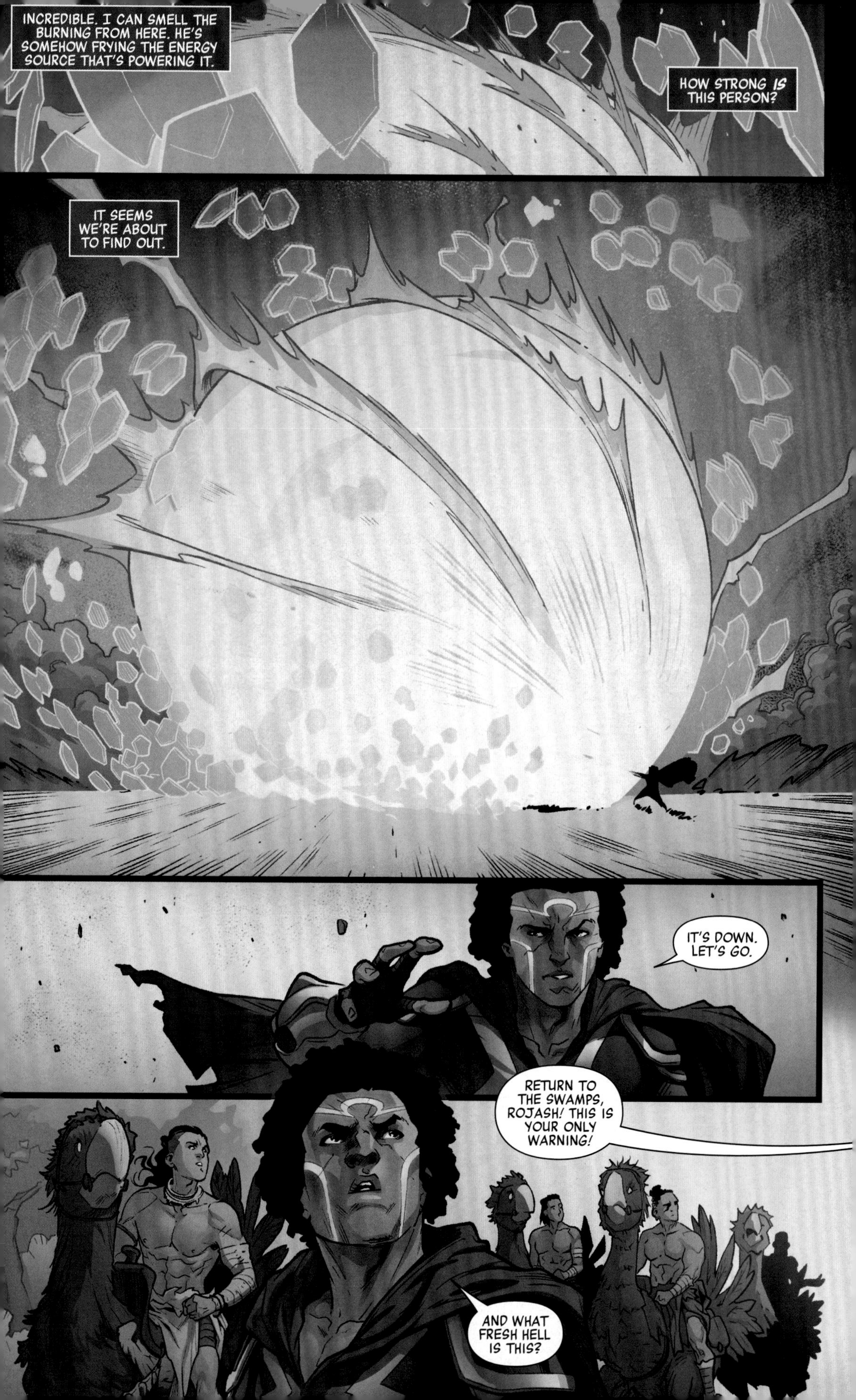
INCREDIBLE. I CAN SMELL THE BURNING FROM HERE. HE'S SOMEHOW FRYING THE ENERGY SOURCE THAT'S POWERING IT.
HOW STRONG IS THIS PERSON?
IT SEEMS WE'RE ABOUT TO FIND OUT.
IT'S DOWN. LET'S GO.
RETURN TO THE SWAMPS, ROJASH! THIS IS YOUR ONLY WARNING!
AND WHAT FRESH HELL IS THIS?

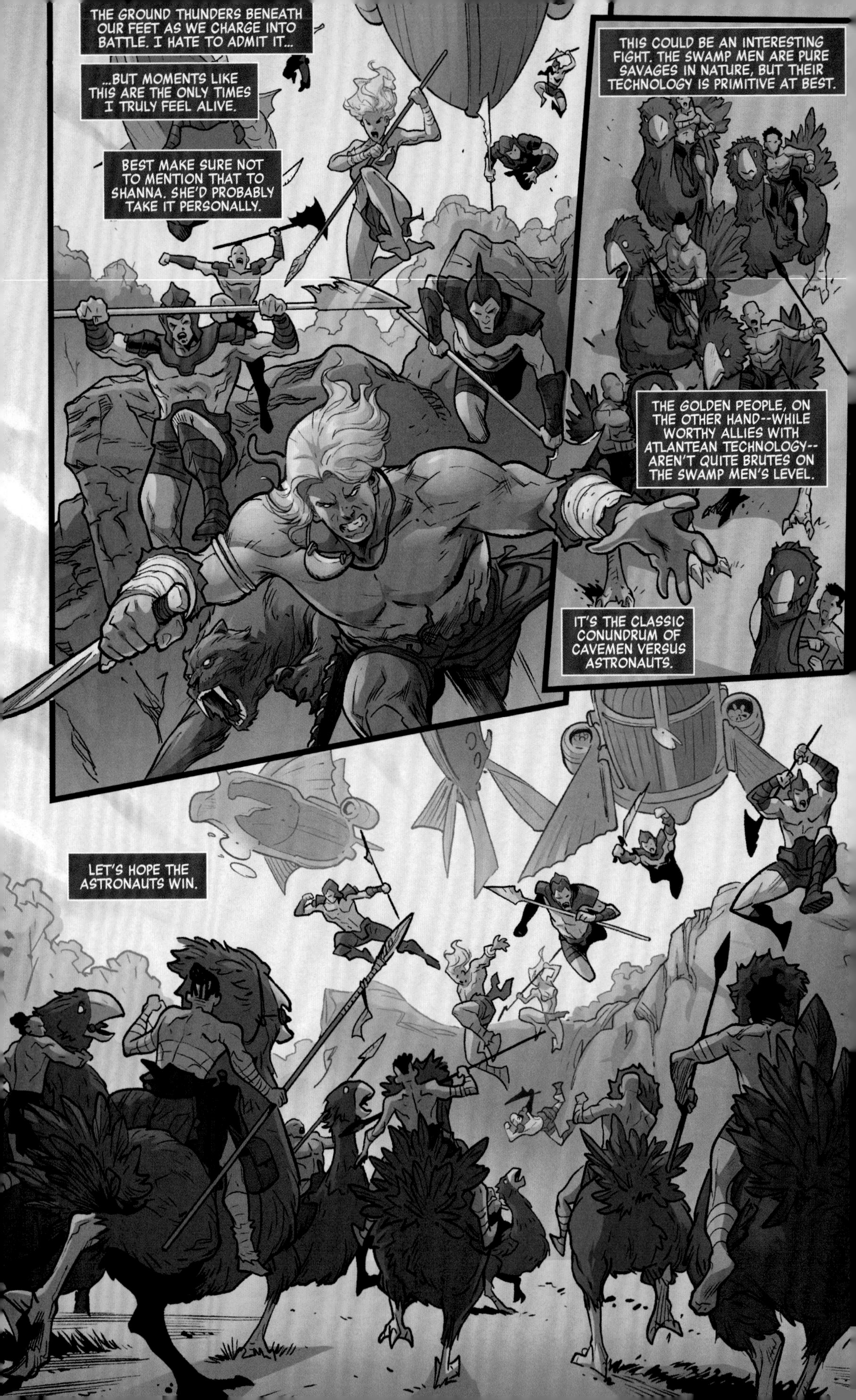
THE GROUND THUNDERS BENEATH OUR FEET AS WE CHARGE INTO BATTLE. I HATE TO ADMIT IT...
...BUT MOMENTS LIKE THIS ARE THE ONLY TIMES I TRULY FEEL ALIVE.
BEST MAKE SURE NOT TO MENTION THAT TO SHANNA. SHE'D PROBABLY TAKE IT PERSONALLY.
THIS COULD BE AN INTERESTING FIGHT. THE SWAMP MEN ARE PURE SAVAGES IN NATURE, BUT THEIR TECHNOLOGY IS PRIMITIVE AT BEST.
THE GOLDEN PEOPLE, ON THE OTHER HAND--WHILE WORTHY ALLIES WITH ATLANTEAN TECHNOLOGY--AREN'T QUITE BRUTES ON THE SWAMP MEN'S LEVEL.
IT'S THE CLASSIC CONUNDRUM OF CAVEMEN VERSUS ASTRONAUTS.
LET'S HOPE THE ASTRONAUTS WIN.

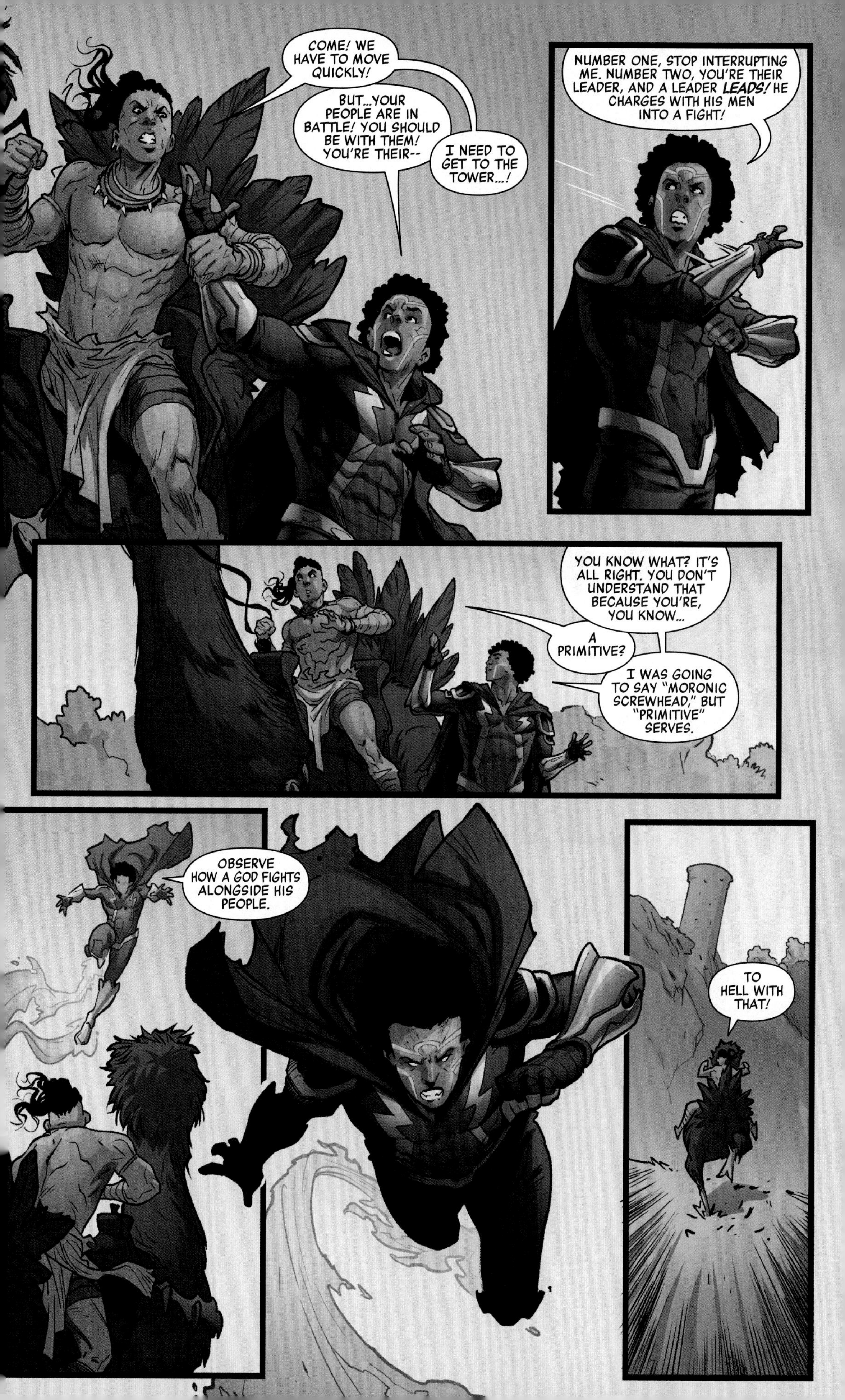
COME! WE HAVE TO MOVE QUICKLY!
BUT...YOUR PEOPLE ARE IN BATTLE! YOU SHOULD BE WITH THEM! YOU'RE THEIR--
I NEED TO GET TO THE TOWER...!
NUMBER ONE, STOP INTERRUPTING ME. NUMBER TWO, YOU'RE THEIR LEADER, AND A LEADER **LEADS!** HE CHARGES WITH HIS MEN INTO A FIGHT!
YOU KNOW WHAT? IT'S ALL RIGHT. YOU DON'T UNDERSTAND THAT BECAUSE YOU'RE, YOU KNOW...
A PRIMITIVE?
I WAS GOING TO SAY "MORONIC SCREWHEAD," BUT "PRIMITIVE" SERVES.
OBSERVE HOW A GOD FIGHTS ALONGSIDE HIS PEOPLE.
TO HELL WITH THAT!

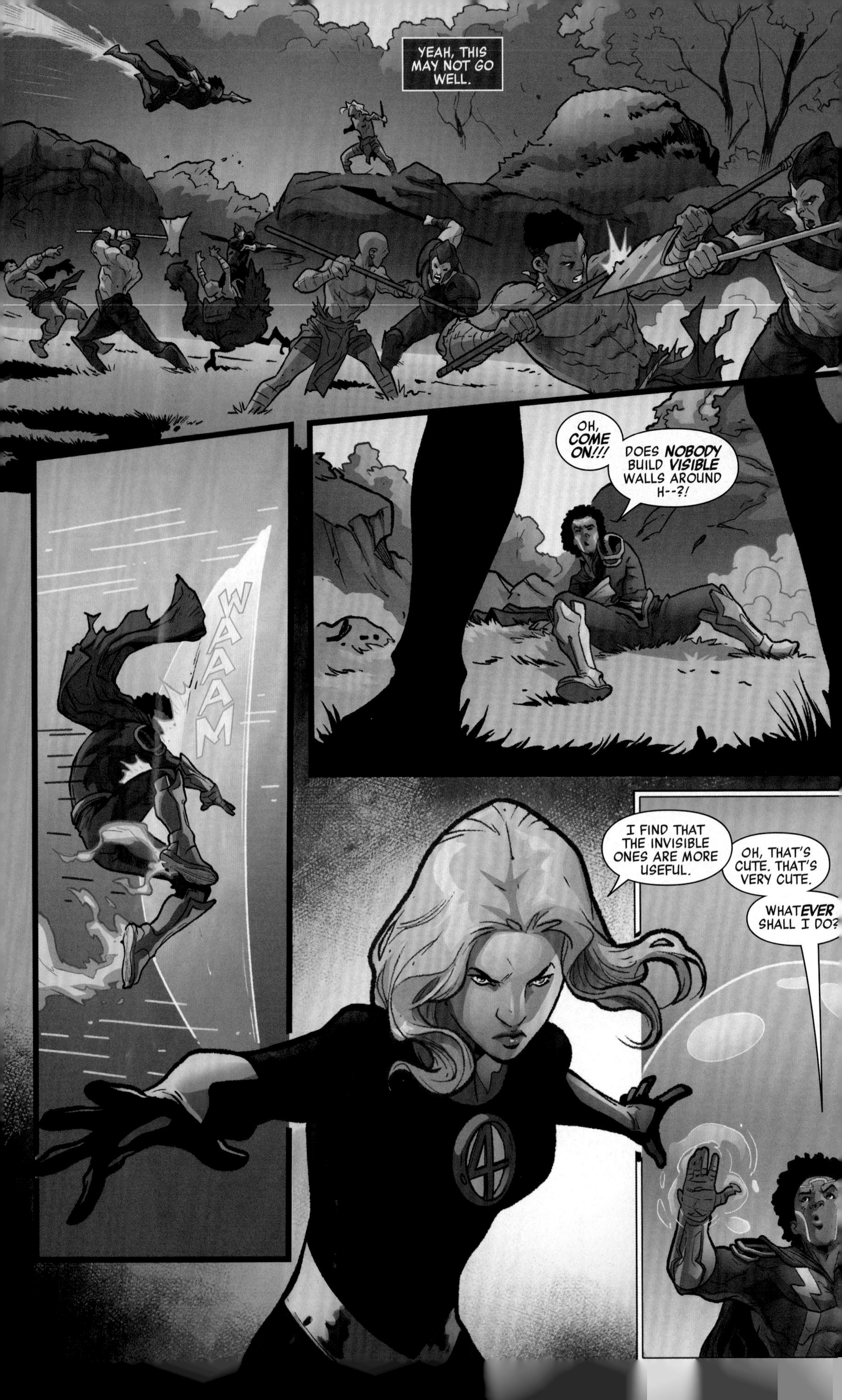

YEAH, THIS MAY NOT GO WELL.
WAAAM
OH, COME ON!!!
DOES NOBODY BUILD VISIBLE WALLS AROUND H--?!
I FIND THAT THE INVISIBLE ONES ARE MORE USEFUL.
OH, THAT'S CUTE. THAT'S VERY CUTE.
WHATEVER SHALL I DO?

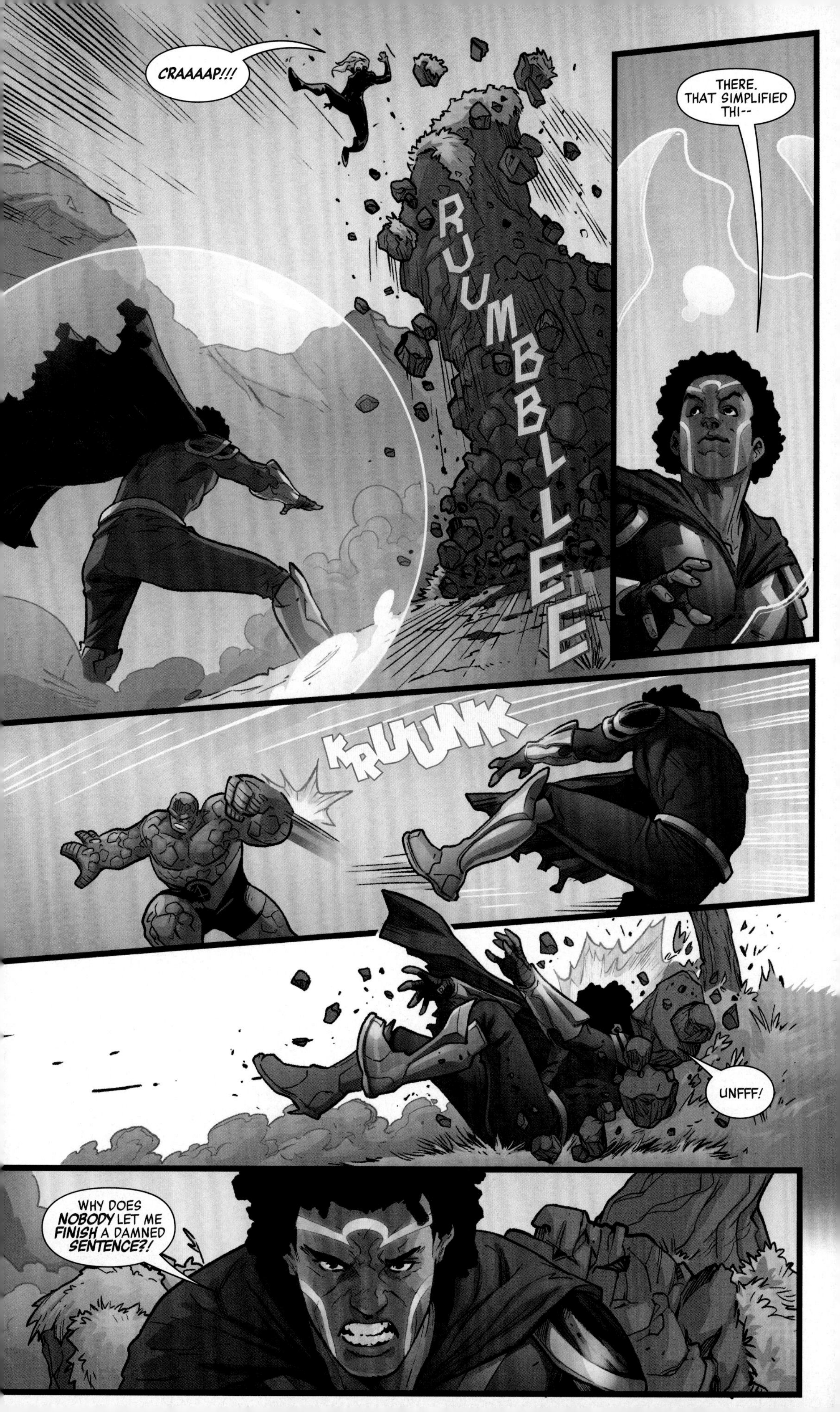

CRAAAAP!!!
RUMBLLE
THERE. THAT SIMPLIFIED THI--
KRUUNK
UNFFF!
WHY DOES NOBODY LET ME FINISH A DAMNED SENTENCE?!

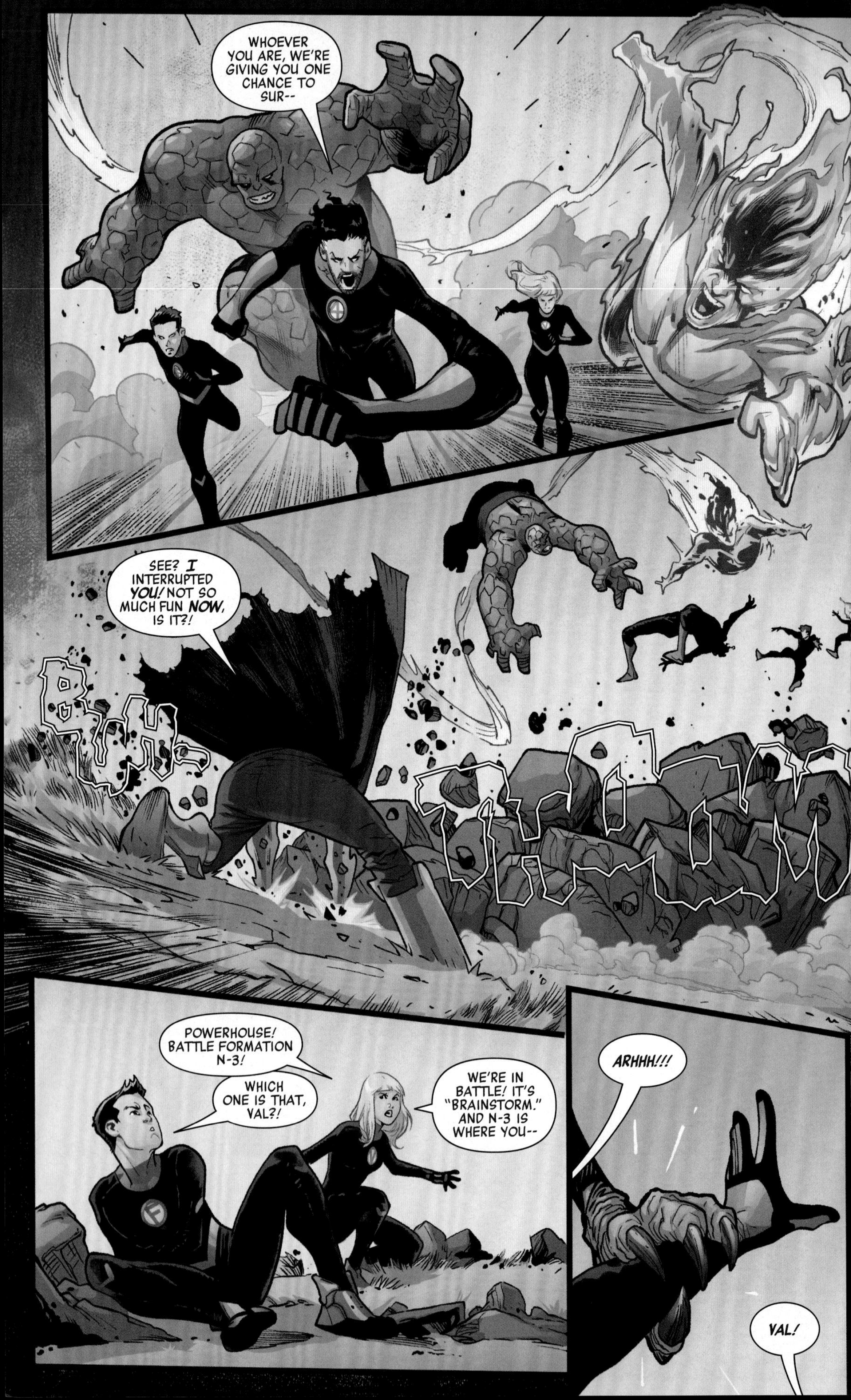
WHOEVER YOU ARE, WE'RE GIVING YOU ONE CHANCE TO SUR--
SEE? I INTERRUPTED YOU! NOT SO MUCH FUN NOW, IS IT?!
POWERHOUSE! BATTLE FORMATION N-3!
WHICH ONE IS THAT, VAL?!
WE'RE IN BATTLE! IT'S "BRAINSTORM." AND N-3 IS WHERE YOU--
ARHHH!!!
VAL!

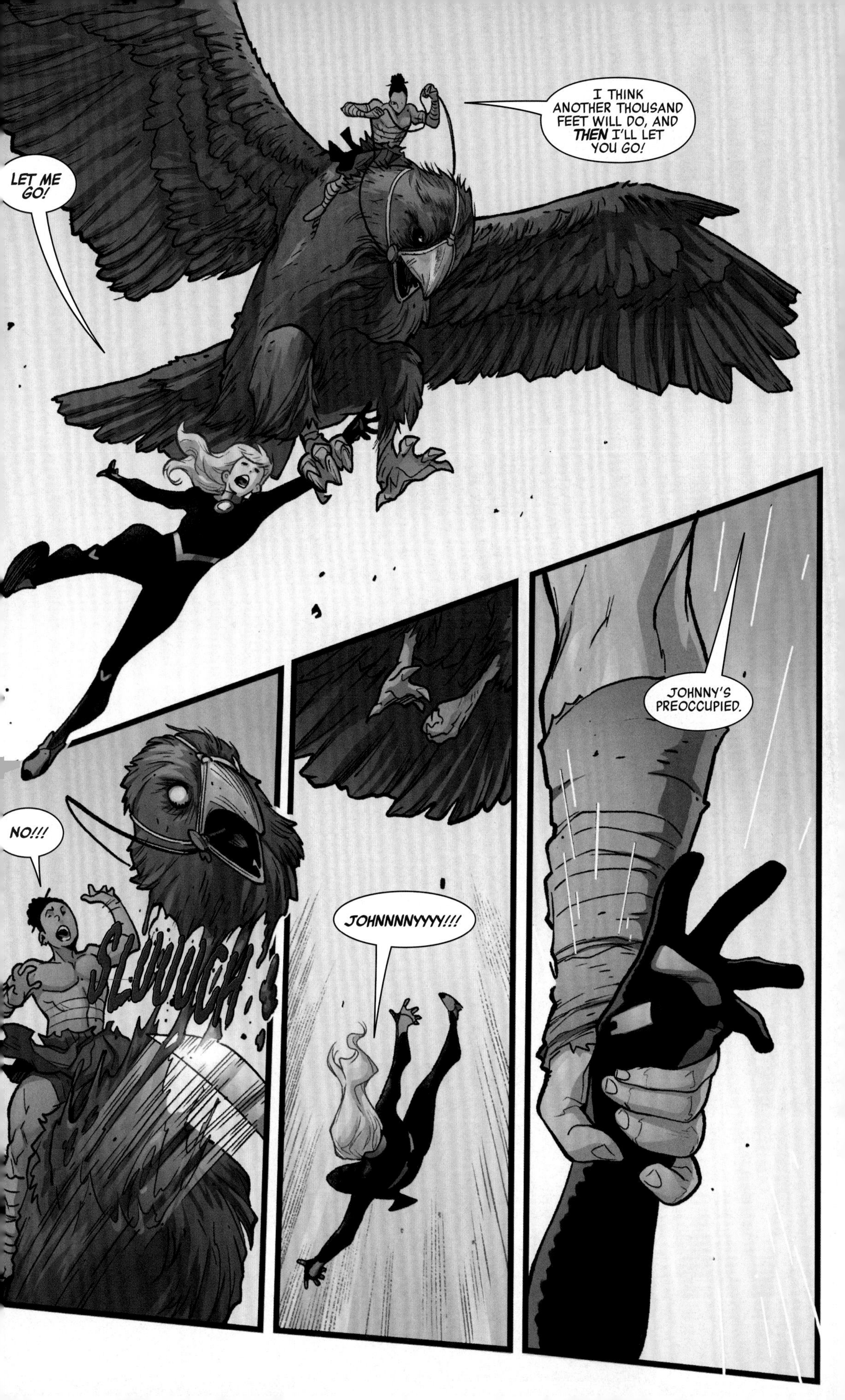
LET ME GO!
I THINK ANOTHER THOUSAND FEET WILL DO, AND THEN I'LL LET YOU GO!
NO!!!
SLUUUCH
JOHNNNNYYYY!!!
JOHNNY'S PREOCCUPIED.

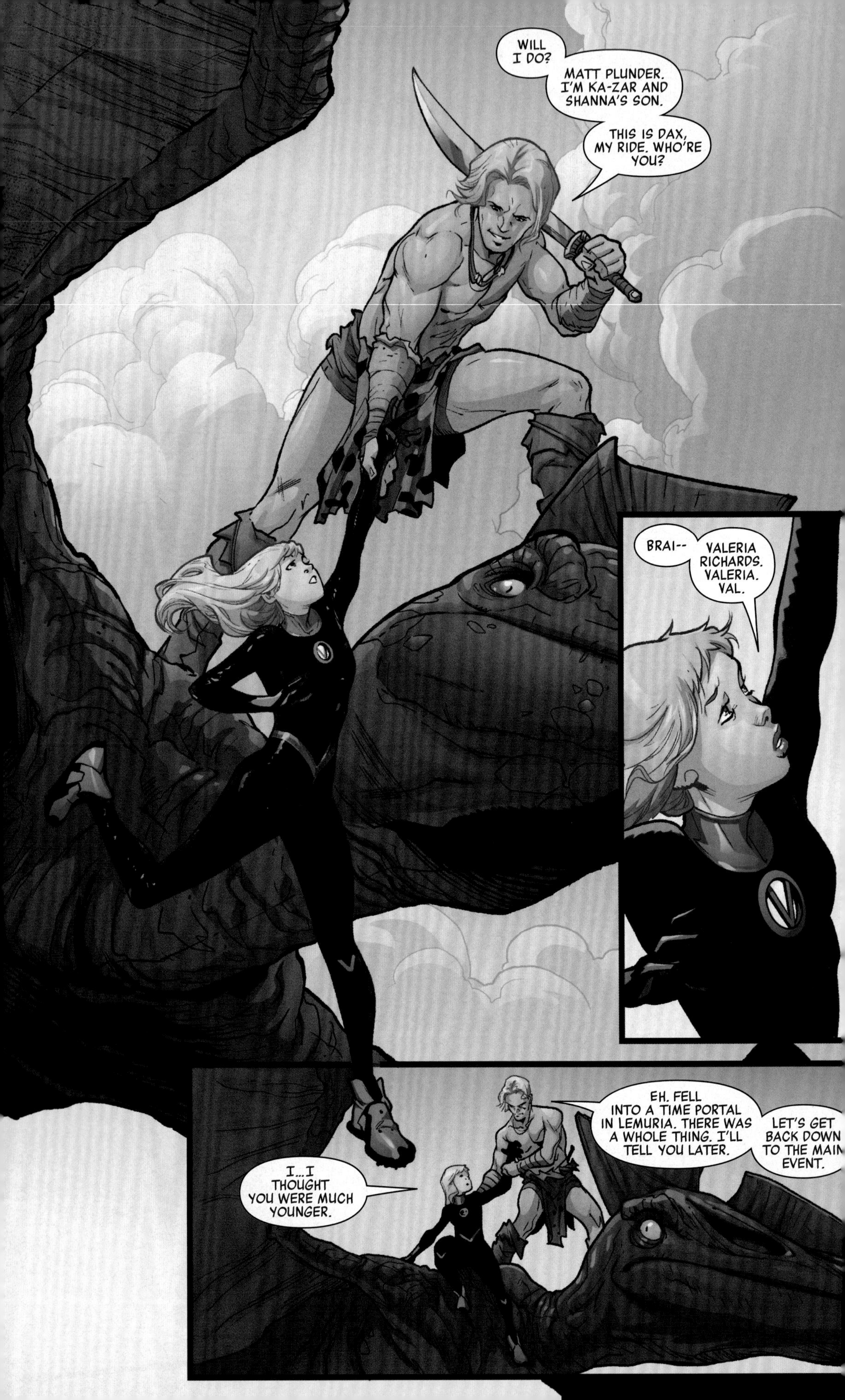
WILL I DO?
MATT PLUNDER. I'M KA-ZAR AND SHANNA'S SON.
THIS IS DAX, MY RIDE. WHO'RE YOU?
BRAI--
VALERIA RICHARDS. VALERIA. VAL.
I...I THOUGHT YOU WERE MUCH YOUNGER.
EH. FELL INTO A TIME PORTAL IN LEMURIA. THERE WAS A WHOLE THING. I'LL TELL YOU LATER.
LET'S GET BACK DOWN TO THE MAIN EVENT.

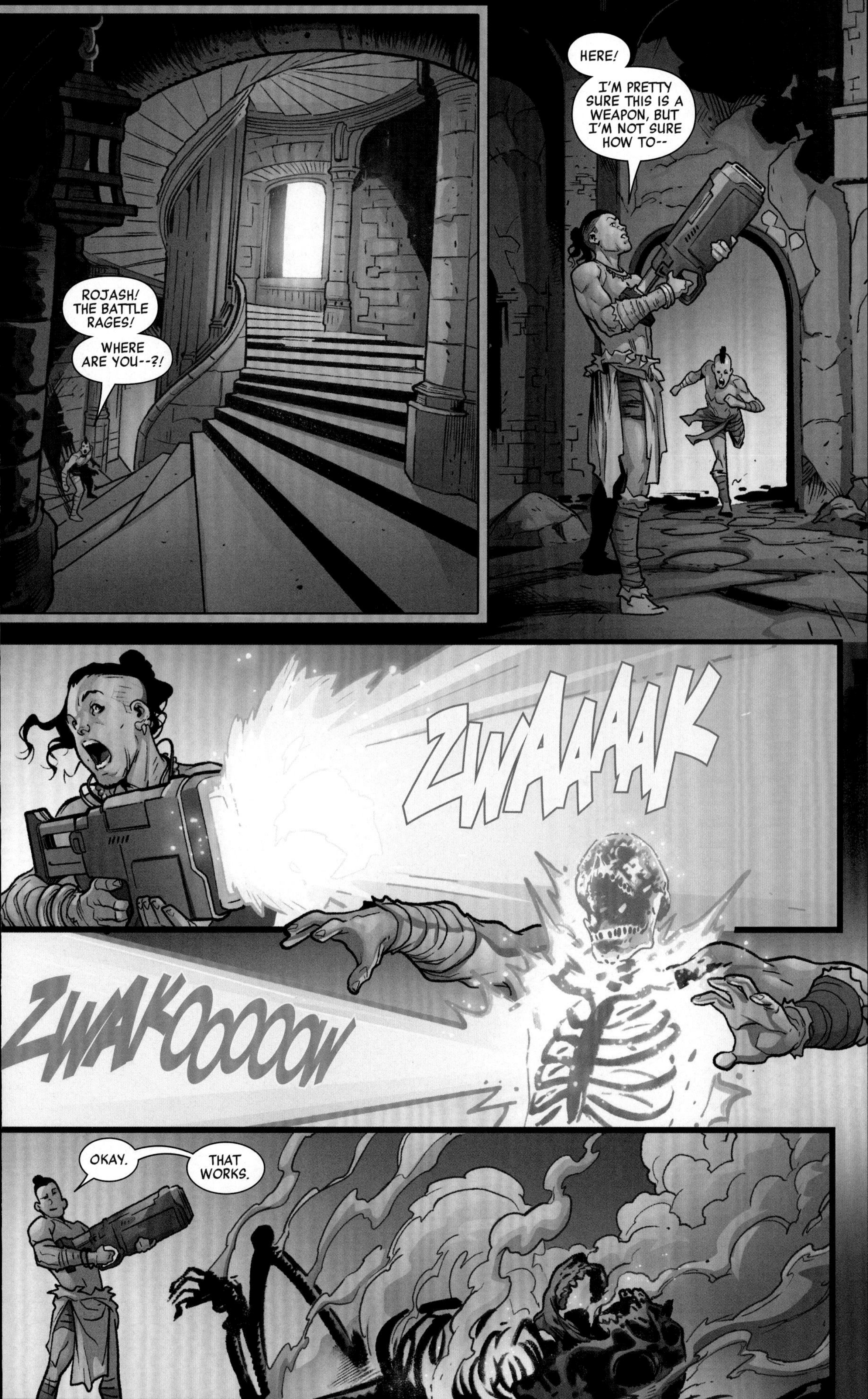
ROJASH! THE BATTLE RAGES!
WHERE ARE YOU--?!
HERE!
I'M PRETTY SURE THIS IS A WEAPON, BUT I'M NOT SURE HOW TO--
ZWAAAAK
ZWAKOOOOOW
OKAY.
THAT WORKS.

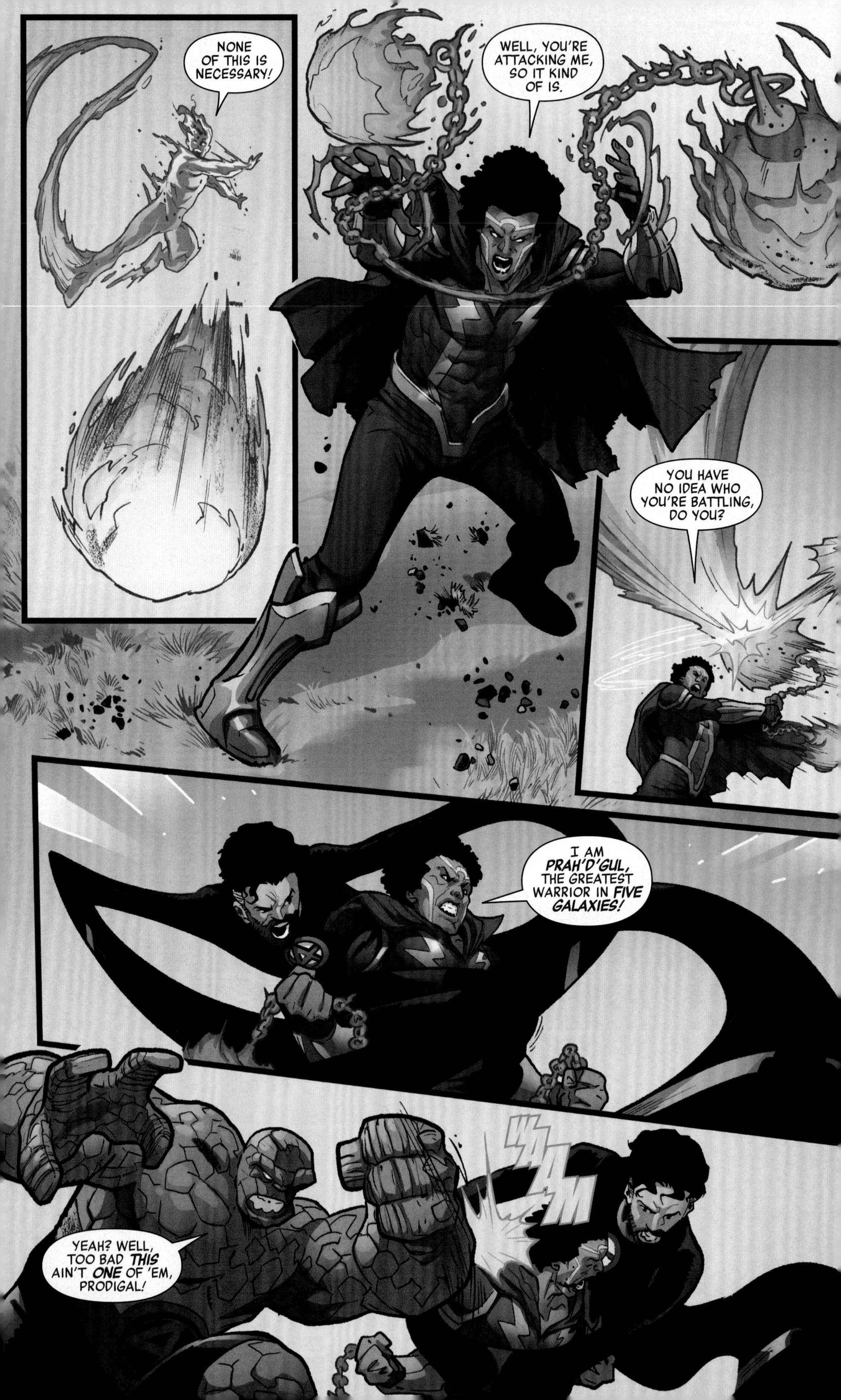
NONE OF THIS IS NECESSARY!
WELL, YOU'RE ATTACKING ME, SO IT KIND OF IS.
YOU HAVE NO IDEA WHO YOU'RE BATTLING, DO YOU?
I AM PRAH'D'GUL, THE GREATEST WARRIOR IN FIVE GALAXIES!
YEAH? WELL, TOO BAD THIS AIN'T ONE OF 'EM, PRODIGAL!
WHAM

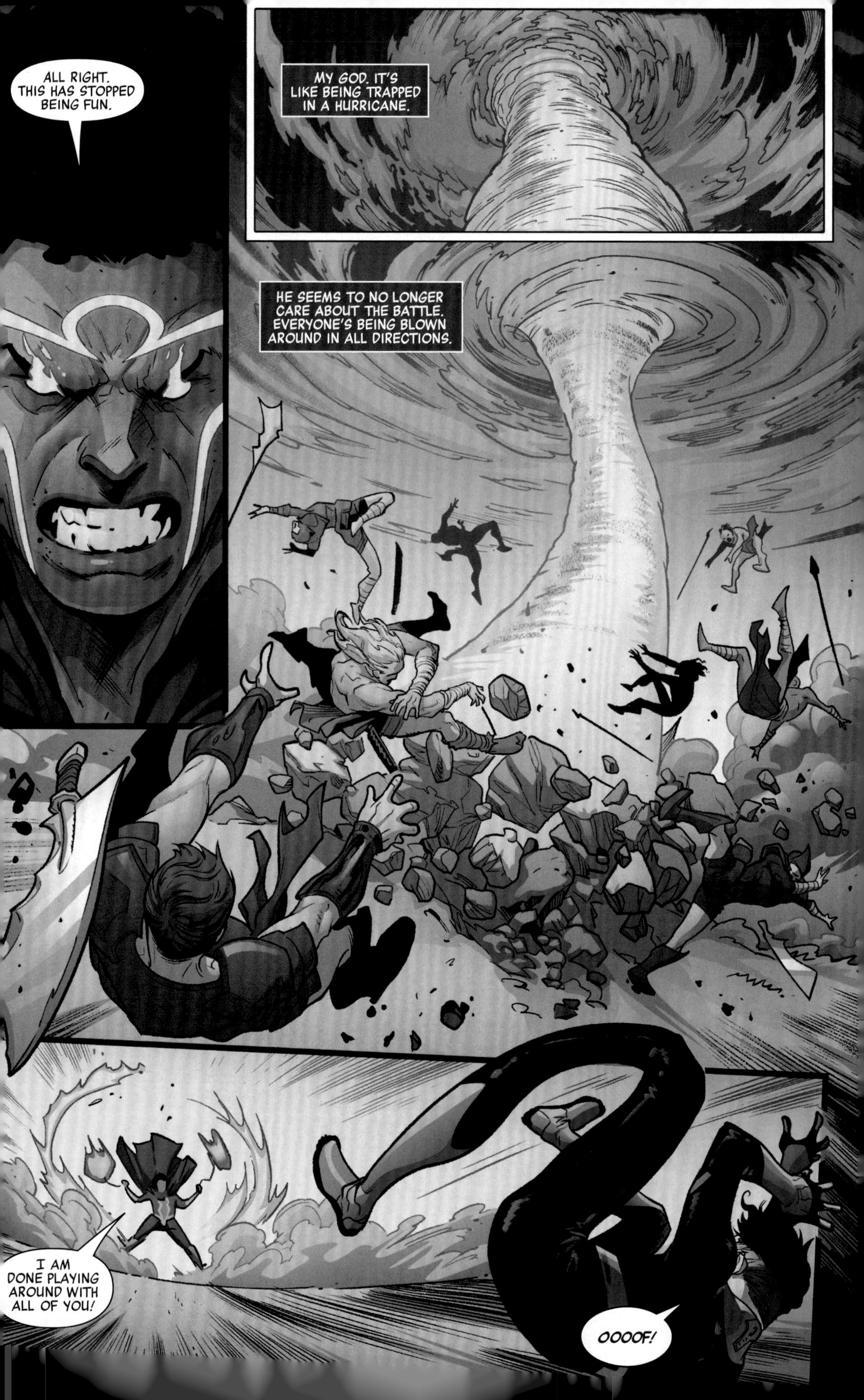

ALL RIGHT. THIS HAS STOPPED BEING FUN.
MY GOD. IT'S LIKE BEING TRAPPED IN A HURRICANE.
HE SEEMS TO NO LONGER CARE ABOUT THE BATTLE. EVERYONE'S BEING BLOWN AROUND IN ALL DIRECTIONS.
I AM DONE PLAYING AROUND WITH ALL OF YOU!
OOOOF!

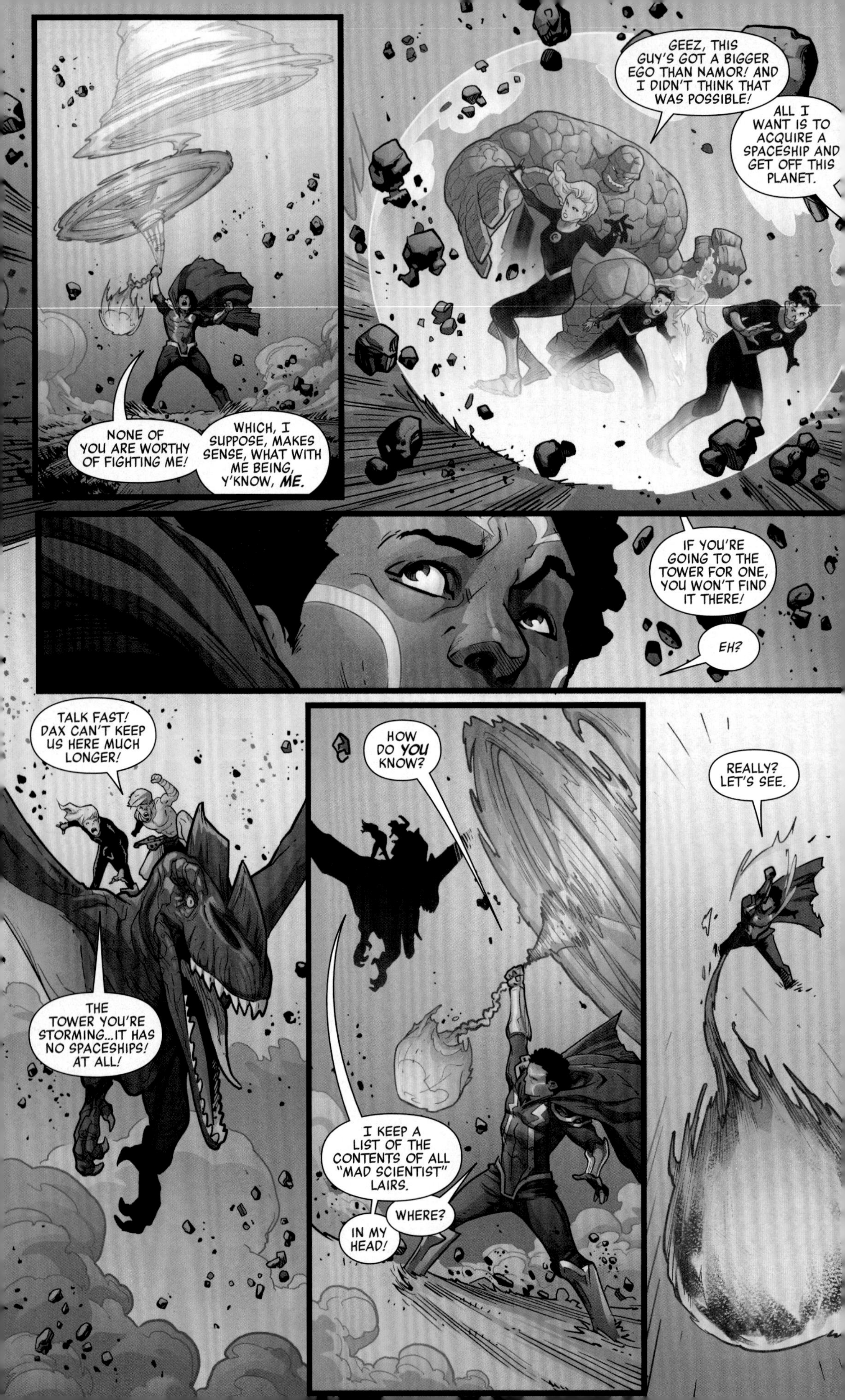
NONE OF YOU ARE WORTHY OF FIGHTING ME!
WHICH, I SUPPOSE, MAKES SENSE, WHAT WITH ME BEING, Y'KNOW, ***ME.***
GEEZ, THIS GUY'S GOT A BIGGER EGO THAN NAMOR! AND I DIDN'T THINK THAT WAS POSSIBLE!
ALL I WANT IS TO ACQUIRE A SPACESHIP AND GET OFF THIS PLANET.
IF YOU'RE GOING TO THE TOWER FOR ONE, YOU WON'T FIND IT THERE!
EH?
TALK FAST! DAX CAN'T KEEP US HERE MUCH LONGER!
THE TOWER YOU'RE STORMING...IT HAS NO SPACESHIPS! AT ALL!
HOW DO ***YOU*** KNOW?
I KEEP A LIST OF THE CONTENTS OF ALL "MAD SCIENTIST" LAIRS.
WHERE?
IN MY HEAD!
REALLY? LET'S SEE.

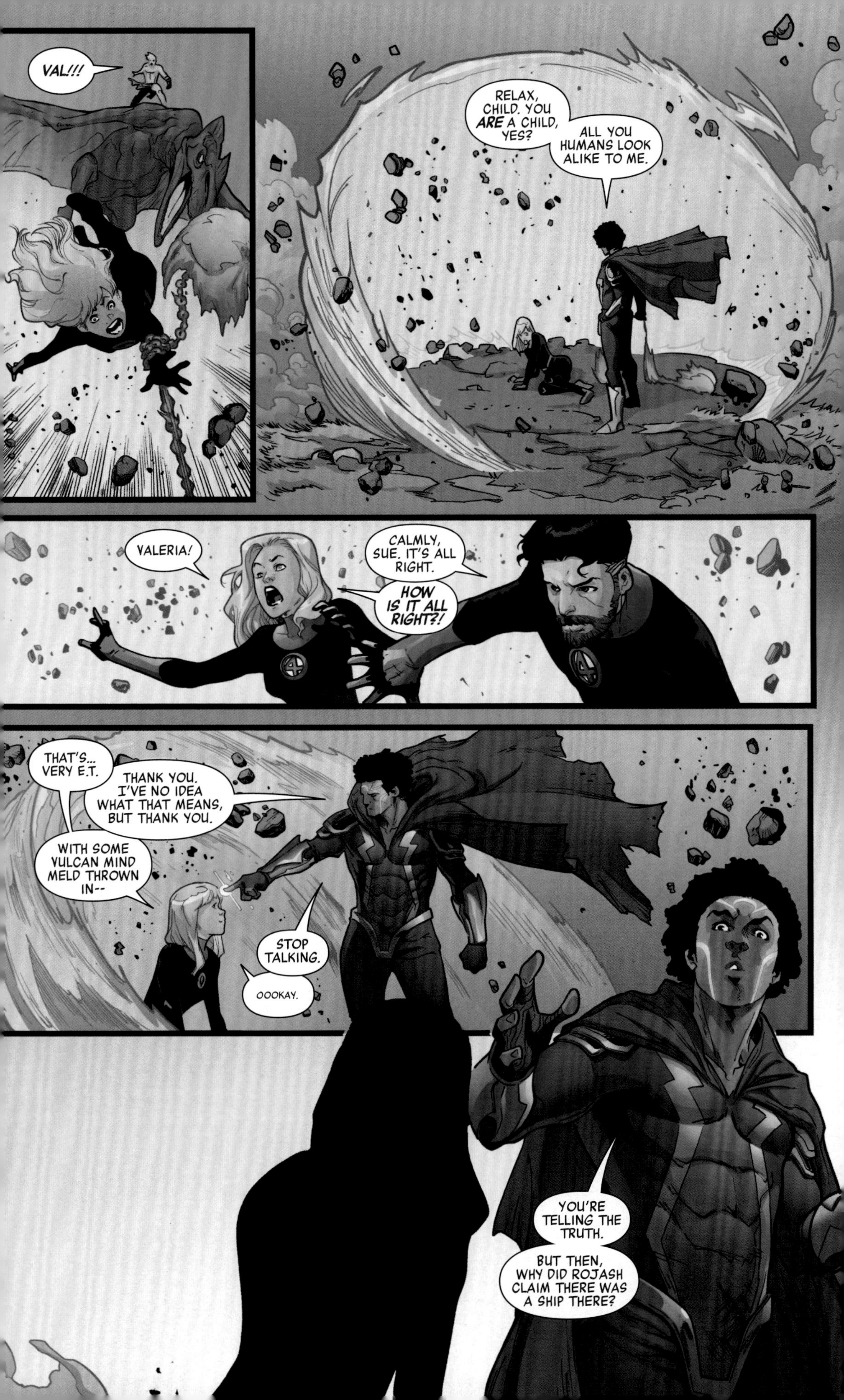
VAL!!!
RELAX, CHILD. YOU ARE A CHILD, YES?
ALL YOU HUMANS LOOK ALIKE TO ME.
VALERIA!
CALMLY, SUE. IT'S ALL RIGHT.
HOW IS IT ALL RIGHT?!
THAT'S... VERY E.T.
THANK YOU. I'VE NO IDEA WHAT THAT MEANS, BUT THANK YOU.
WITH SOME VULCAN MIND MELD THROWN IN--
STOP TALKING.
OOOKAY.
YOU'RE TELLING THE TRUTH.
BUT THEN, WHY DID ROJASH CLAIM THERE WAS A SHIP THERE?

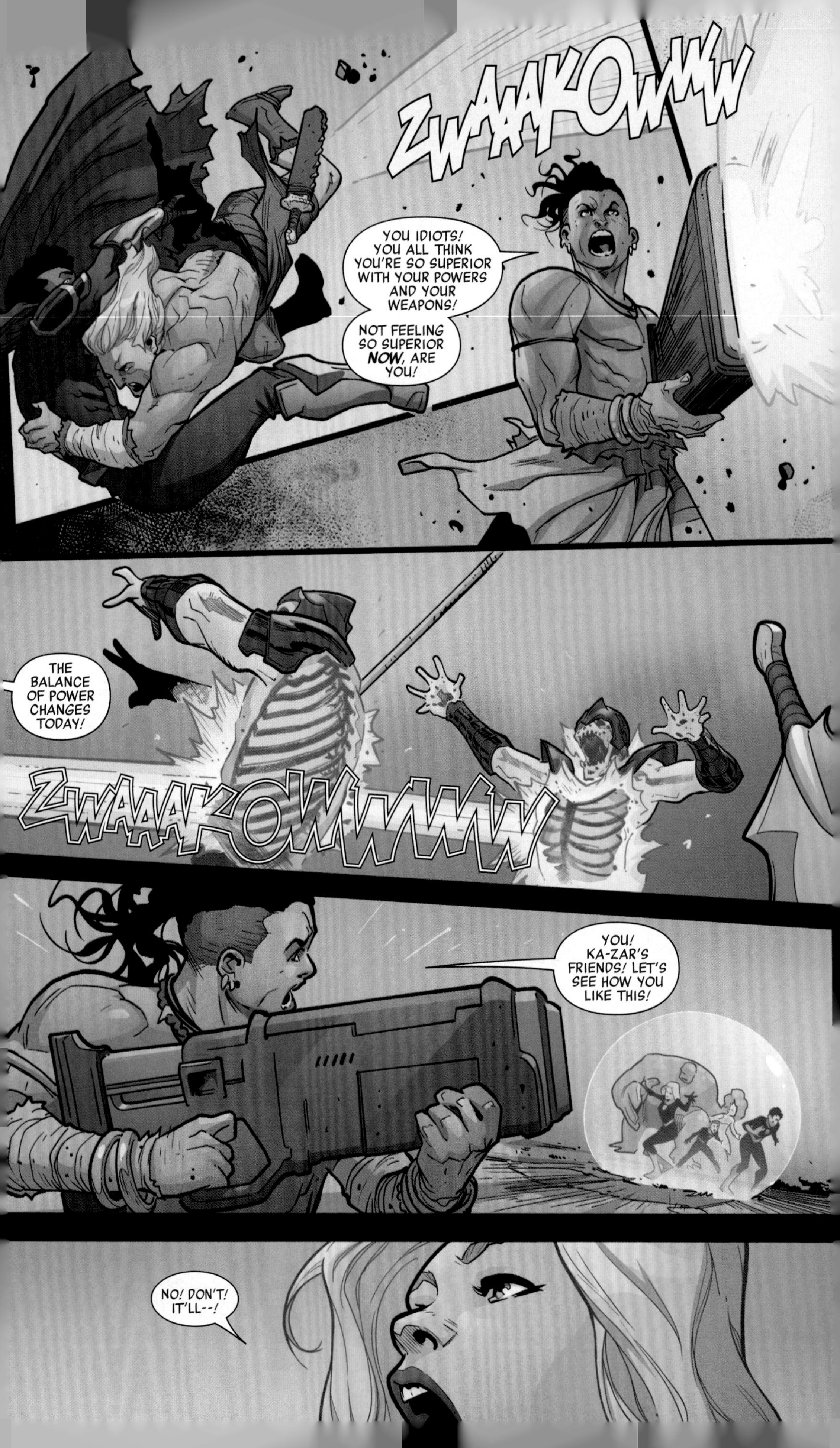
ZWAAAKOWWW
YOU IDIOTS! YOU ALL THINK YOU'RE SO SUPERIOR WITH YOUR POWERS AND YOUR WEAPONS!
NOT FEELING SO SUPERIOR NOW, ARE YOU!
THE BALANCE OF POWER CHANGES TODAY!
ZWAAAKOWWWWW
YOU! KA-ZAR'S FRIENDS! LET'S SEE HOW YOU LIKE THIS!
NO! DON'T! IT'LL--!

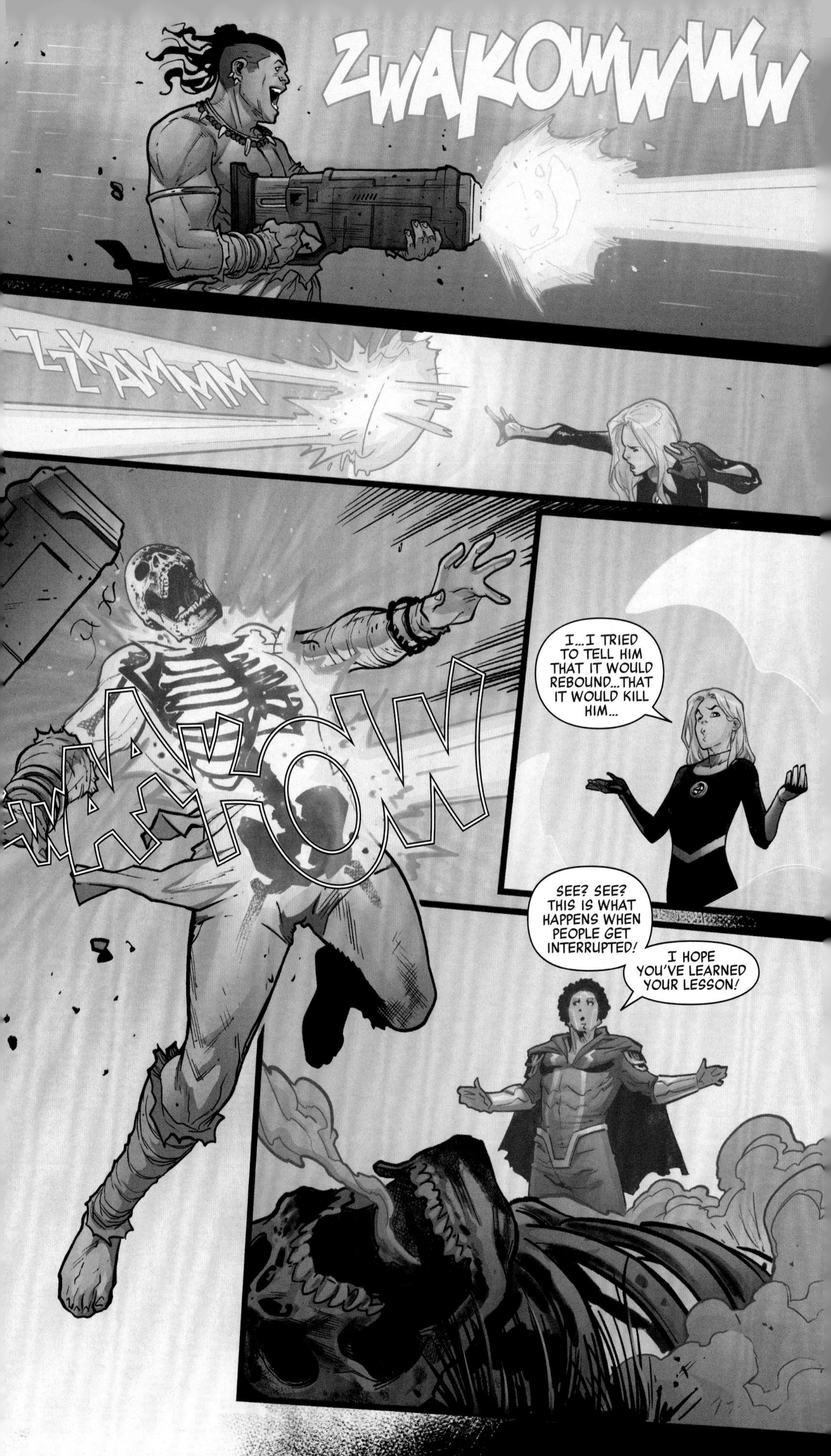
ZWAKOWWWW
ZZKAMMM
I...I TRIED TO TELL HIM THAT IT WOULD REBOUND...THAT IT WOULD KILL HIM...
WAKOW
SEE? SEE? THIS IS WHAT HAPPENS WHEN PEOPLE GET INTERRUPTED!
I HOPE YOU'VE LEARNED YOUR LESSON!

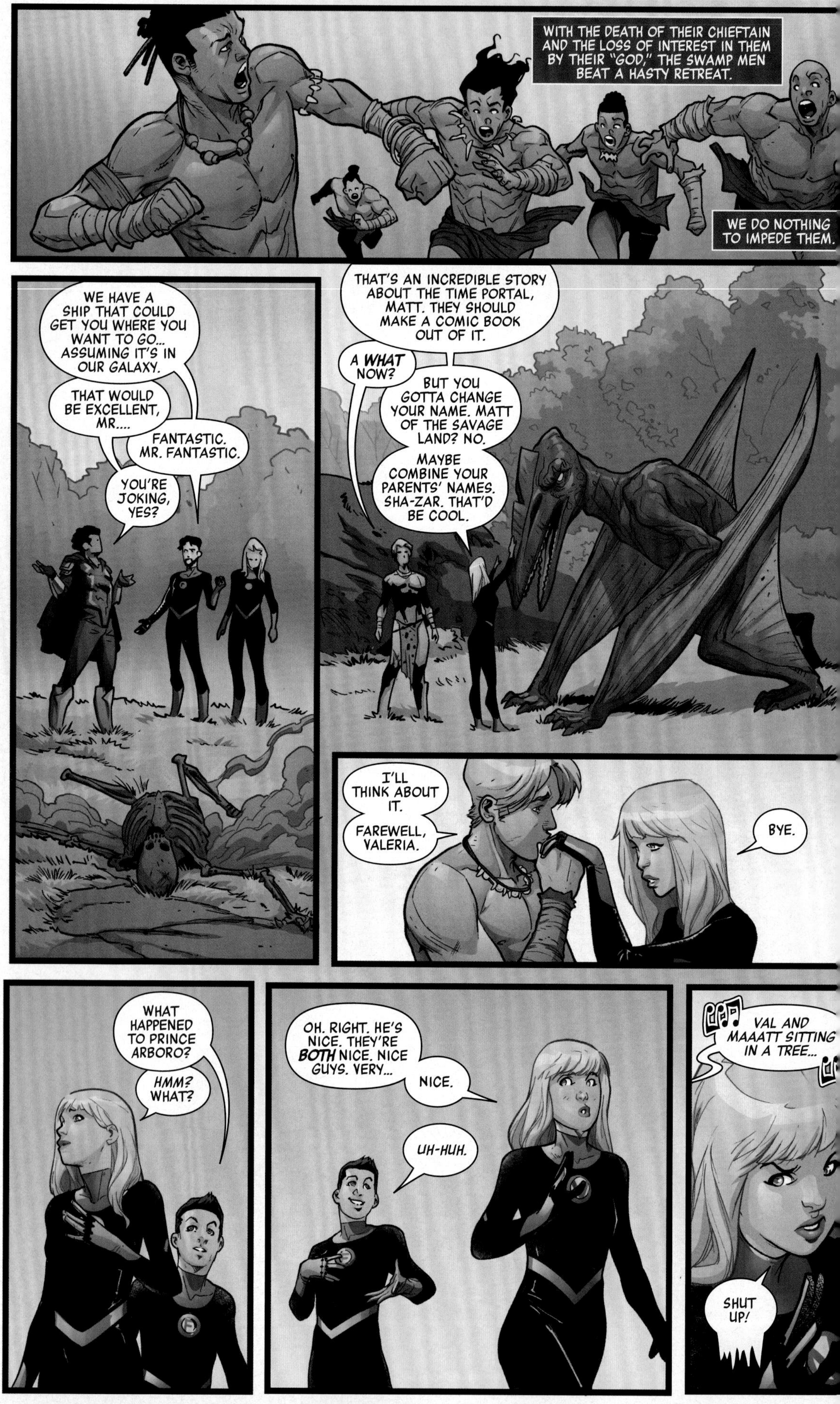
WITH THE DEATH OF THEIR CHIEFTAIN AND THE LOSS OF INTEREST IN THEM BY THEIR "GOD," THE SWAMP MEN BEAT A HASTY RETREAT.
WE DO NOTHING TO IMPEDE THEM.
WE HAVE A SHIP THAT COULD GET YOU WHERE YOU WANT TO GO... ASSUMING IT'S IN OUR GALAXY.
THAT WOULD BE EXCELLENT, MR....
FANTASTIC. MR. FANTASTIC.
YOU'RE JOKING, YES?
THAT'S AN INCREDIBLE STORY ABOUT THE TIME PORTAL, MATT. THEY SHOULD MAKE A COMIC BOOK OUT OF IT.
A *WHAT* NOW?
BUT YOU GOTTA CHANGE YOUR NAME. MATT OF THE SAVAGE LAND? NO.
MAYBE COMBINE YOUR PARENTS' NAMES. SHA-ZAR. THAT'D BE COOL.
I'LL THINK ABOUT IT.
FAREWELL, VALERIA.
BYE.
WHAT HAPPENED TO PRINCE ARBORO?
HMM? WHAT?
OH. RIGHT. HE'S NICE. THEY'RE *BOTH* NICE. NICE GUYS. VERY...
NICE.
UH-HUH.
VAL AND MAAATT SITTING IN A TREE...
SHUT UP!

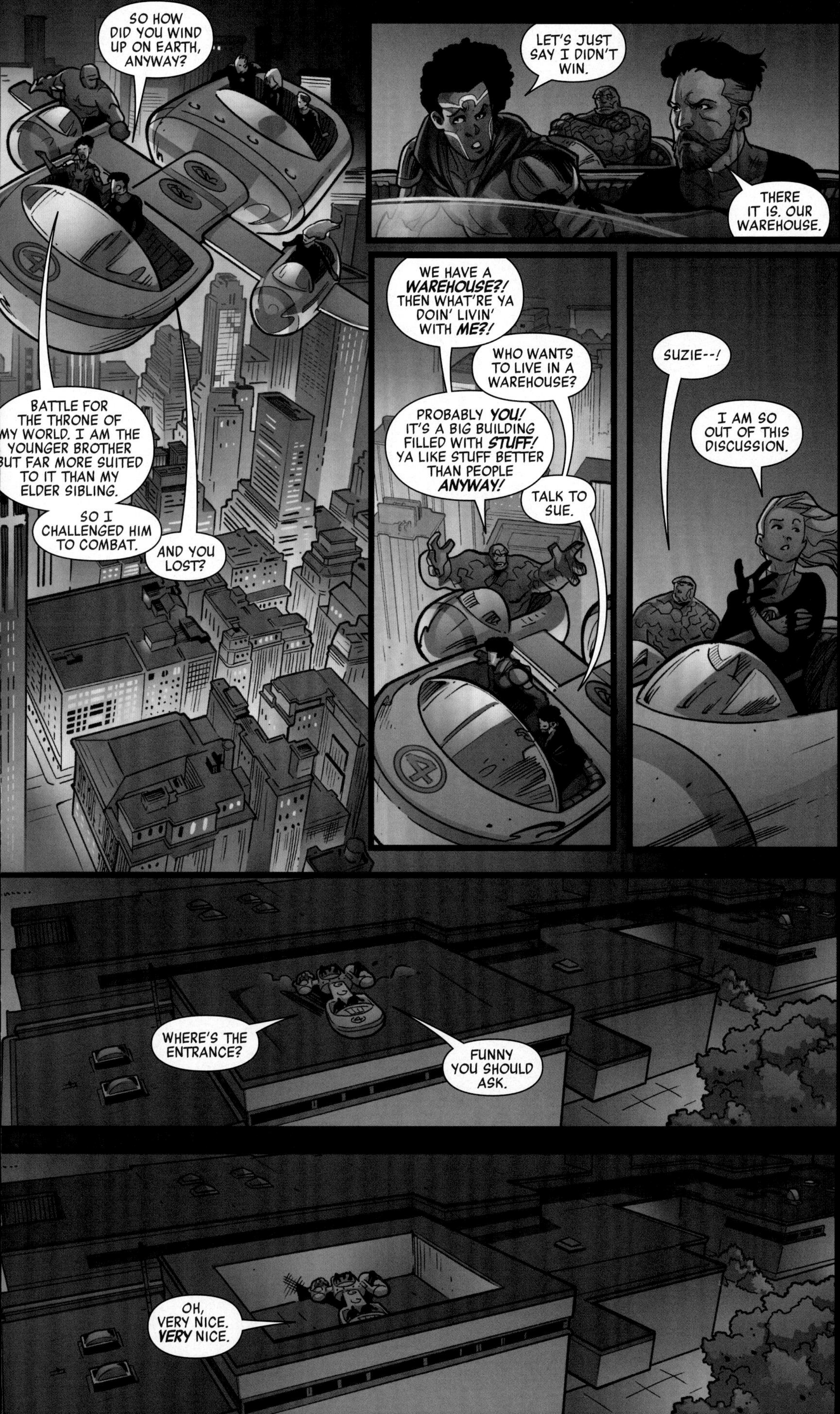
SO HOW DID YOU WIND UP ON EARTH, ANYWAY?
BATTLE FOR THE THRONE OF MY WORLD. I AM THE YOUNGER BROTHER BUT FAR MORE SUITED TO IT THAN MY ELDER SIBLING.
SO I CHALLENGED HIM TO COMBAT.
AND YOU LOST?
LET'S JUST SAY I DIDN'T WIN.
THERE IT IS. OUR WAREHOUSE.
WE HAVE A WAREHOUSE?! THEN WHAT'RE YA DOIN' LIVIN' WITH ME?!
WHO WANTS TO LIVE IN A WAREHOUSE?
PROBABLY YOU! IT'S A BIG BUILDING FILLED WITH STUFF! YA LIKE STUFF BETTER THAN PEOPLE ANYWAY!
TALK TO SUE.
SUZIE--!
I AM SO OUT OF THIS DISCUSSION.
WHERE'S THE ENTRANCE?
FUNNY YOU SHOULD ASK.
OH, VERY NICE. VERY NICE.

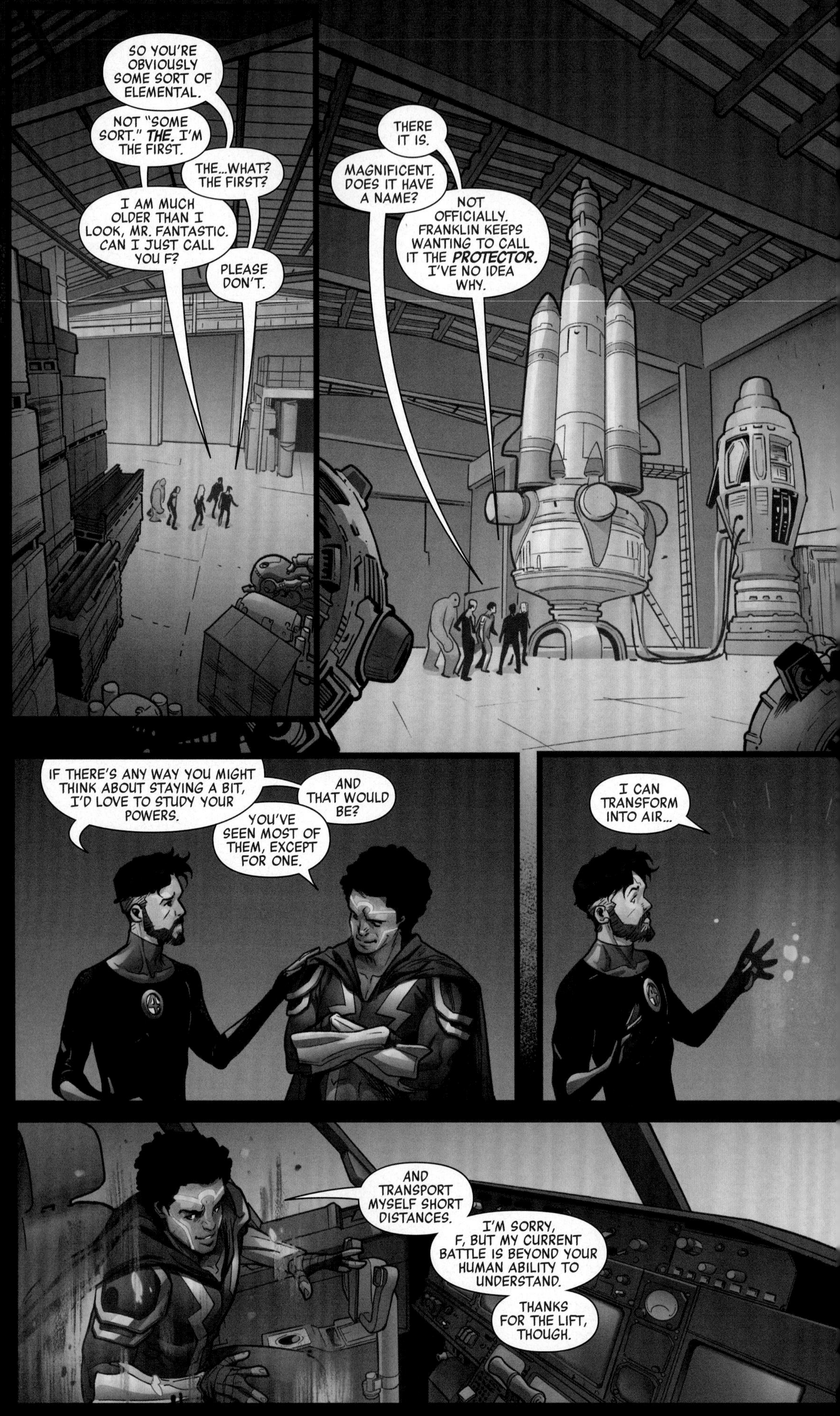
SO YOU'RE OBVIOUSLY SOME SORT OF ELEMENTAL.
NOT "SOME SORT." THE. I'M THE FIRST.
THE...WHAT? THE FIRST?
I AM MUCH OLDER THAN I LOOK, MR. FANTASTIC. CAN I JUST CALL YOU F?
PLEASE DON'T.
THERE IT IS.
MAGNIFICENT. DOES IT HAVE A NAME?
NOT OFFICIALLY. FRANKLIN KEEPS WANTING TO CALL IT THE PROTECTOR. I'VE NO IDEA WHY.
IF THERE'S ANY WAY YOU MIGHT THINK ABOUT STAYING A BIT, I'D LOVE TO STUDY YOUR POWERS.
YOU'VE SEEN MOST OF THEM, EXCEPT FOR ONE.
AND THAT WOULD BE?
I CAN TRANSFORM INTO AIR...
AND TRANSPORT MYSELF SHORT DISTANCES.
I'M SORRY, F, BUT MY CURRENT BATTLE IS BEYOND YOUR HUMAN ABILITY TO UNDERSTAND.
THANKS FOR THE LIFT, THOUGH.

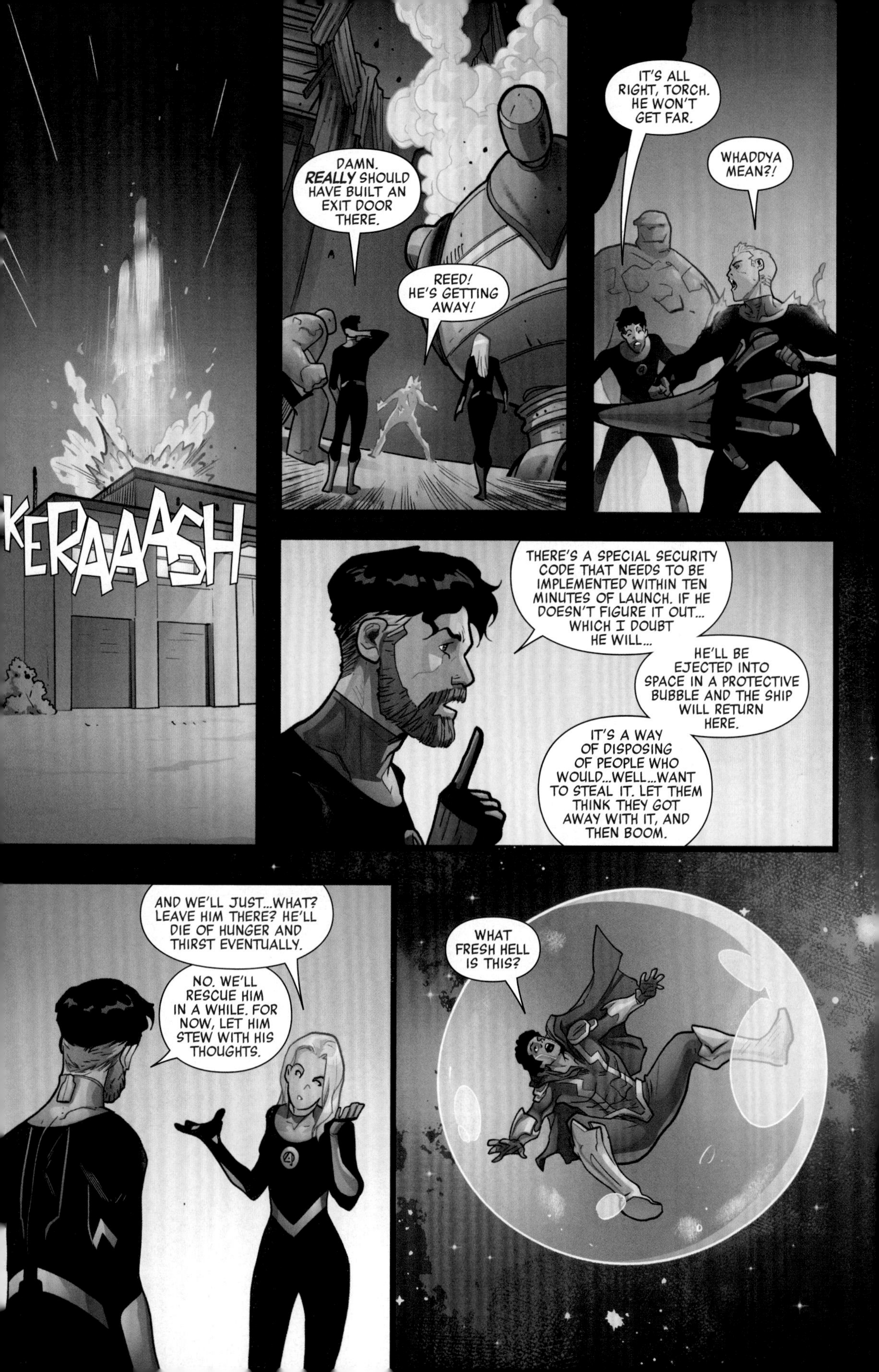
KERAAASH
DAMN. **REALLY** SHOULD HAVE BUILT AN EXIT DOOR THERE.
REED! HE'S GETTING AWAY!
IT'S ALL RIGHT, TORCH. HE WON'T GET FAR.
WHADDYA MEAN?!
THERE'S A SPECIAL SECURITY CODE THAT NEEDS TO BE IMPLEMENTED WITHIN TEN MINUTES OF LAUNCH. IF HE DOESN'T FIGURE IT OUT... WHICH I DOUBT HE WILL...
HE'LL BE EJECTED INTO SPACE IN A PROTECTIVE BUBBLE AND THE SHIP WILL RETURN HERE.
IT'S A WAY OF DISPOSING OF PEOPLE WHO WOULD...WELL...WANT TO STEAL IT. LET THEM THINK THEY GOT AWAY WITH IT, AND THEN BOOM.
AND WE'LL JUST...WHAT? LEAVE HIM THERE? HE'LL DIE OF HUNGER AND THIRST EVENTUALLY.
NO. WE'LL RESCUE HIM IN A WHILE. FOR NOW, LET HIM STEW WITH HIS THOUGHTS.
WHAT FRESH HELL IS THIS?

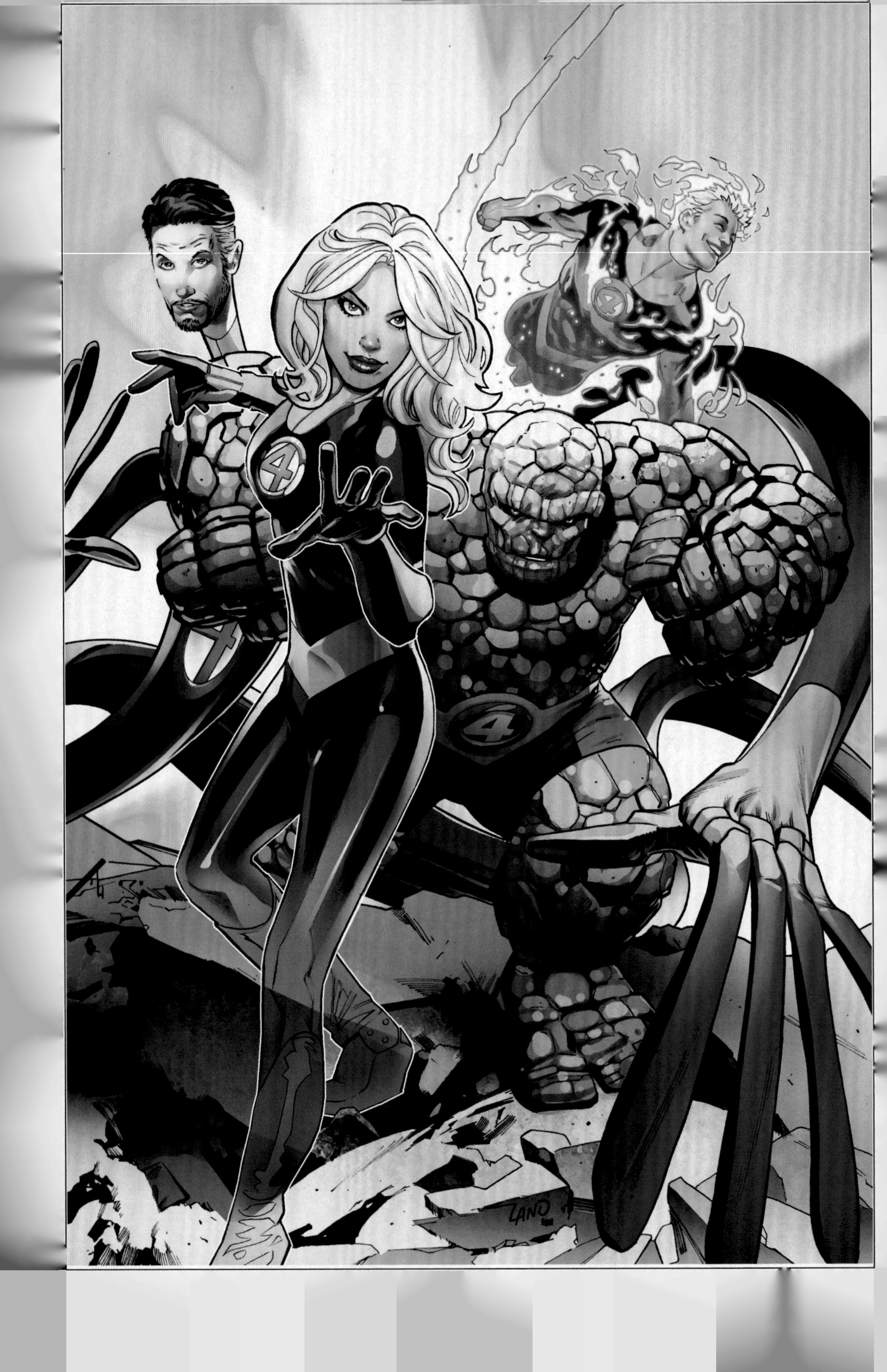

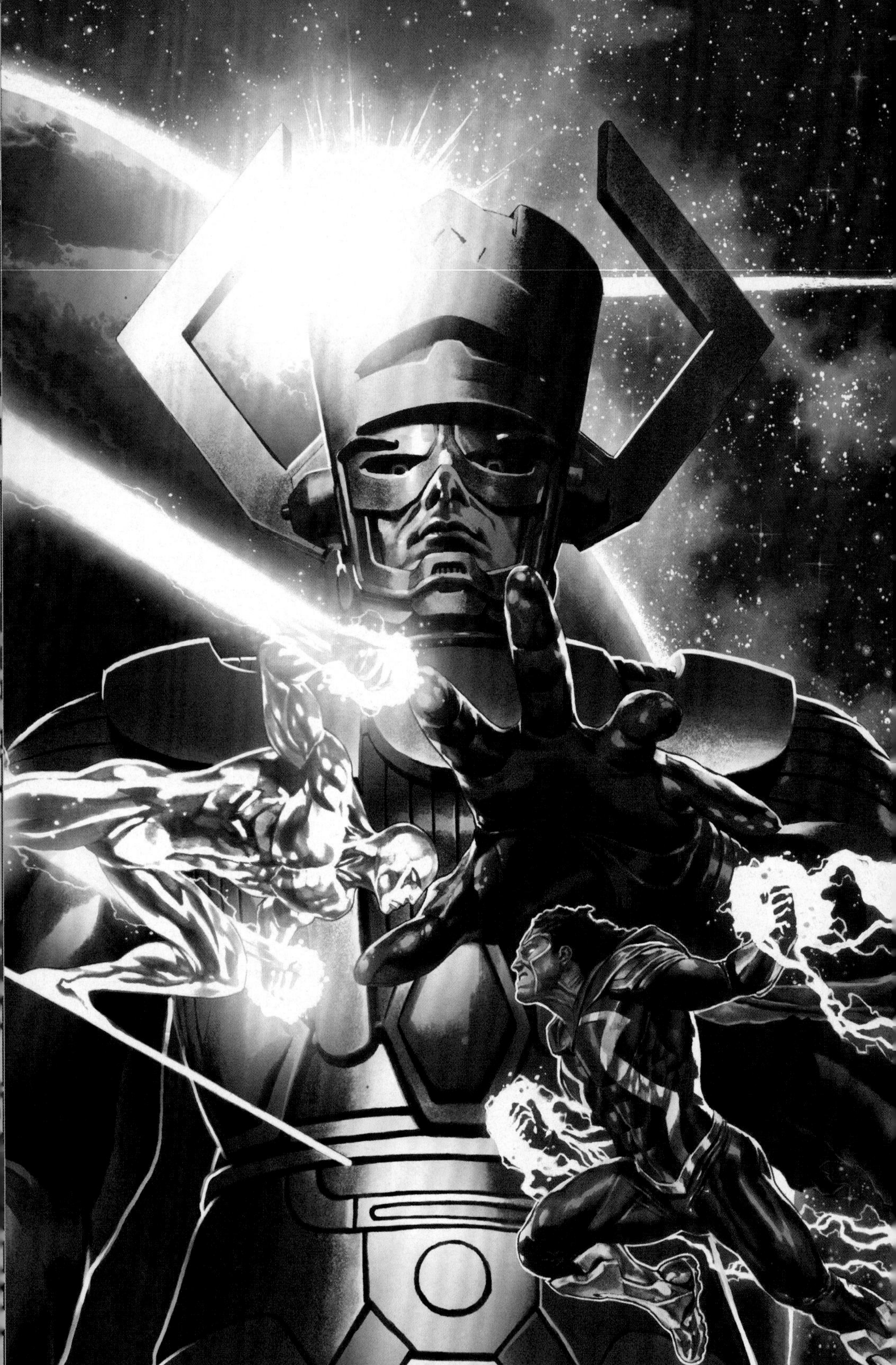

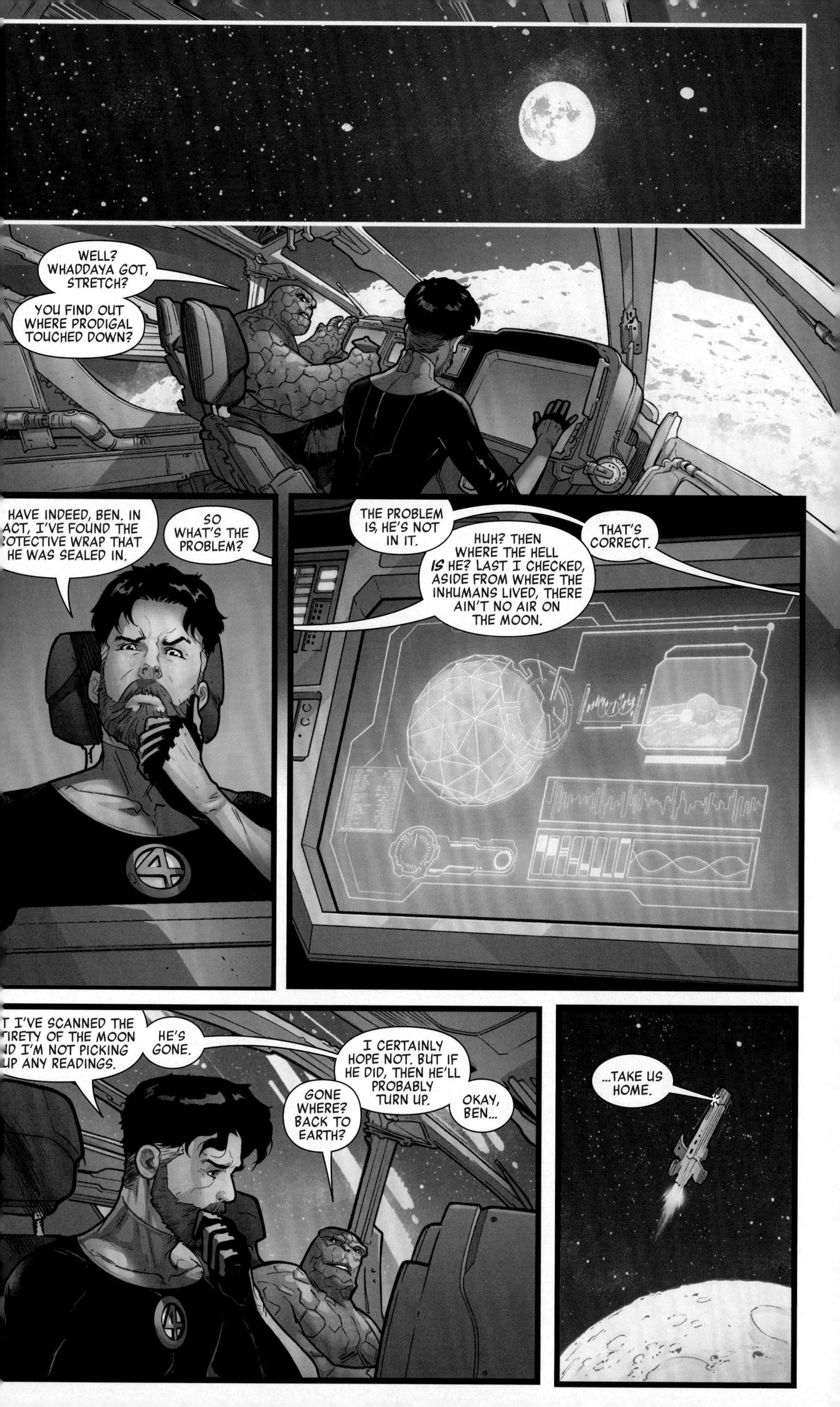
WELL? WHADDAYA GOT, STRETCH?
YOU FIND OUT WHERE PRODIGAL TOUCHED DOWN?
HAVE INDEED, BEN. IN ACT, I'VE FOUND THE OTECTIVE WRAP THAT HE WAS SEALED IN.
SO WHAT'S THE PROBLEM?
THE PROBLEM IS, HE'S NOT IN IT.
HUH? THEN WHERE THE HELL *IS* HE? LAST I CHECKED, ASIDE FROM WHERE THE INHUMANS LIVED, THERE AIN'T NO AIR ON THE MOON.
THAT'S CORRECT.
T I'VE SCANNED THE TIRETY OF THE MOON D I'M NOT PICKING UP ANY READINGS.
HE'S GONE.
GONE WHERE? BACK TO EARTH?
I CERTAINLY HOPE NOT. BUT IF HE DID, THEN HE'LL PROBABLY TURN UP.
OKAY, BEN...
...TAKE US HOME.

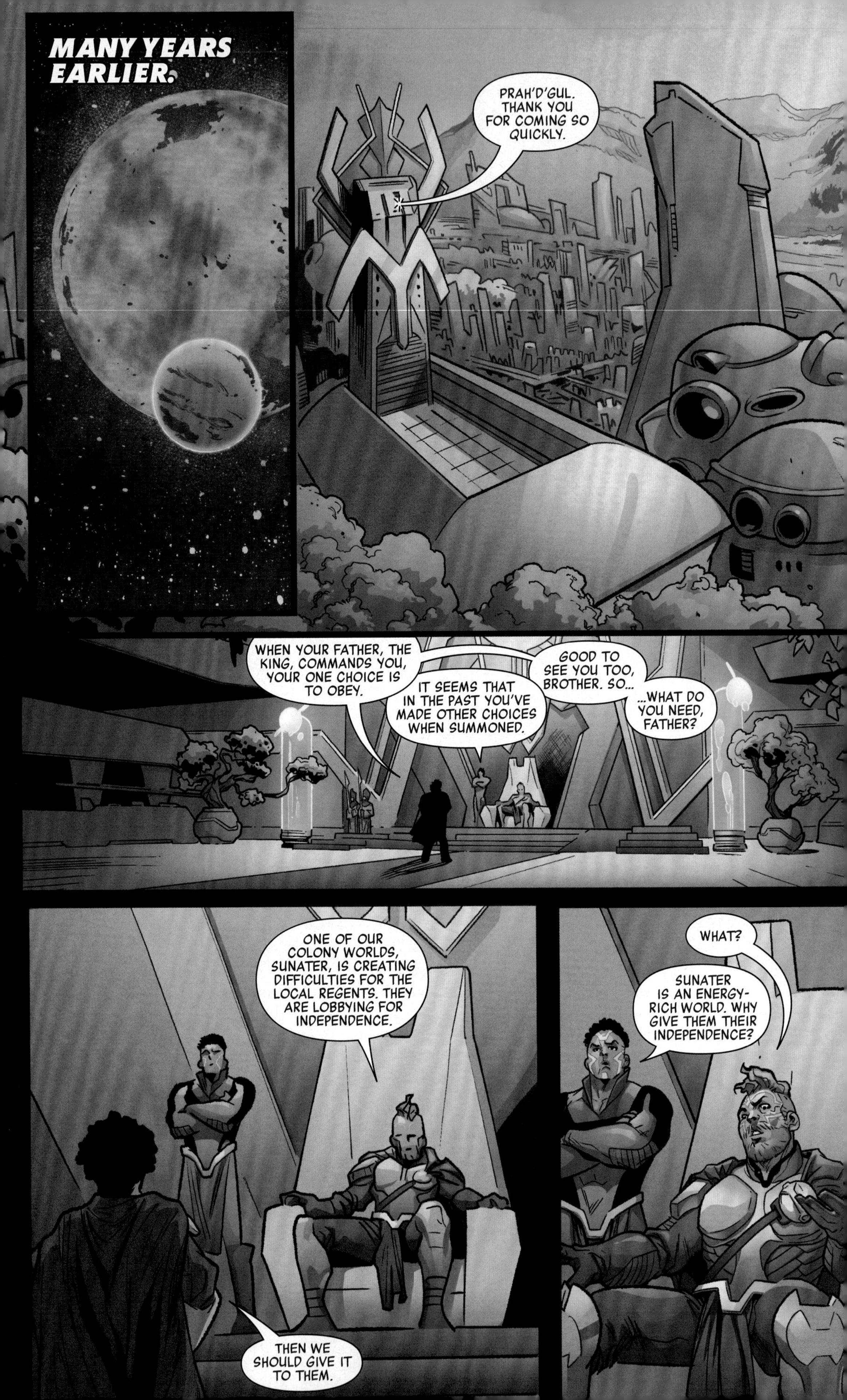
MANY YEARS EARLIER.
PRAH'D'GUL. THANK YOU FOR COMING SO QUICKLY.
WHEN YOUR FATHER, THE KING, COMMANDS YOU, YOUR ONE CHOICE IS TO OBEY.
IT SEEMS THAT IN THE PAST YOU'VE MADE OTHER CHOICES WHEN SUMMONED.
GOOD TO SEE YOU TOO, BROTHER. SO...
...WHAT DO YOU NEED, FATHER?
ONE OF OUR COLONY WORLDS, SUNATER, IS CREATING DIFFICULTIES FOR THE LOCAL REGENTS. THEY ARE LOBBYING FOR INDEPENDENCE.
THEN WE SHOULD GIVE IT TO THEM.
WHAT?
SUNATER IS AN ENERGY-RICH WORLD. WHY GIVE THEM THEIR INDEPENDENCE?

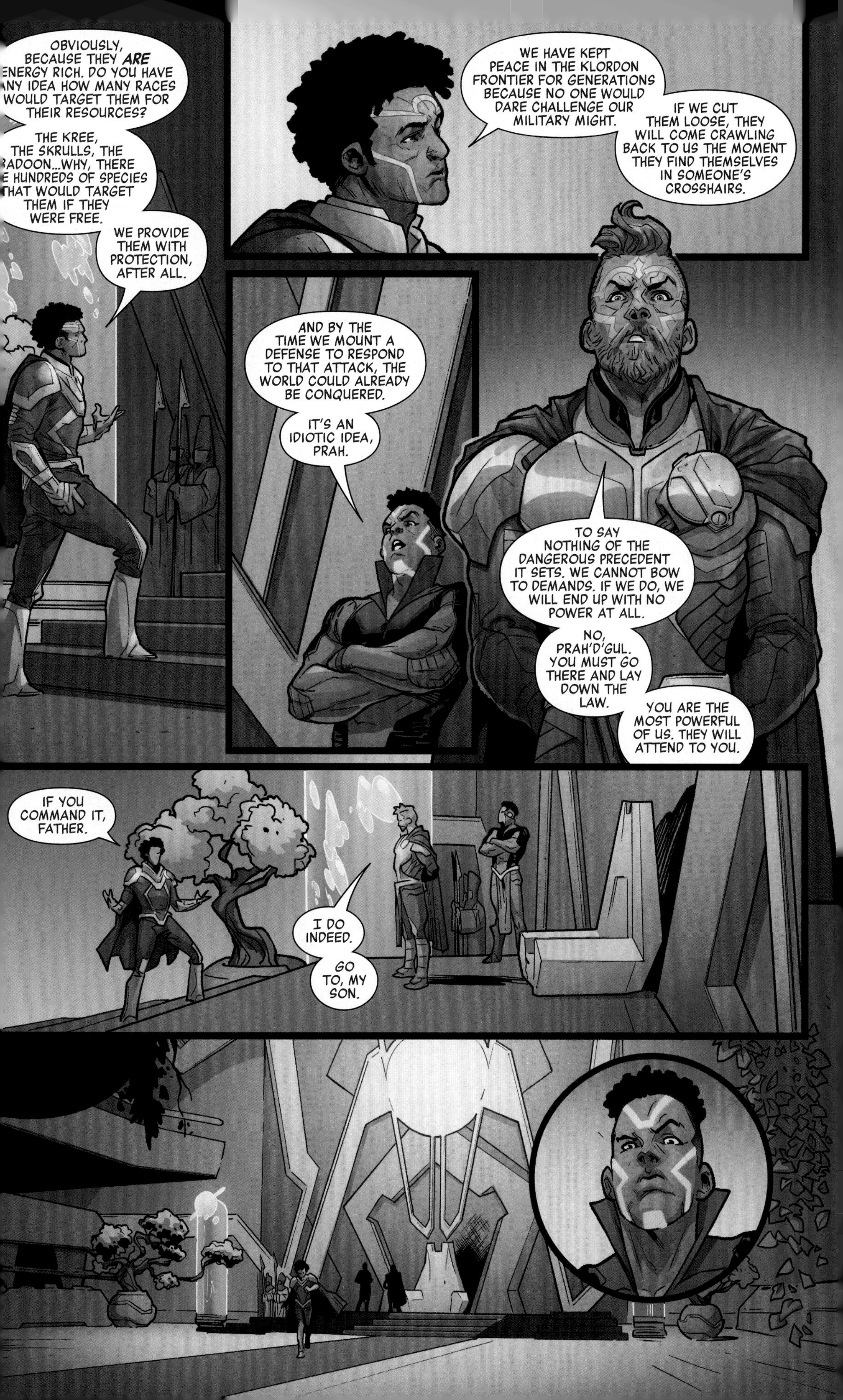
OBVIOUSLY, BECAUSE THEY ARE ENERGY RICH. DO YOU HAVE ANY IDEA HOW MANY RACES WOULD TARGET THEM FOR THEIR RESOURCES?
THE KREE, THE SKRULLS, THE BADOON...WHY, THERE ARE HUNDREDS OF SPECIES THAT WOULD TARGET THEM IF THEY WERE FREE.
WE PROVIDE THEM WITH PROTECTION, AFTER ALL.
WE HAVE KEPT PEACE IN THE KLORDON FRONTIER FOR GENERATIONS BECAUSE NO ONE WOULD DARE CHALLENGE OUR MILITARY MIGHT.
IF WE CUT THEM LOOSE, THEY WILL COME CRAWLING BACK TO US THE MOMENT THEY FIND THEMSELVES IN SOMEONE'S CROSSHAIRS.
AND BY THE TIME WE MOUNT A DEFENSE TO RESPOND TO THAT ATTACK, THE WORLD COULD ALREADY BE CONQUERED.
IT'S AN IDIOTIC IDEA, PRAH.
TO SAY NOTHING OF THE DANGEROUS PRECEDENT IT SETS. WE CANNOT BOW TO DEMANDS. IF WE DO, WE WILL END UP WITH NO POWER AT ALL.
NO, PRAH'D'GUL. YOU MUST GO THERE AND LAY DOWN THE LAW.
YOU ARE THE MOST POWERFUL OF US. THEY WILL ATTEND TO YOU.
IF YOU COMMAND IT, FATHER.
I DO INDEED.
GO TO, MY SON.

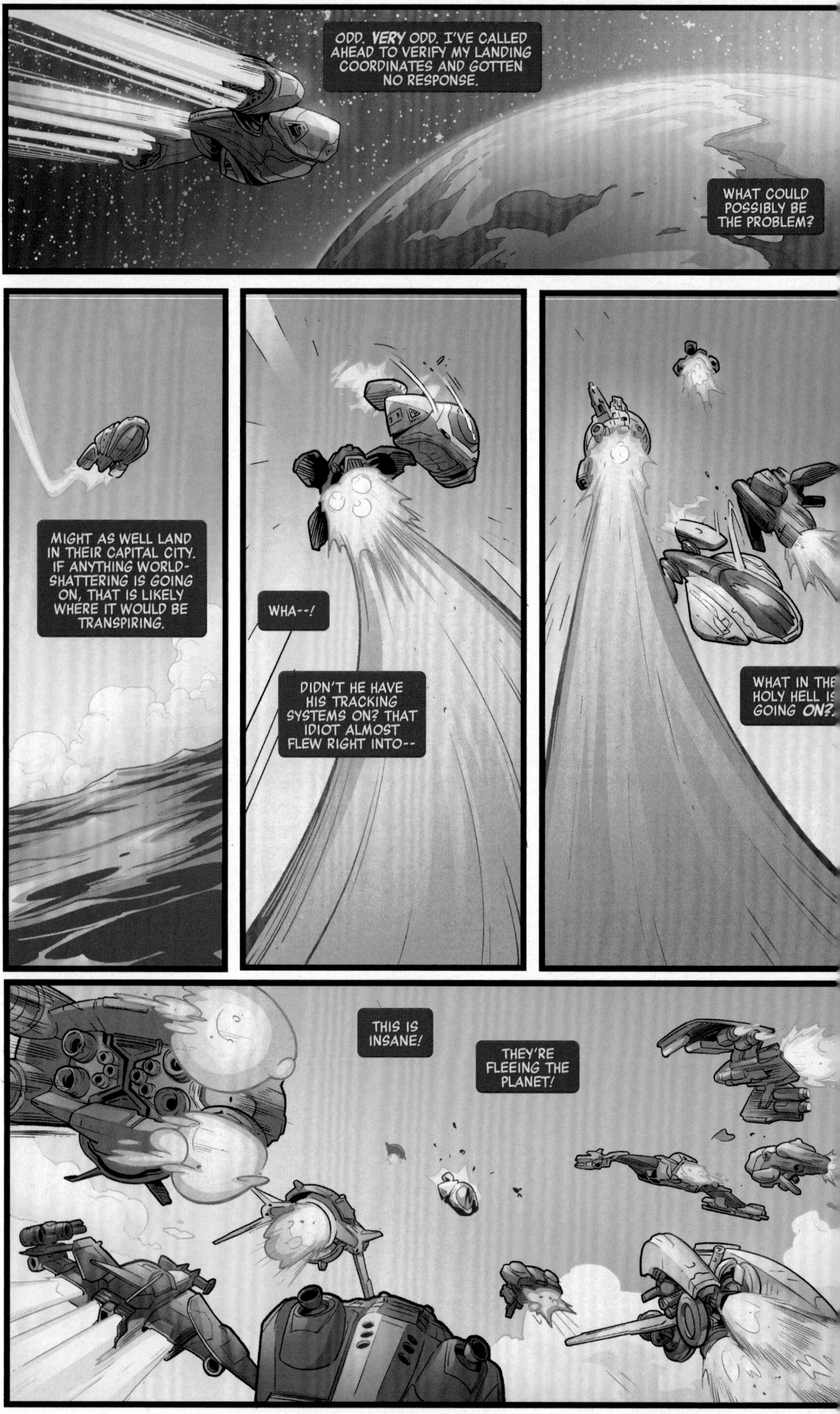
ODD. VERY ODD. I'VE CALLED AHEAD TO VERIFY MY LANDING COORDINATES AND GOTTEN NO RESPONSE.
WHAT COULD POSSIBLY BE THE PROBLEM?
MIGHT AS WELL LAND IN THEIR CAPITAL CITY. IF ANYTHING WORLD-SHATTERING IS GOING ON, THAT IS LIKELY WHERE IT WOULD BE TRANSPIRING.
WHA--!
DIDN'T HE HAVE HIS TRACKING SYSTEMS ON? THAT IDIOT ALMOST FLEW RIGHT INTO--
WHAT IN THE HOLY HELL IS GOING ON?!
THIS IS INSANE!
THEY'RE FLEEING THE PLANET!

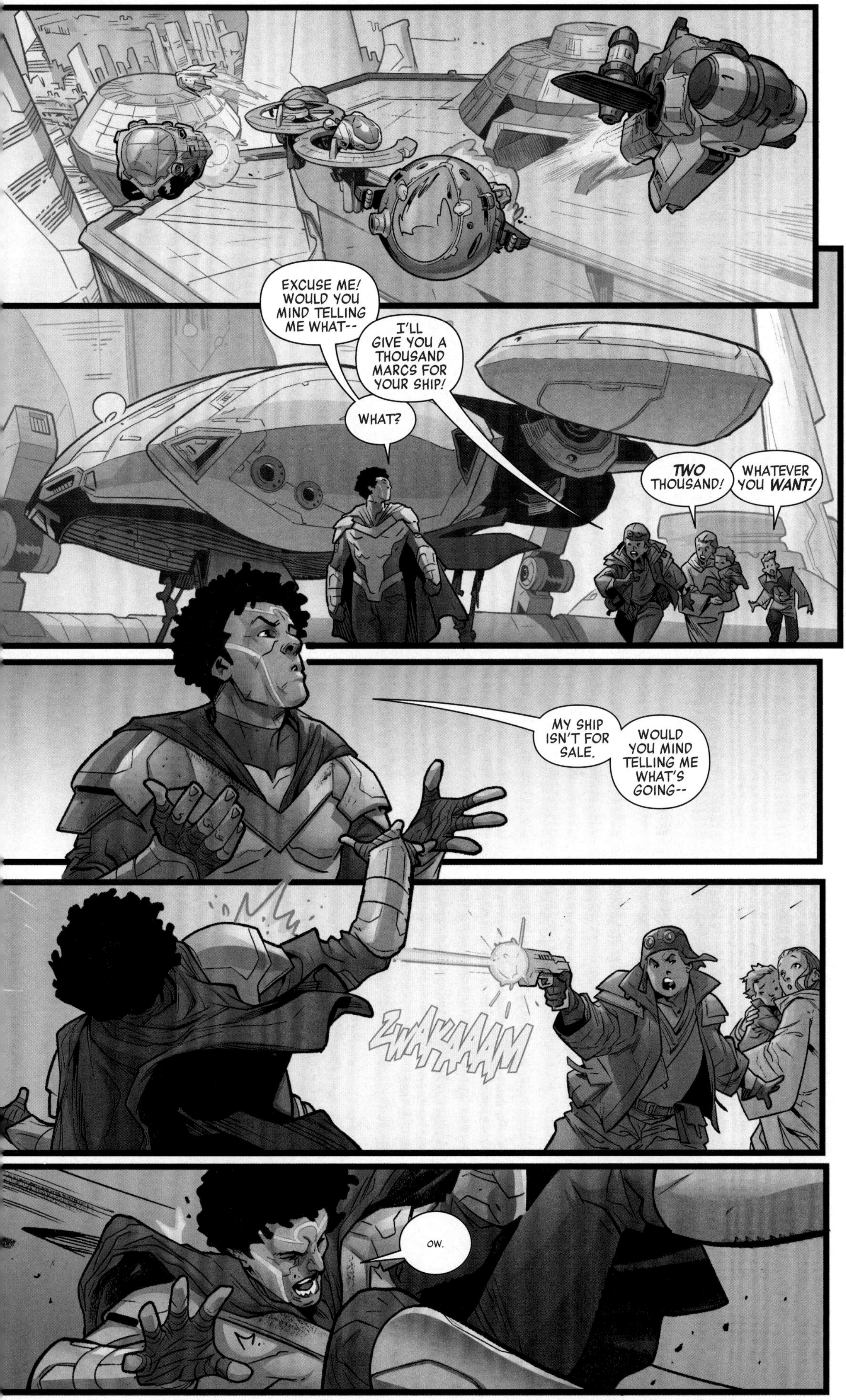
EXCUSE ME! WOULD YOU MIND TELLING ME WHAT--
I'LL GIVE YOU A THOUSAND MARCS FOR YOUR SHIP!
WHAT?
TWO THOUSAND!
WHATEVER YOU WANT!
MY SHIP ISN'T FOR SALE.
WOULD YOU MIND TELLING ME WHAT'S GOING--
ZWAKAAAM
OW.

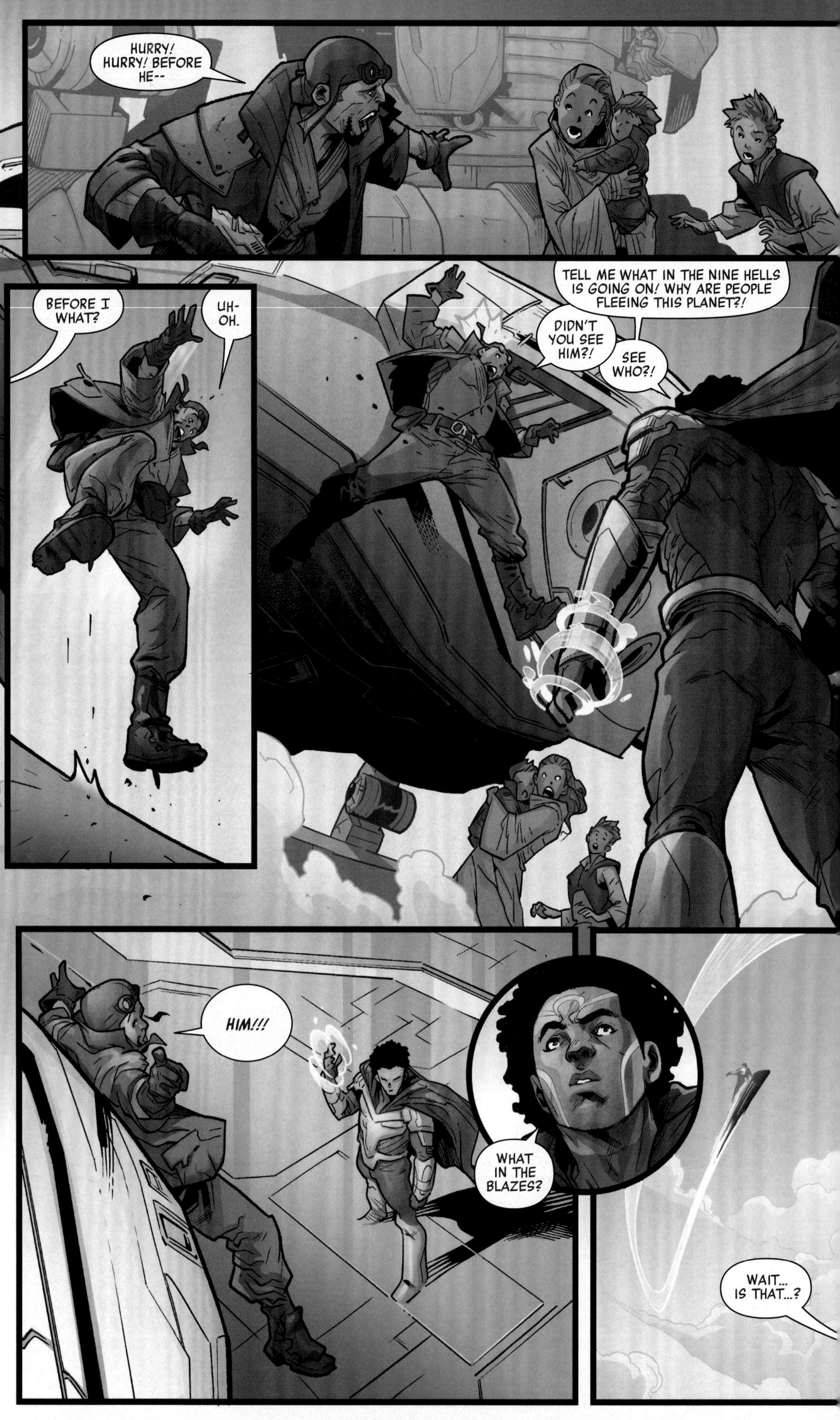
HURRY! HURRY! BEFORE HE--
BEFORE I WHAT?
UH-OH.
TELL ME WHAT IN THE NINE HELLS IS GOING ON! WHY ARE PEOPLE FLEEING THIS PLANET?!
DIDN'T YOU SEE HIM?!
SEE WHO?!
HIM!!!
WHAT IN THE BLAZES?
WAIT... IS THAT...?

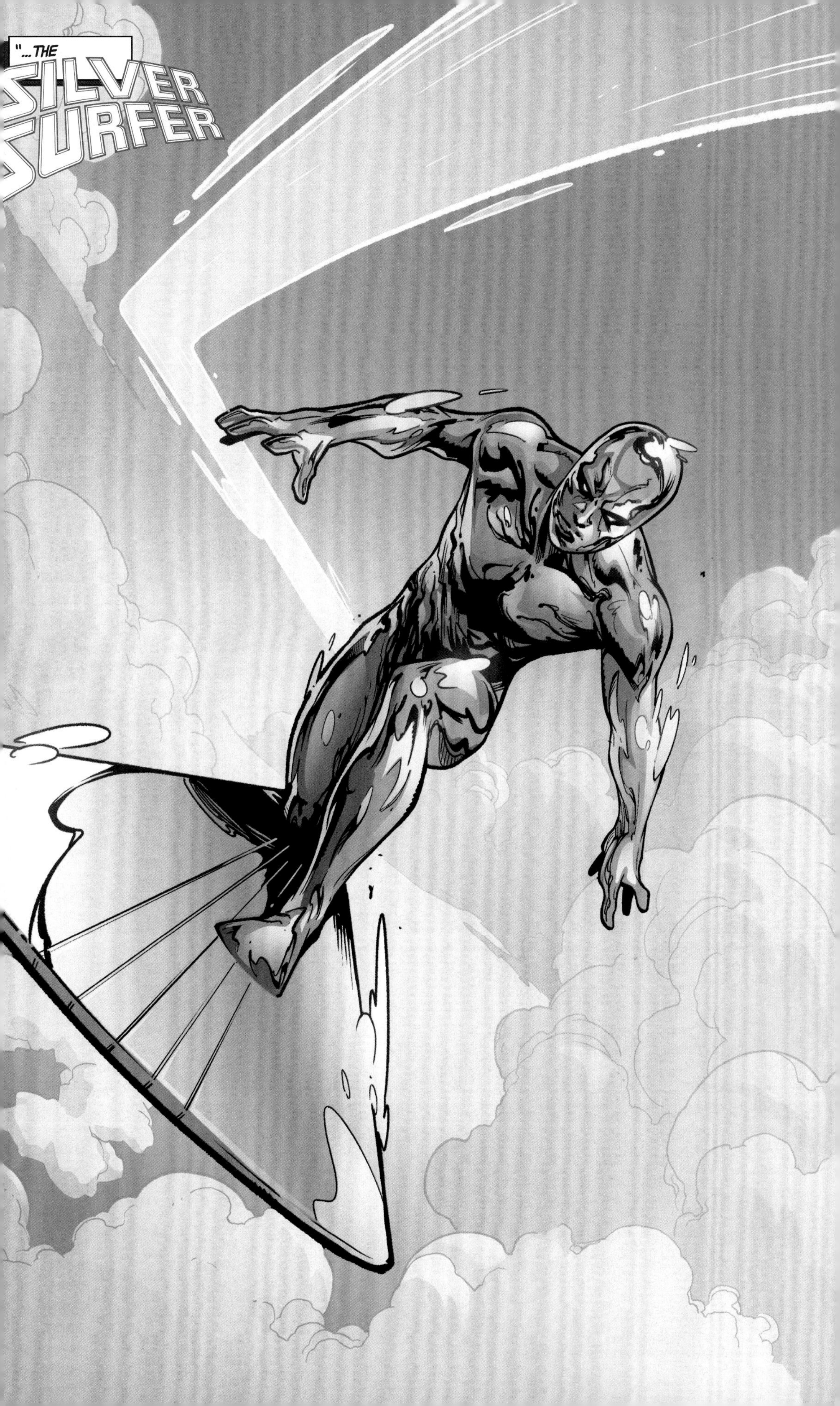
"...THE
SILVER SURFER

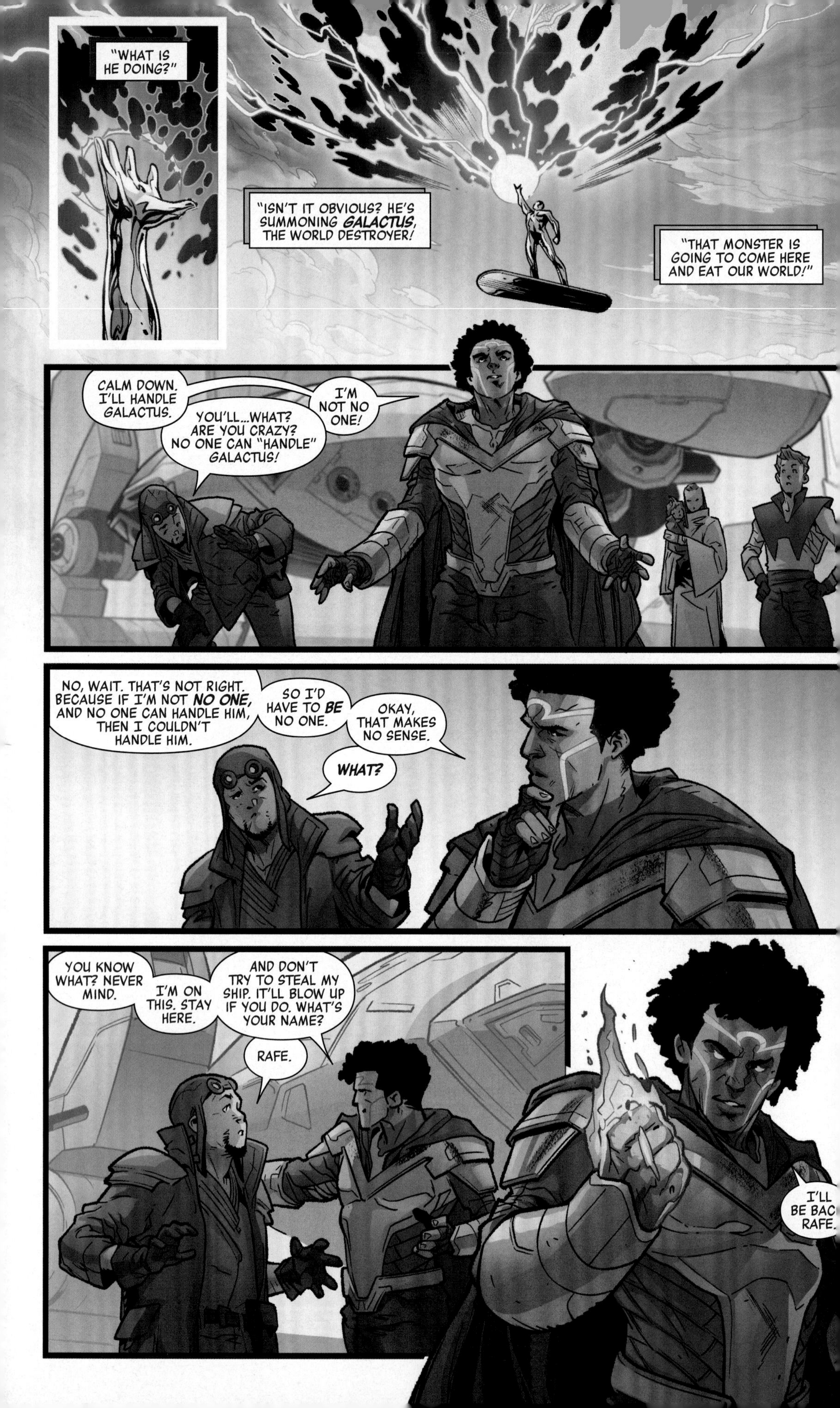
"WHAT IS HE DOING?"
"ISN'T IT OBVIOUS? HE'S SUMMONING GALACTUS, THE WORLD DESTROYER!
"THAT MONSTER IS GOING TO COME HERE AND EAT OUR WORLD!"
CALM DOWN. I'LL HANDLE GALACTUS.
YOU'LL...WHAT? ARE YOU CRAZY? NO ONE CAN "HANDLE" GALACTUS!
I'M NOT NO ONE!
NO, WAIT. THAT'S NOT RIGHT. BECAUSE IF I'M NOT NO ONE, AND NO ONE CAN HANDLE HIM, THEN I COULDN'T HANDLE HIM.
SO I'D HAVE TO BE NO ONE.
OKAY, THAT MAKES NO SENSE.
WHAT?
YOU KNOW WHAT? NEVER MIND.
I'M ON THIS. STAY HERE.
AND DON'T TRY TO STEAL MY SHIP. IT'LL BLOW UP IF YOU DO. WHAT'S YOUR NAME?
RAFE.
I'LL BE BAC RAFE.

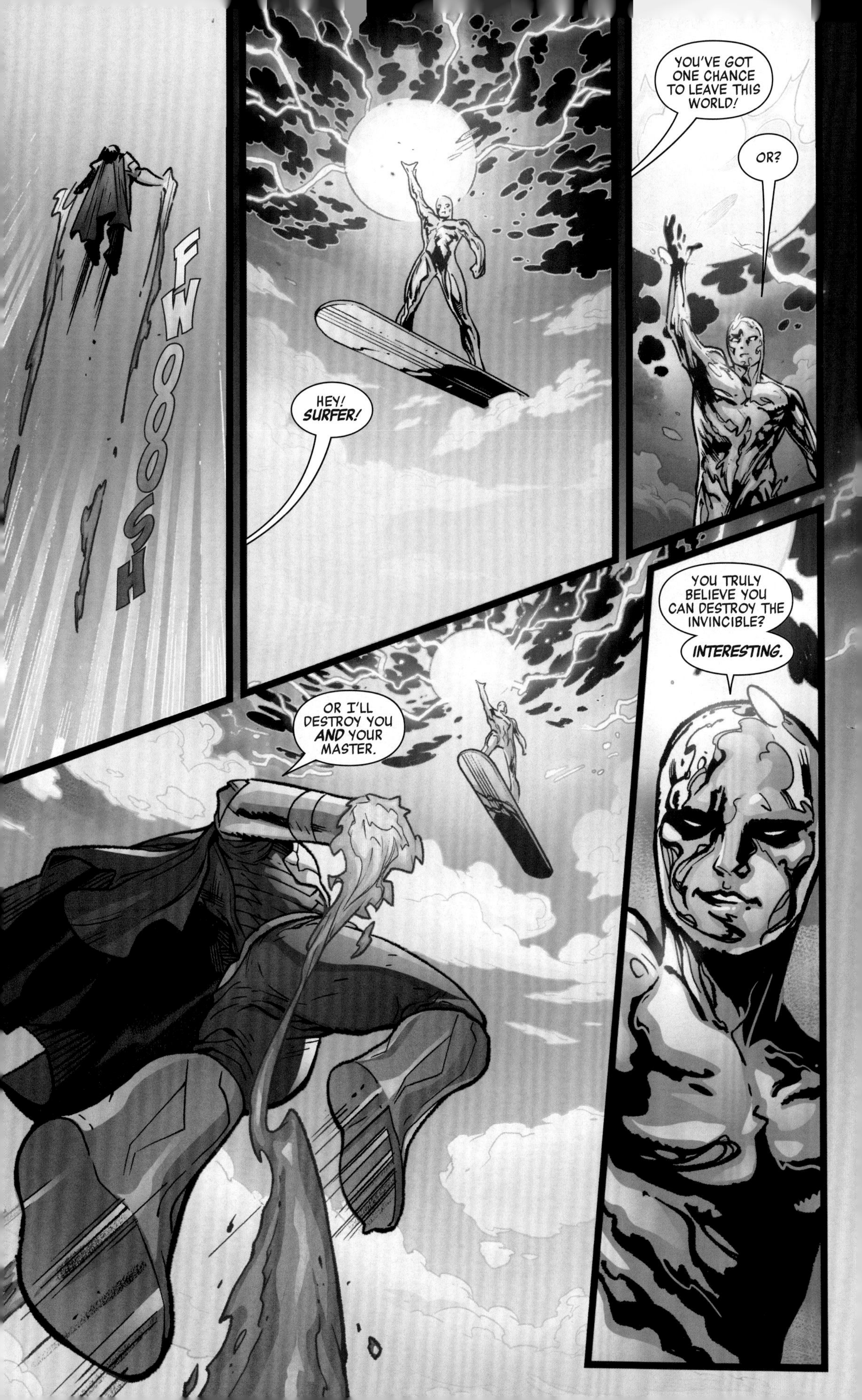
FWOOOSH
HEY! SURFER!
YOU'VE GOT ONE CHANCE TO LEAVE THIS WORLD!
OR?
OR I'LL DESTROY YOU AND YOUR MASTER.
YOU TRULY BELIEVE YOU CAN DESTROY THE INVINCIBLE?
INTERESTING.

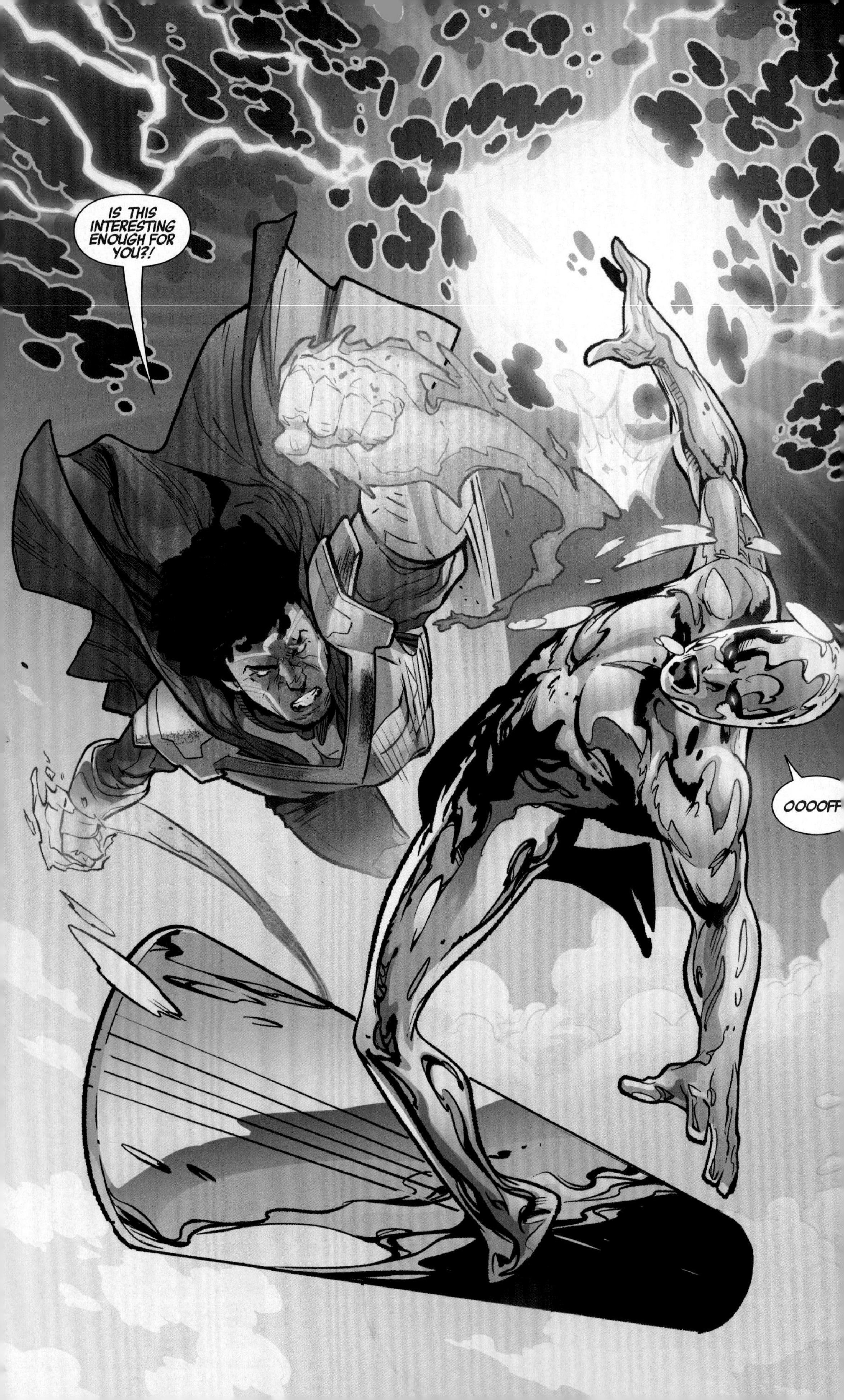
IS THIS INTERESTING ENOUGH FOR YOU?!
OOOOFF

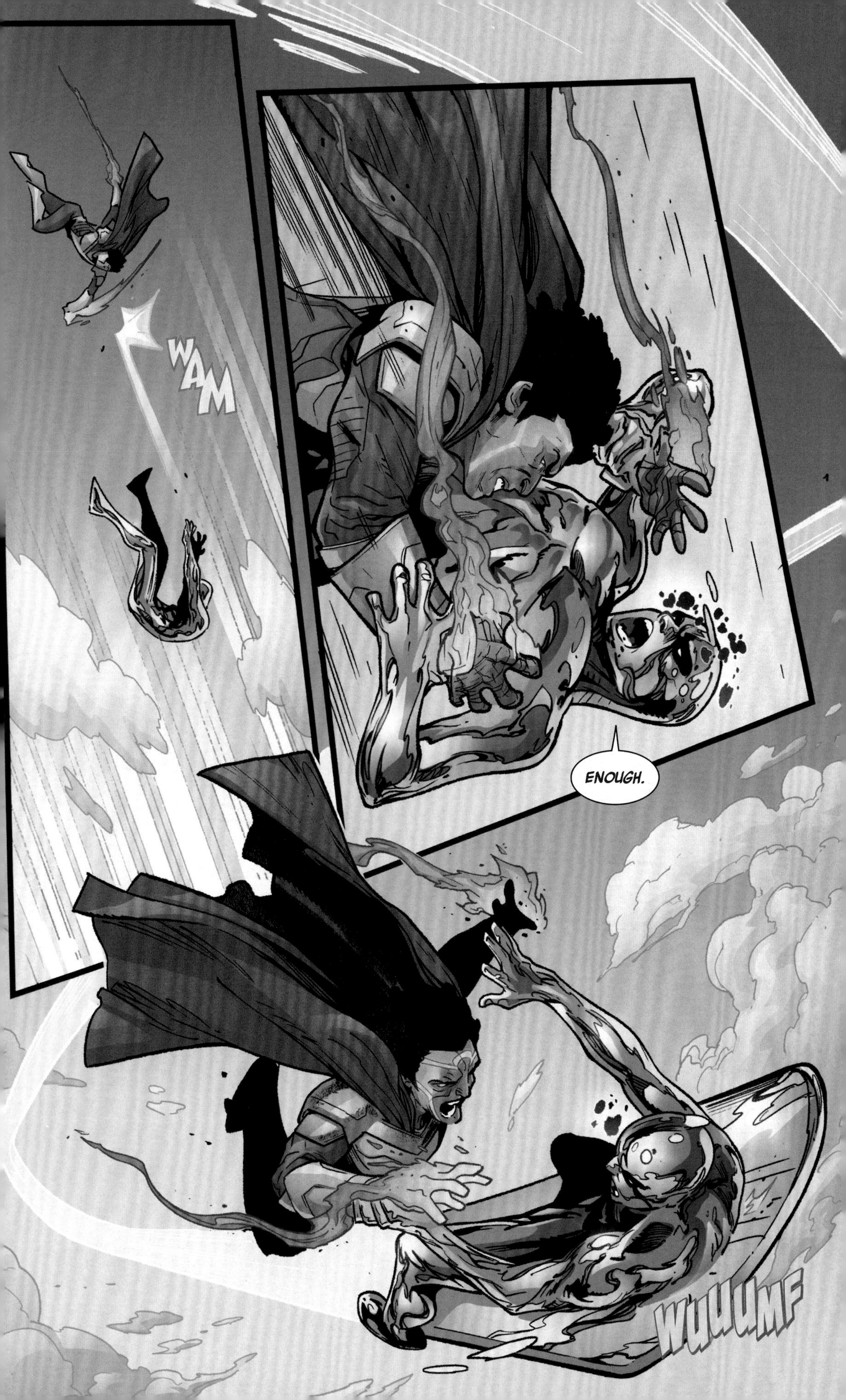
WAM
ENOUGH.
WUUUMF

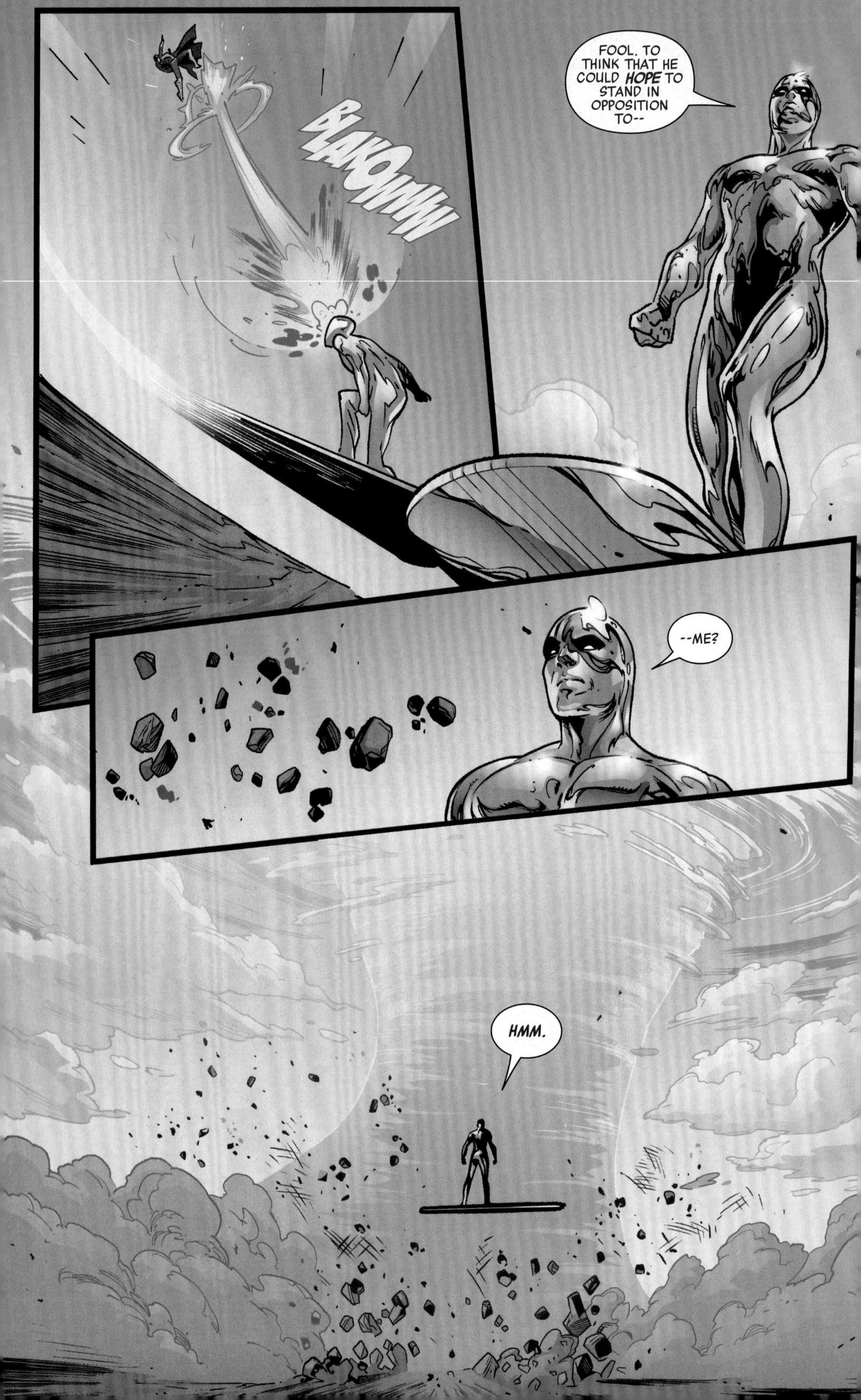
BLAKOWWW
FOOL. TO THINK THAT HE COULD HOPE TO STAND IN OPPOSITION TO--
--ME?
HMM.

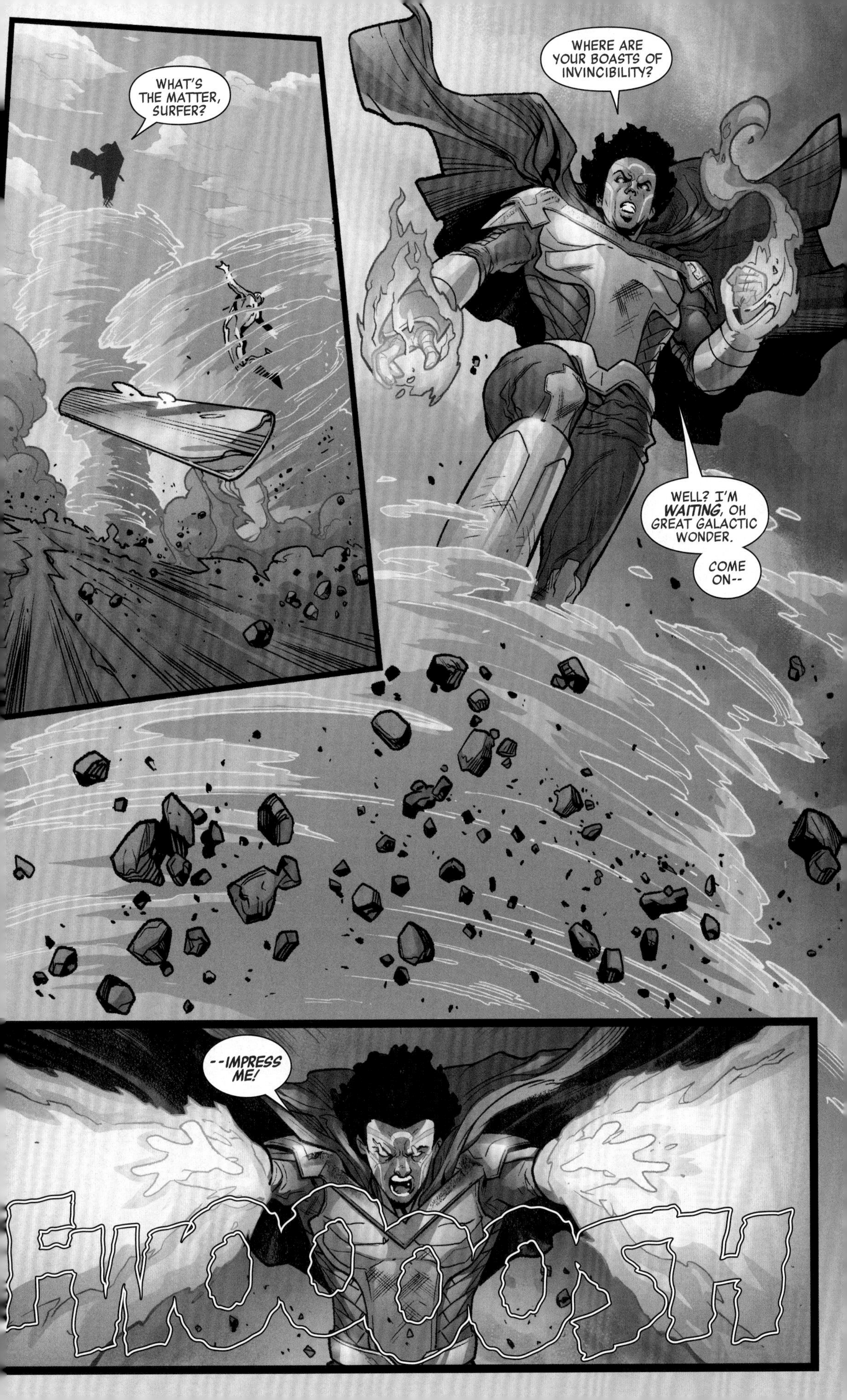
WHAT'S THE MATTER, SURFER?
WHERE ARE YOUR BOASTS OF INVINCIBILITY?
WELL? I'M *WAITING*, OH GREAT GALACTIC WONDER.
COME ON--
--IMPRESS ME!
FWOOOOOSH

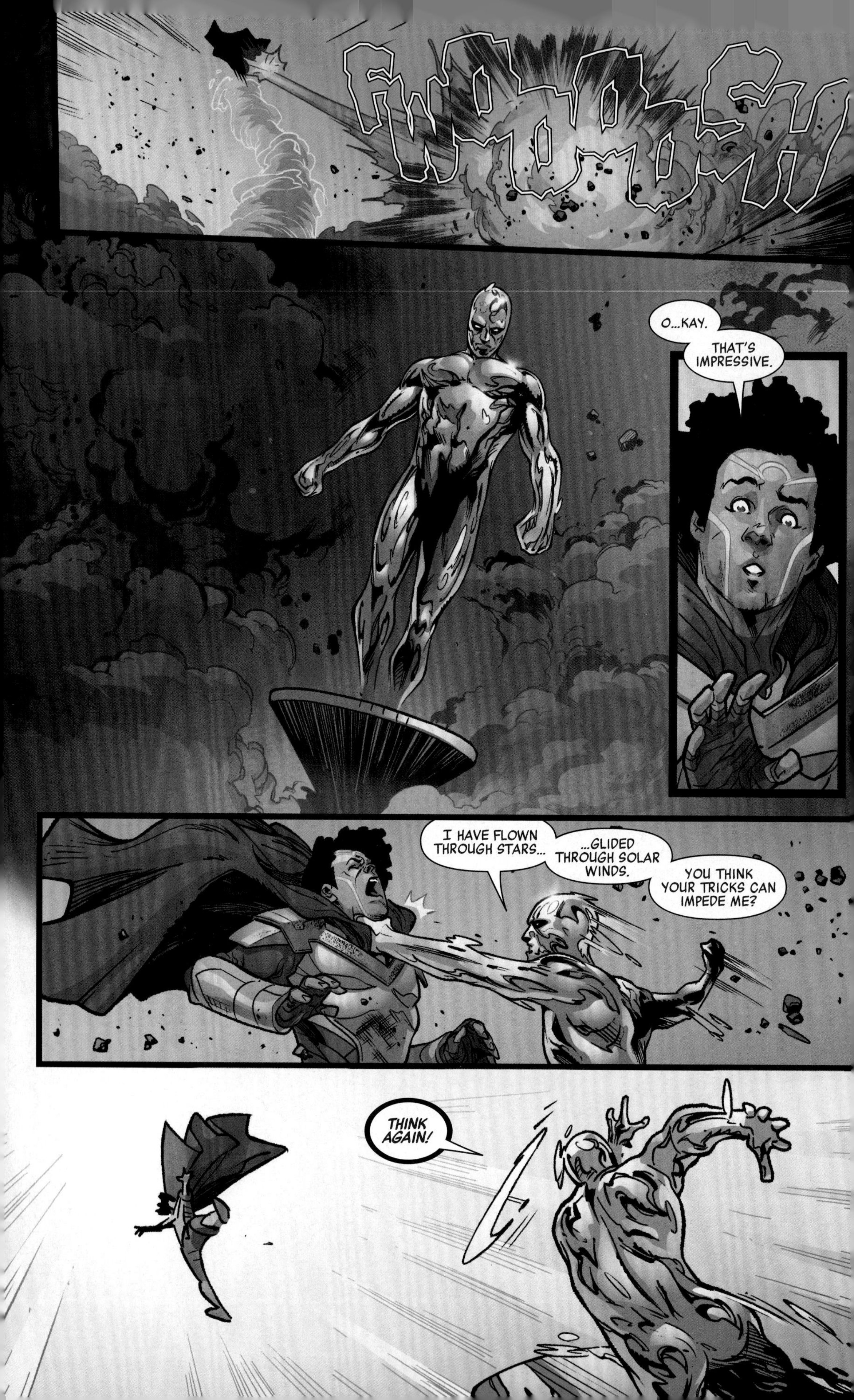

FWOOOOOSH
O...KAY.
THAT'S IMPRESSIVE.
I HAVE FLOWN THROUGH STARS...
...GLIDED THROUGH SOLAR WINDS.
YOU THINK YOUR TRICKS CAN IMPEDE ME?
THINK AGAIN!

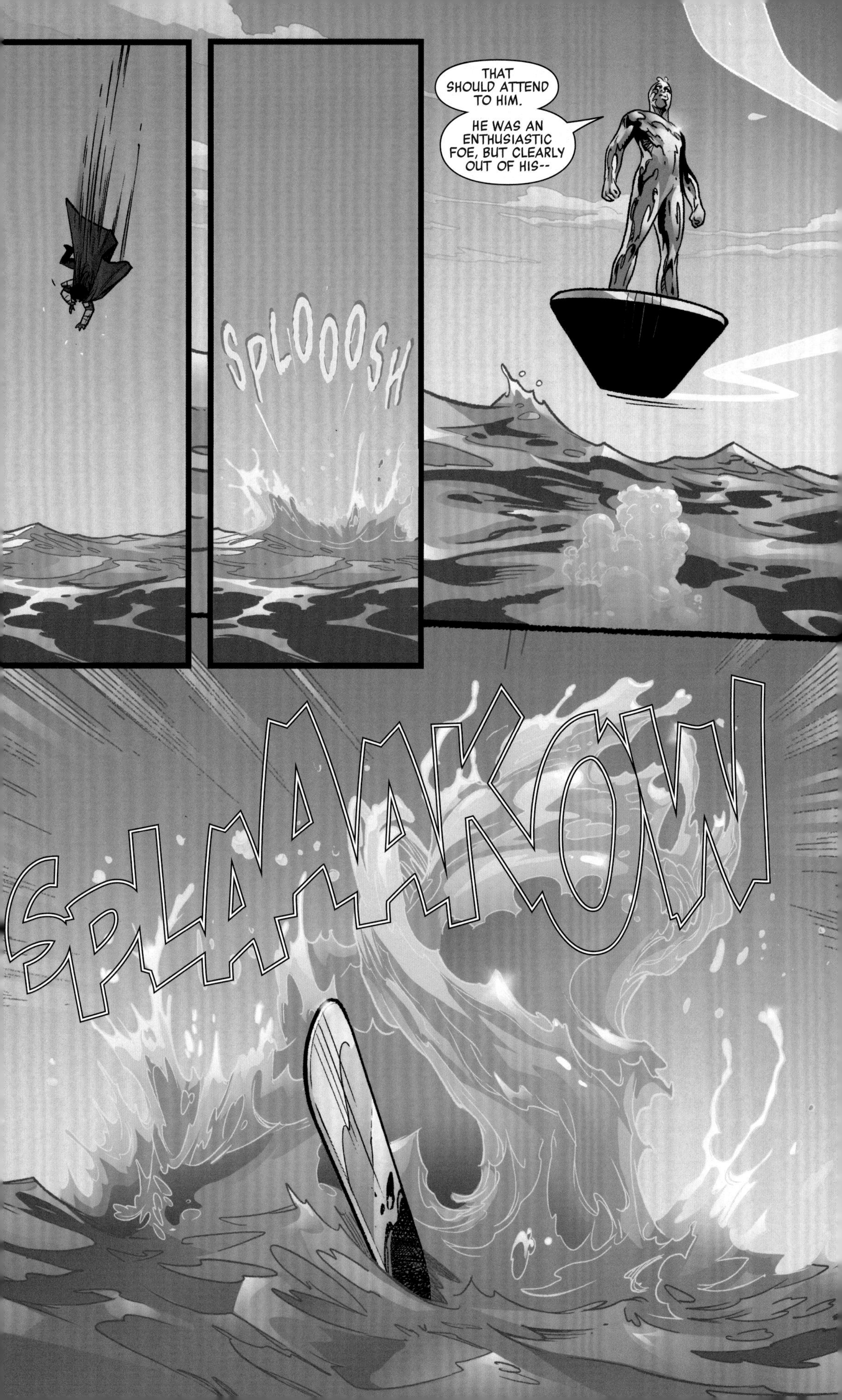
SPLOOOSH
THAT SHOULD ATTEND TO HIM.
HE WAS AN ENTHUSIASTIC FOE, BUT CLEARLY OUT OF HIS--
SPLAAKOW

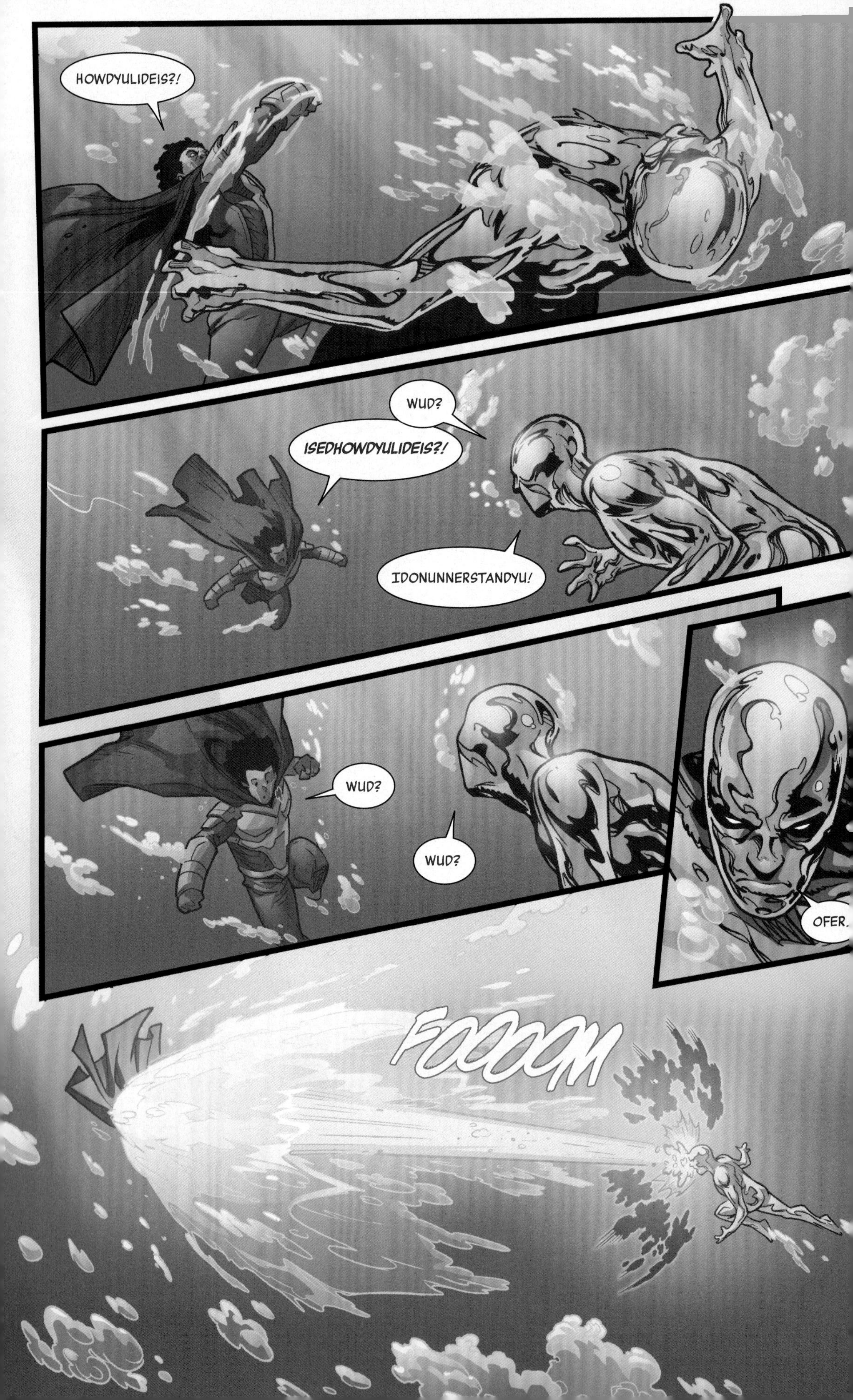
HOWDYULIDEIS?!
WUD?
ISEDHOWDYULIDEIS?!
IDONUNNERSTANDYU!
WUD?
WUD?
OFER.
FOOOOM

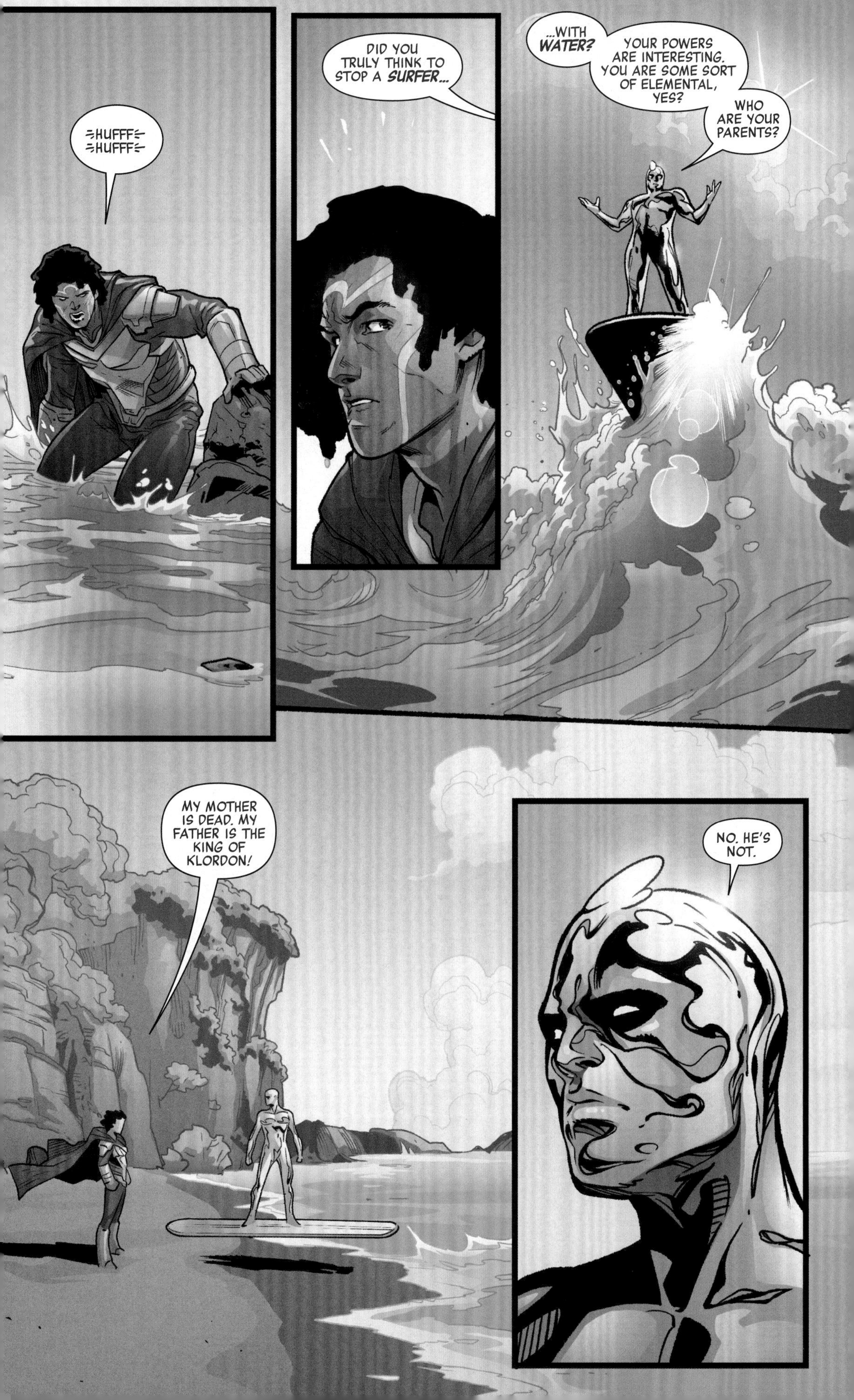

≡HUFFF≡ ≡HUFFF≡
DID YOU TRULY THINK TO STOP A SURFER...
...WITH WATER?
YOUR POWERS ARE INTERESTING. YOU ARE SOME SORT OF ELEMENTAL, YES?
WHO ARE YOUR PARENTS?
MY MOTHER IS DEAD. MY FATHER IS THE KING OF KLORDON!
NO. HE'S NOT.

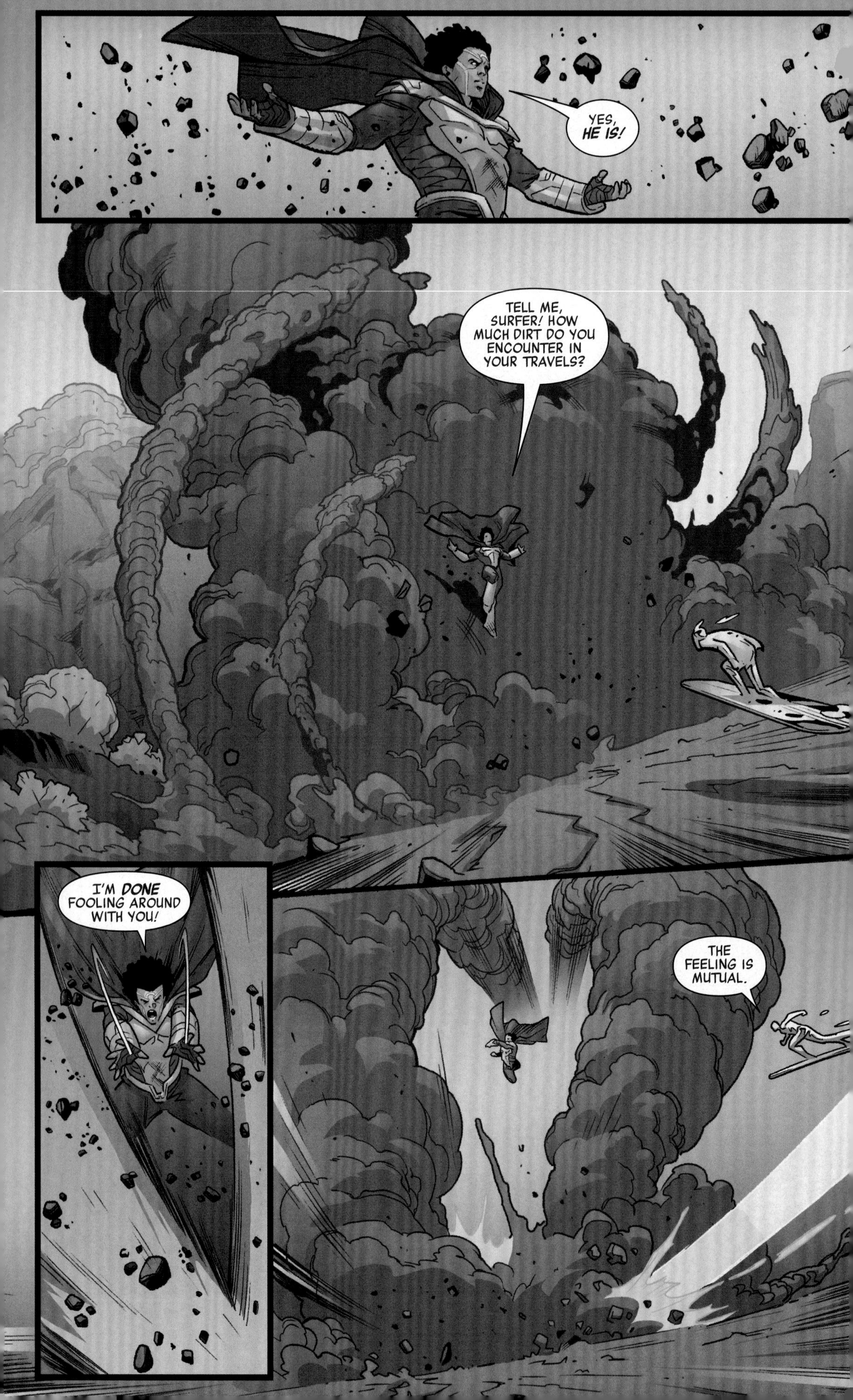
YES, HE IS!
TELL ME, SURFER! HOW MUCH DIRT DO YOU ENCOUNTER IN YOUR TRAVELS?
I'M DONE FOOLING AROUND WITH YOU!
THE FEELING IS MUTUAL.

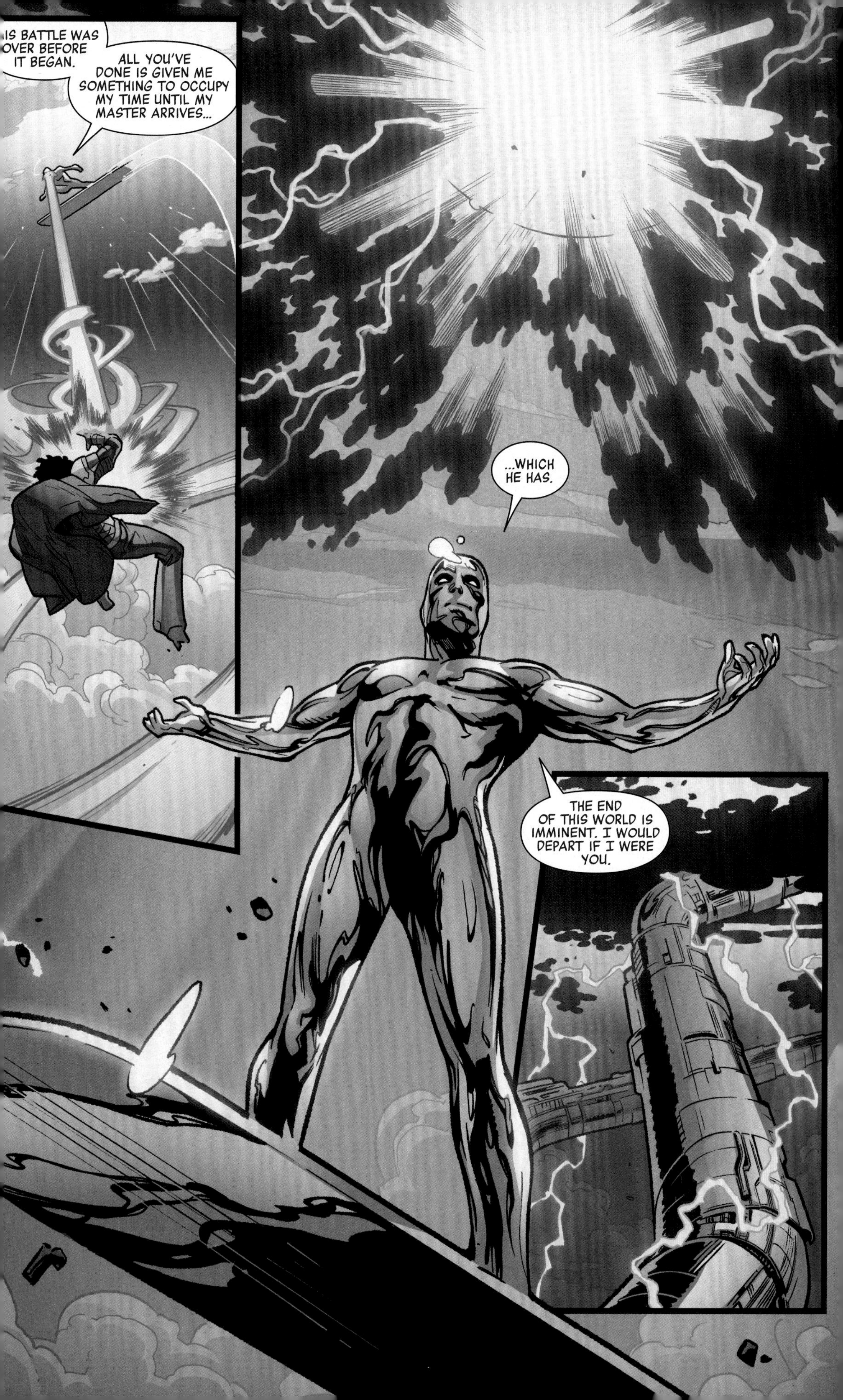
IS BATTLE WAS OVER BEFORE IT BEGAN.
ALL YOU'VE DONE IS GIVEN ME SOMETHING TO OCCUPY MY TIME UNTIL MY MASTER ARRIVES...
...WHICH HE HAS.
THE END OF THIS WORLD IS IMMINENT. I WOULD DEPART IF I WERE YOU.

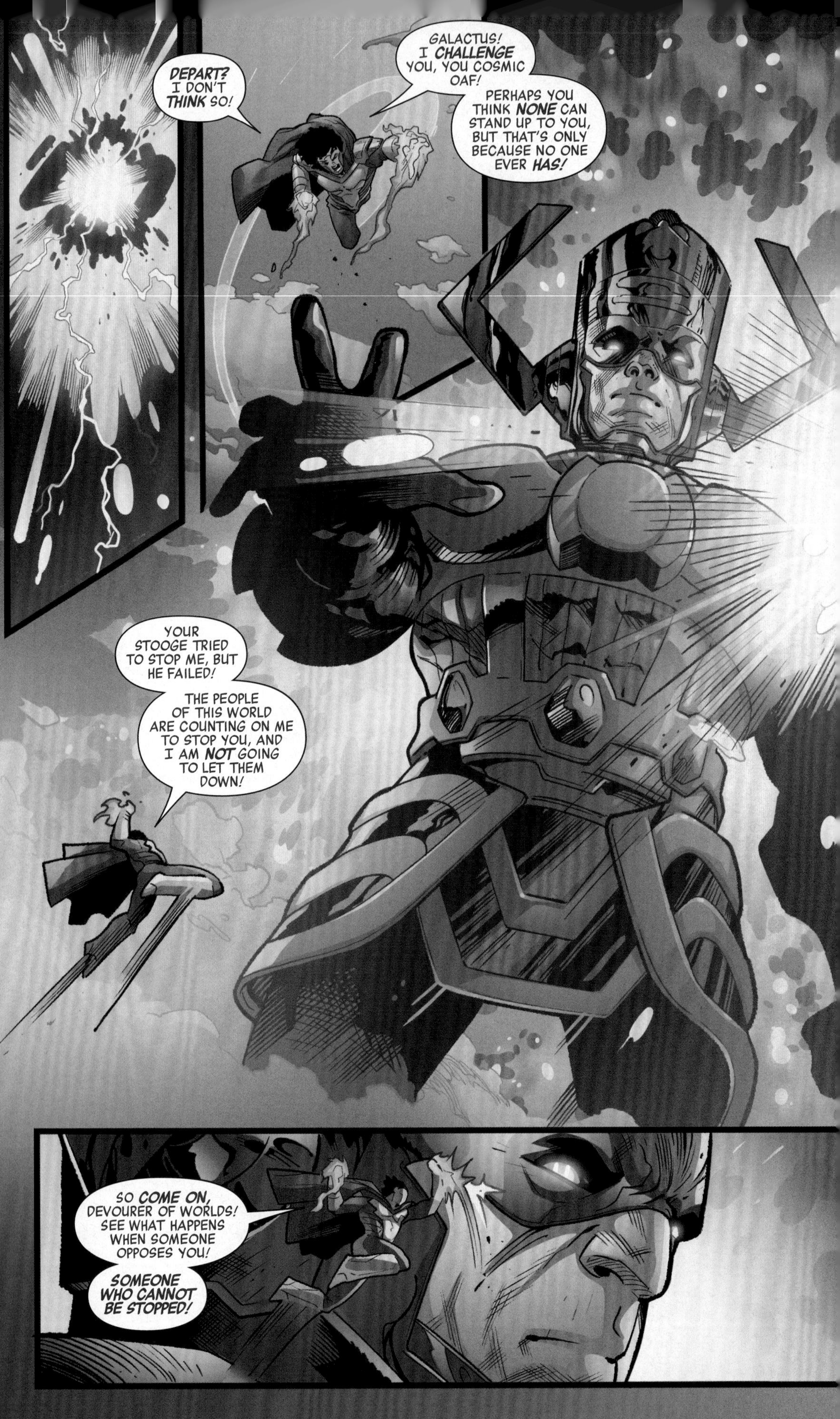
DEPART? I DON'T THINK SO!
GALACTUS! I CHALLENGE YOU, YOU COSMIC OAF!
PERHAPS YOU THINK NONE CAN STAND UP TO YOU, BUT THAT'S ONLY BECAUSE NO ONE EVER HAS!
YOUR STOOGE TRIED TO STOP ME, BUT HE FAILED!
THE PEOPLE OF THIS WORLD ARE COUNTING ON ME TO STOP YOU, AND I AM NOT GOING TO LET THEM DOWN!
SO COME ON, DEVOURER OF WORLDS! SEE WHAT HAPPENS WHEN SOMEONE OPPOSES YOU!
SOMEONE WHO CANNOT BE STOPPED!

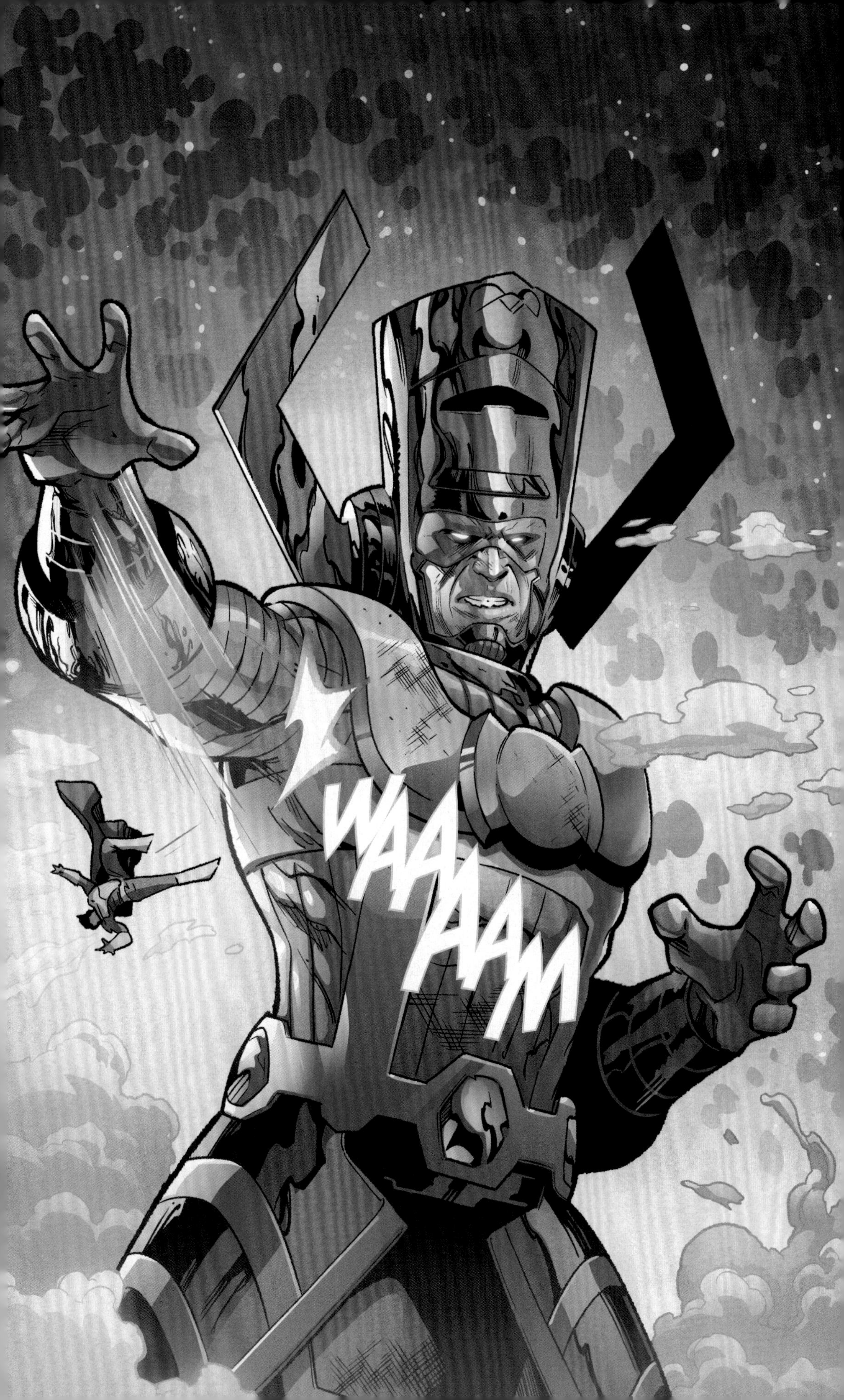
WAAAAAM

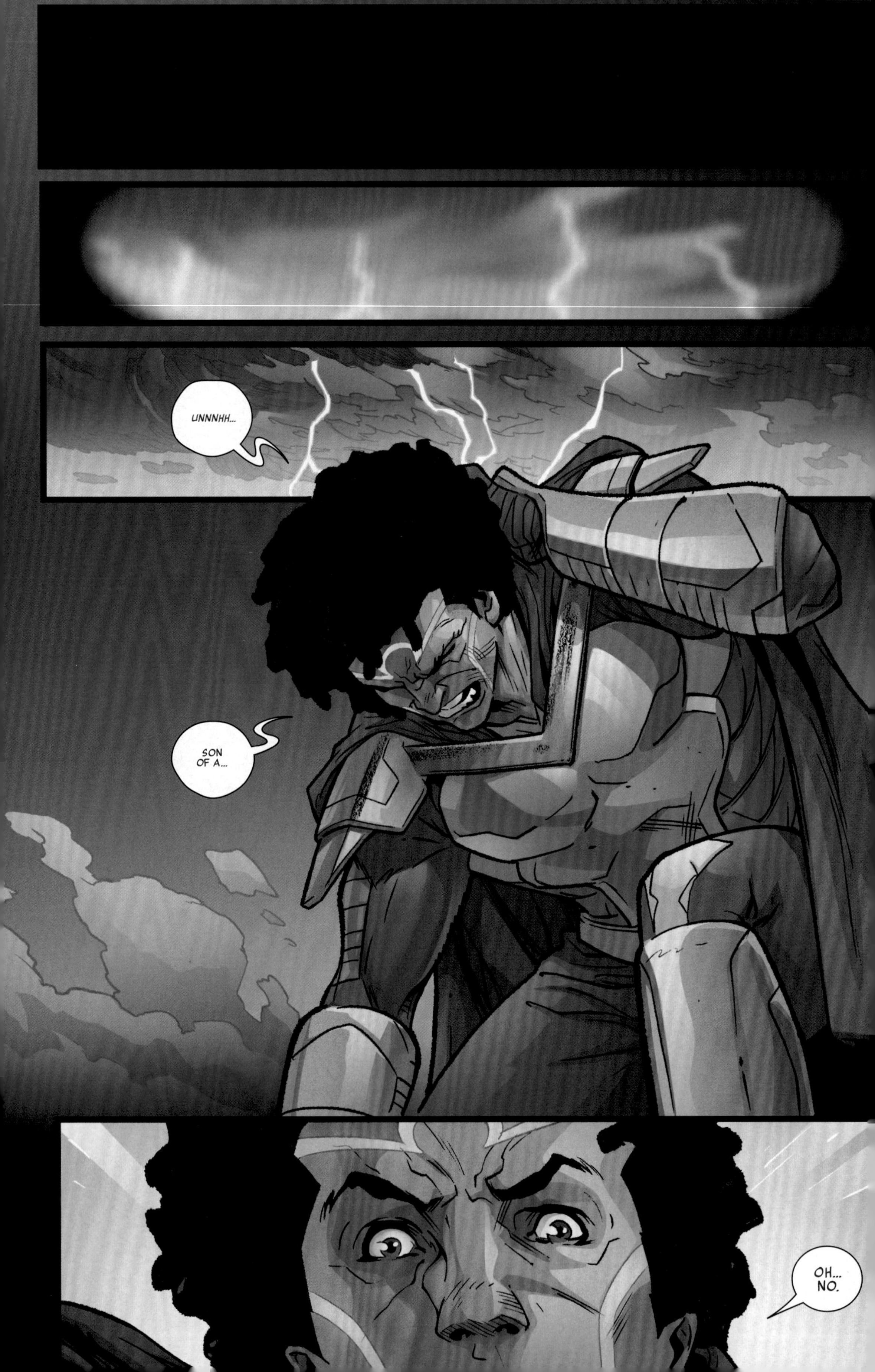
UNNNHH...
SON OF A...
OH... NO.

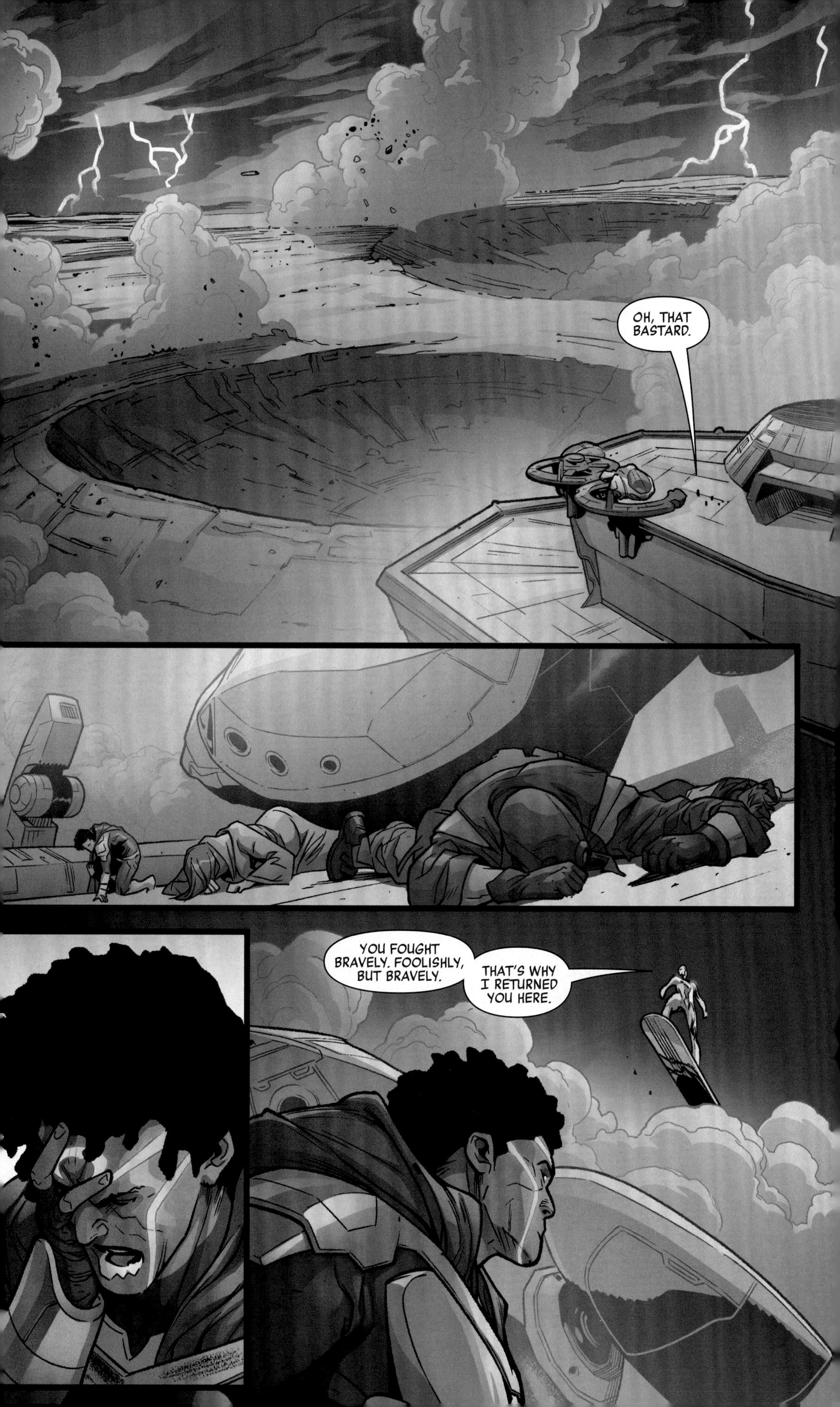
OH, THAT BASTARD.
YOU FOUGHT BRAVELY. FOOLISHLY, BUT BRAVELY.
THAT'S WHY I RETURNED YOU HERE.

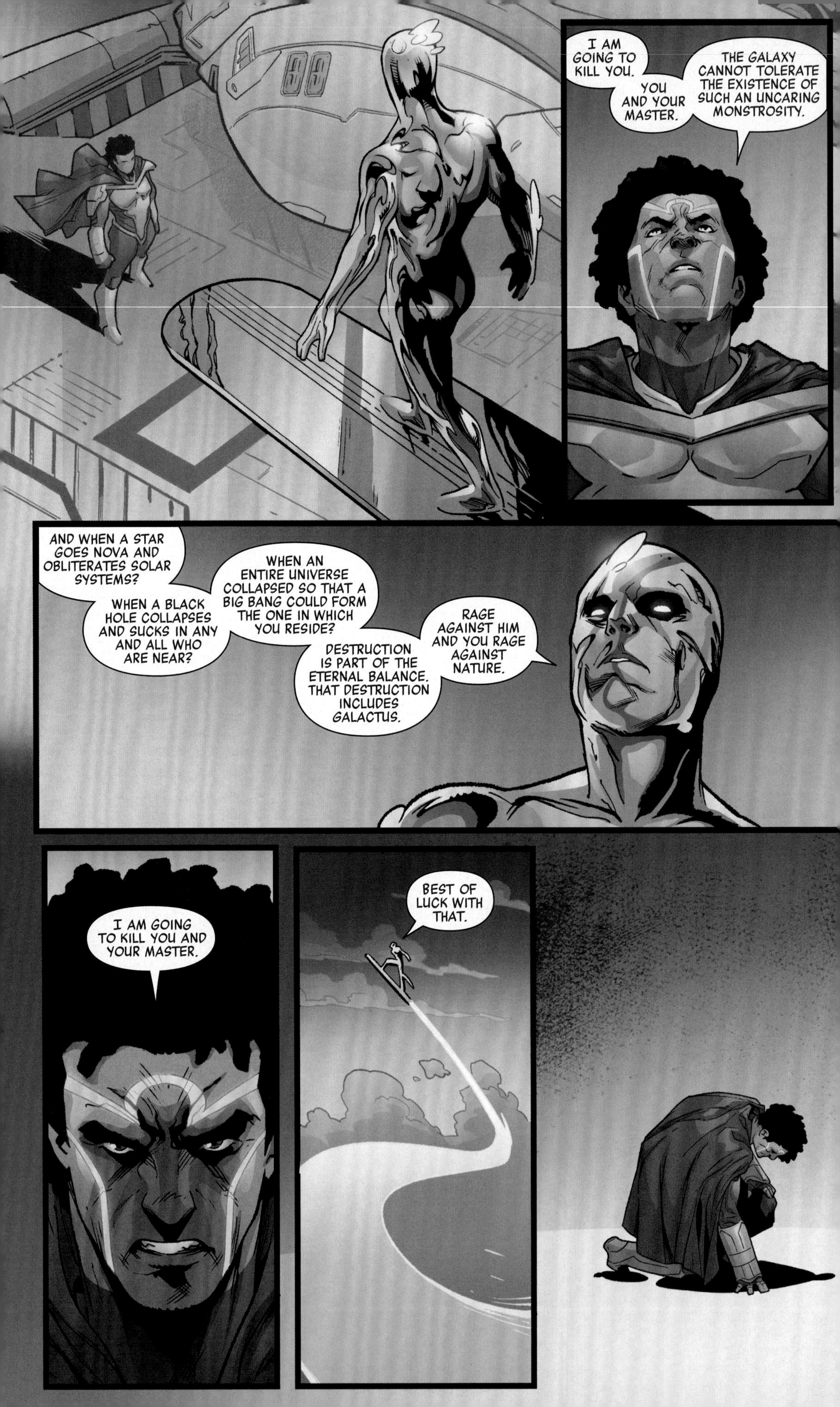
I AM GOING TO KILL YOU.
YOU AND YOUR MASTER.
THE GALAXY CANNOT TOLERATE THE EXISTENCE OF SUCH AN UNCARING MONSTROSITY.
AND WHEN A STAR GOES NOVA AND OBLITERATES SOLAR SYSTEMS?
WHEN A BLACK HOLE COLLAPSES AND SUCKS IN ANY AND ALL WHO ARE NEAR?
WHEN AN ENTIRE UNIVERSE COLLAPSED SO THAT A BIG BANG COULD FORM THE ONE IN WHICH YOU RESIDE?
DESTRUCTION IS PART OF THE ETERNAL BALANCE. THAT DESTRUCTION INCLUDES GALACTUS.
RAGE AGAINST HIM AND YOU RAGE AGAINST NATURE.
I AM GOING TO KILL YOU AND YOUR MASTER.
BEST OF LUCK WITH THAT.

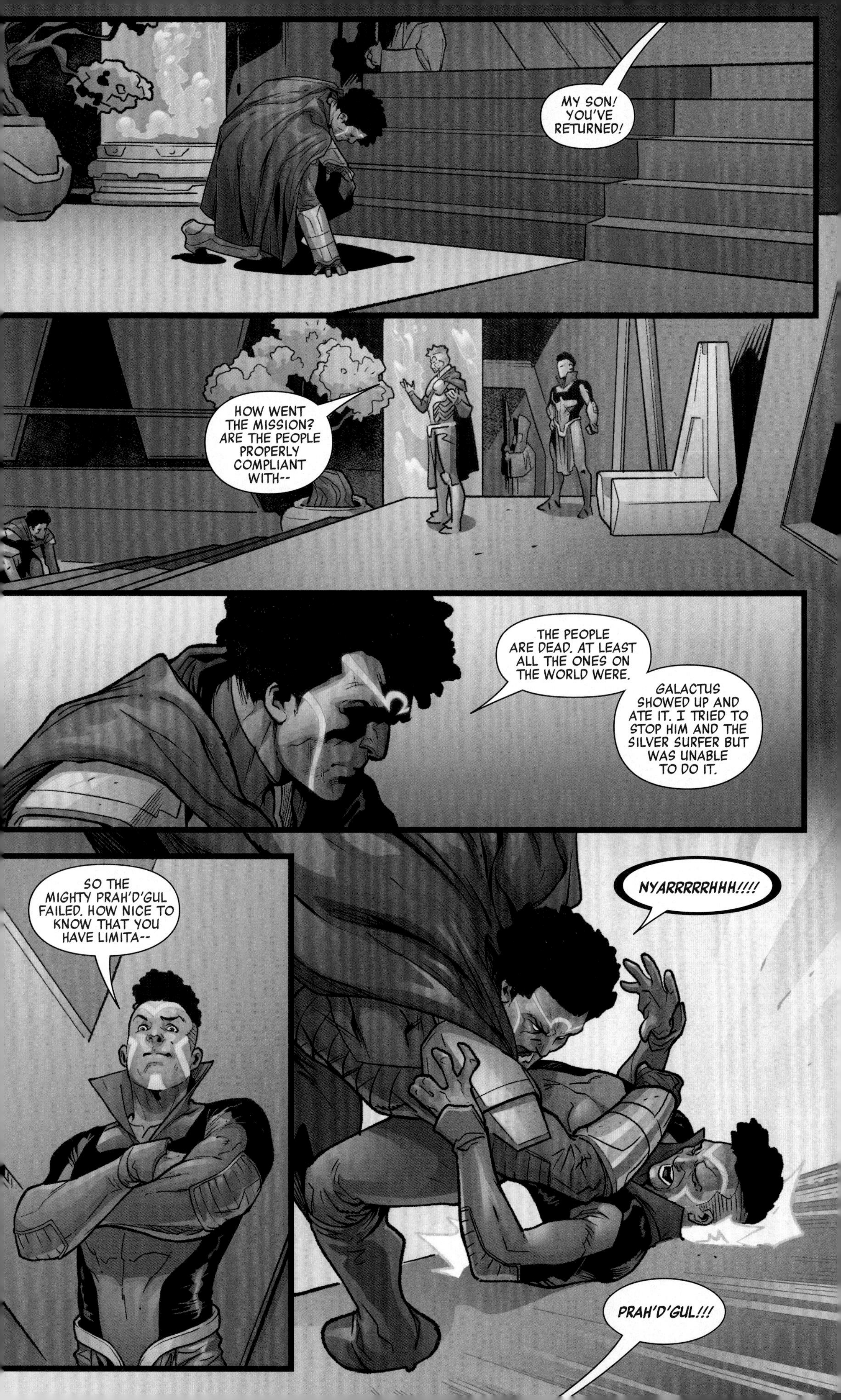
MY SON! YOU'VE RETURNED!
HOW WENT THE MISSION? ARE THE PEOPLE PROPERLY COMPLIANT WITH--
THE PEOPLE ARE DEAD. AT LEAST ALL THE ONES ON THE WORLD WERE.
GALACTUS SHOWED UP AND ATE IT. I TRIED TO STOP HIM AND THE SILVER SURFER BUT WAS UNABLE TO DO IT.
SO THE MIGHTY PRAH'D'GUL FAILED. HOW NICE TO KNOW THAT YOU HAVE LIMITA--
NYARRRRRHHH!!!!
PRAH'D'GUL!!!

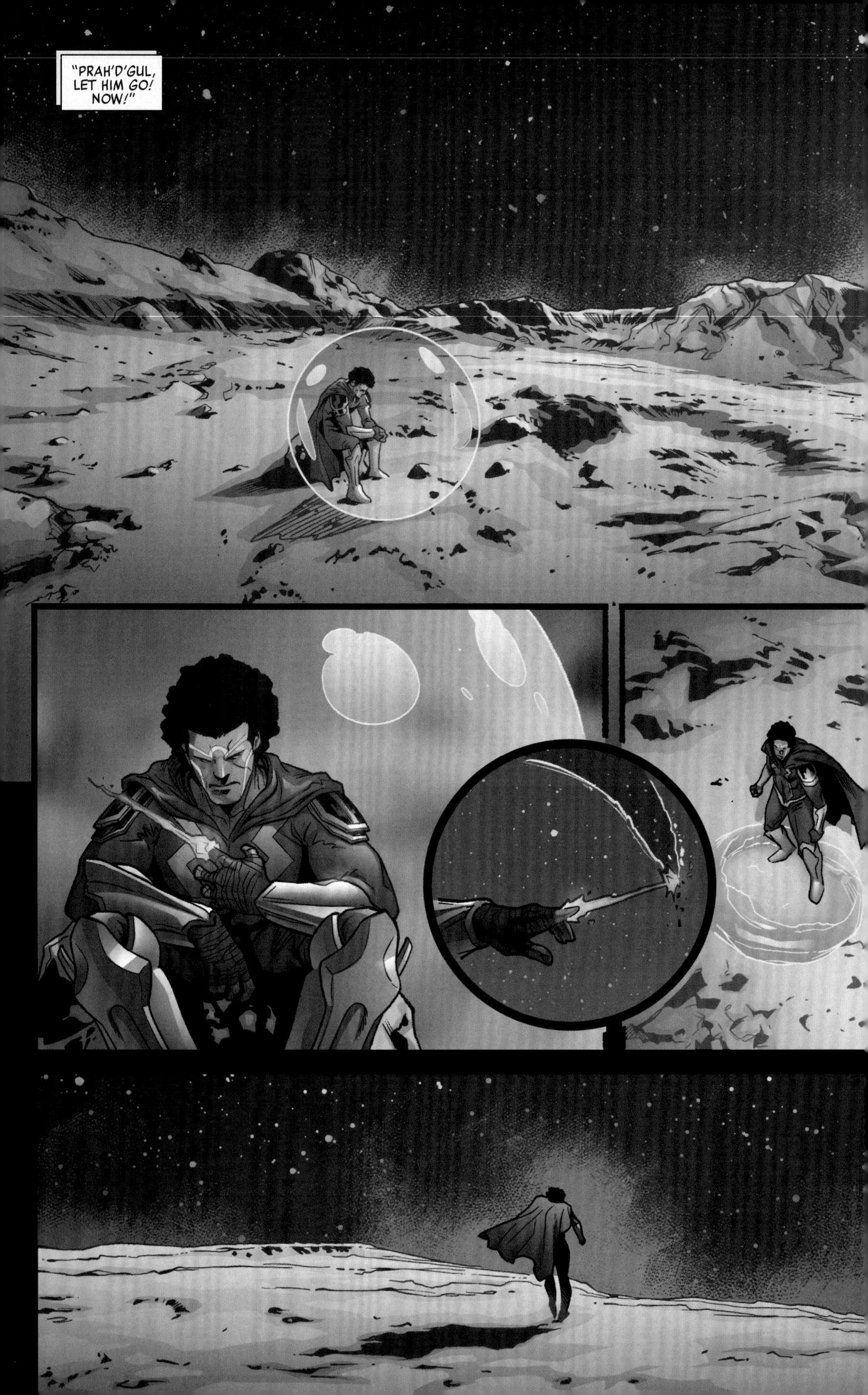
"PRAH'D'GUL, LET HIM GO! NOW!"

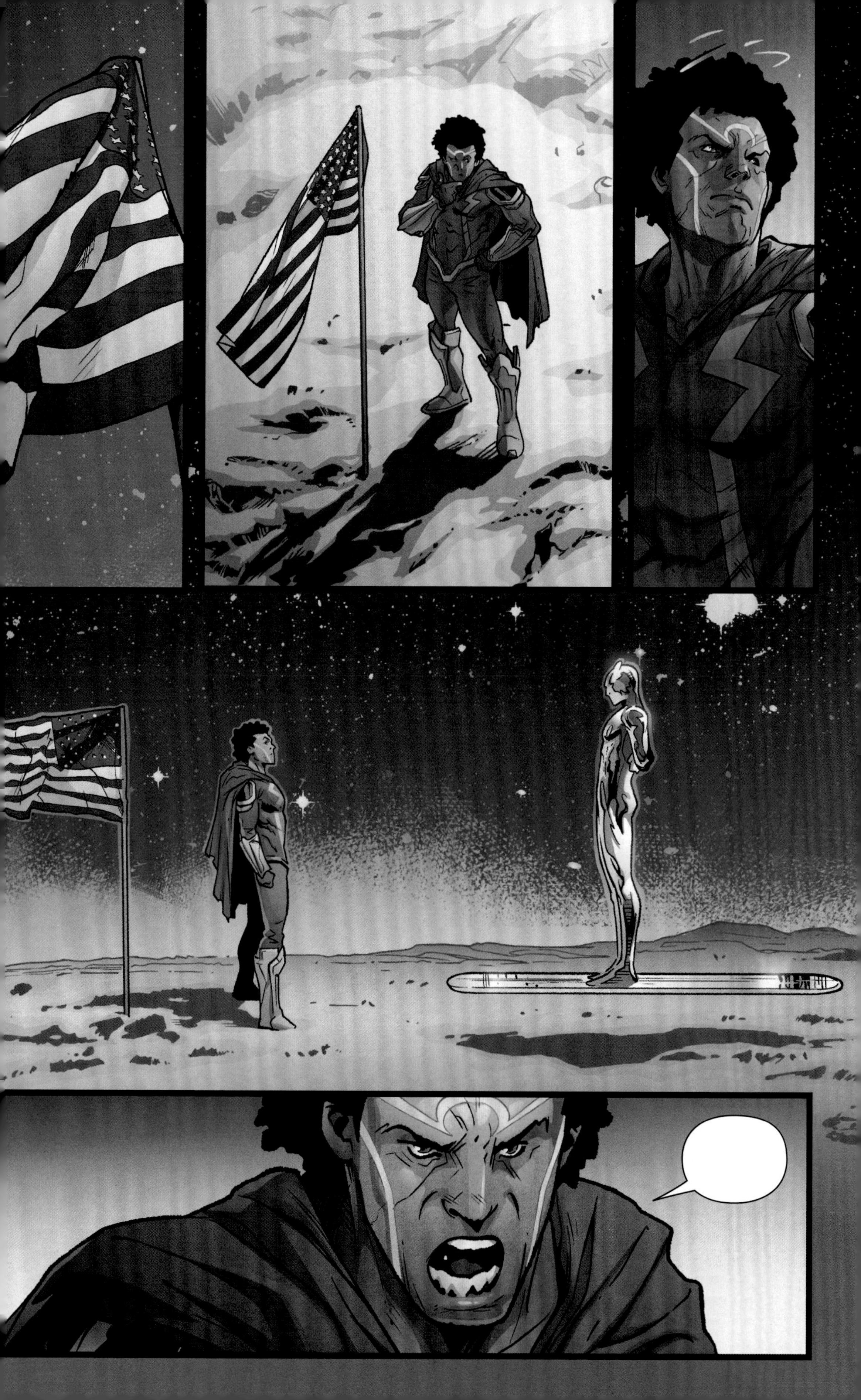

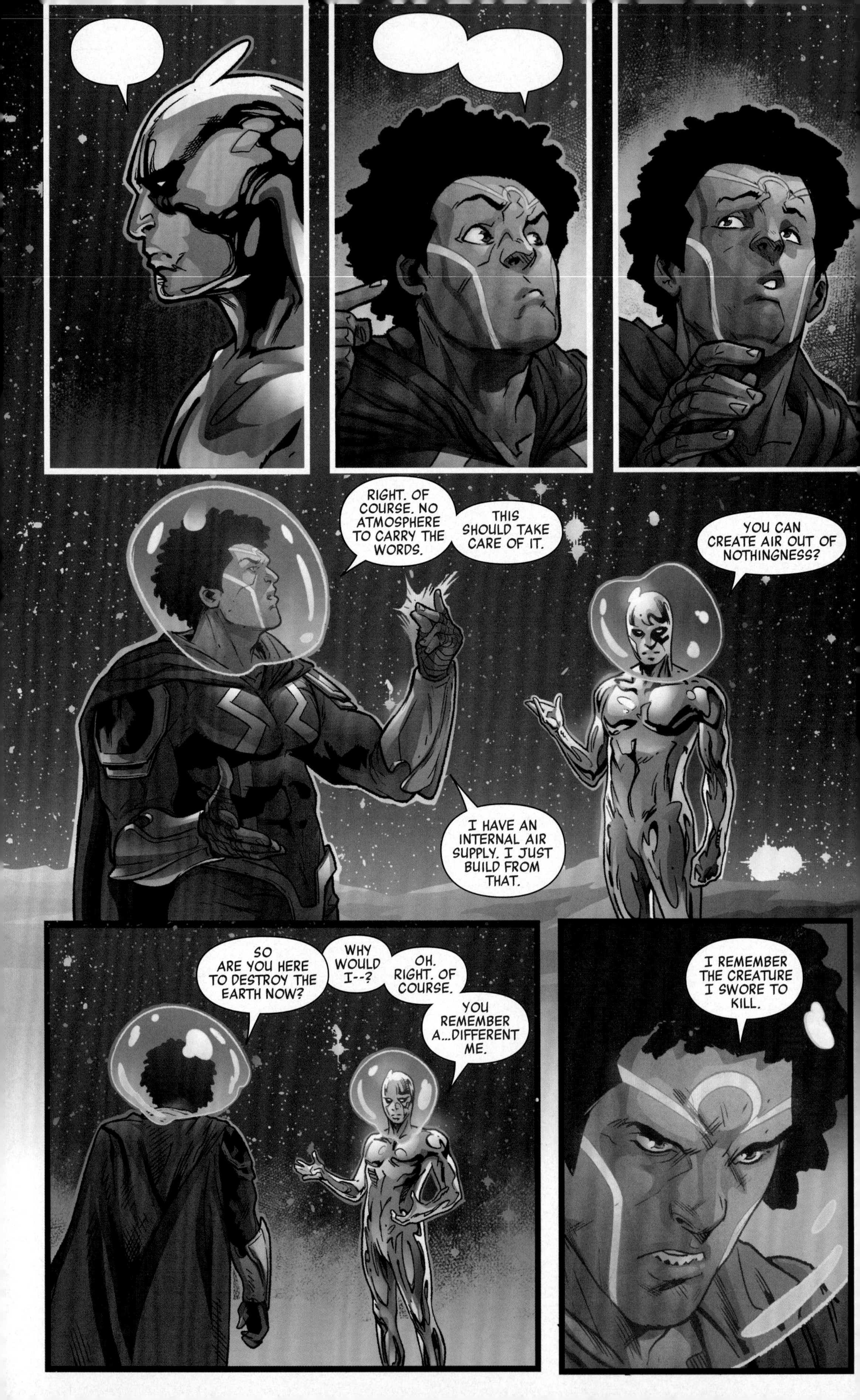
RIGHT. OF COURSE. NO ATMOSPHERE TO CARRY THE WORDS.
THIS SHOULD TAKE CARE OF IT.
YOU CAN CREATE AIR OUT OF NOTHINGNESS?
I HAVE AN INTERNAL AIR SUPPLY. I JUST BUILD FROM THAT.
SO ARE YOU HERE TO DESTROY THE EARTH NOW?
WHY WOULD I--?
OH. RIGHT. OF COURSE.
YOU REMEMBER A...DIFFERENT ME.
I REMEMBER THE CREATURE I SWORE TO KILL.

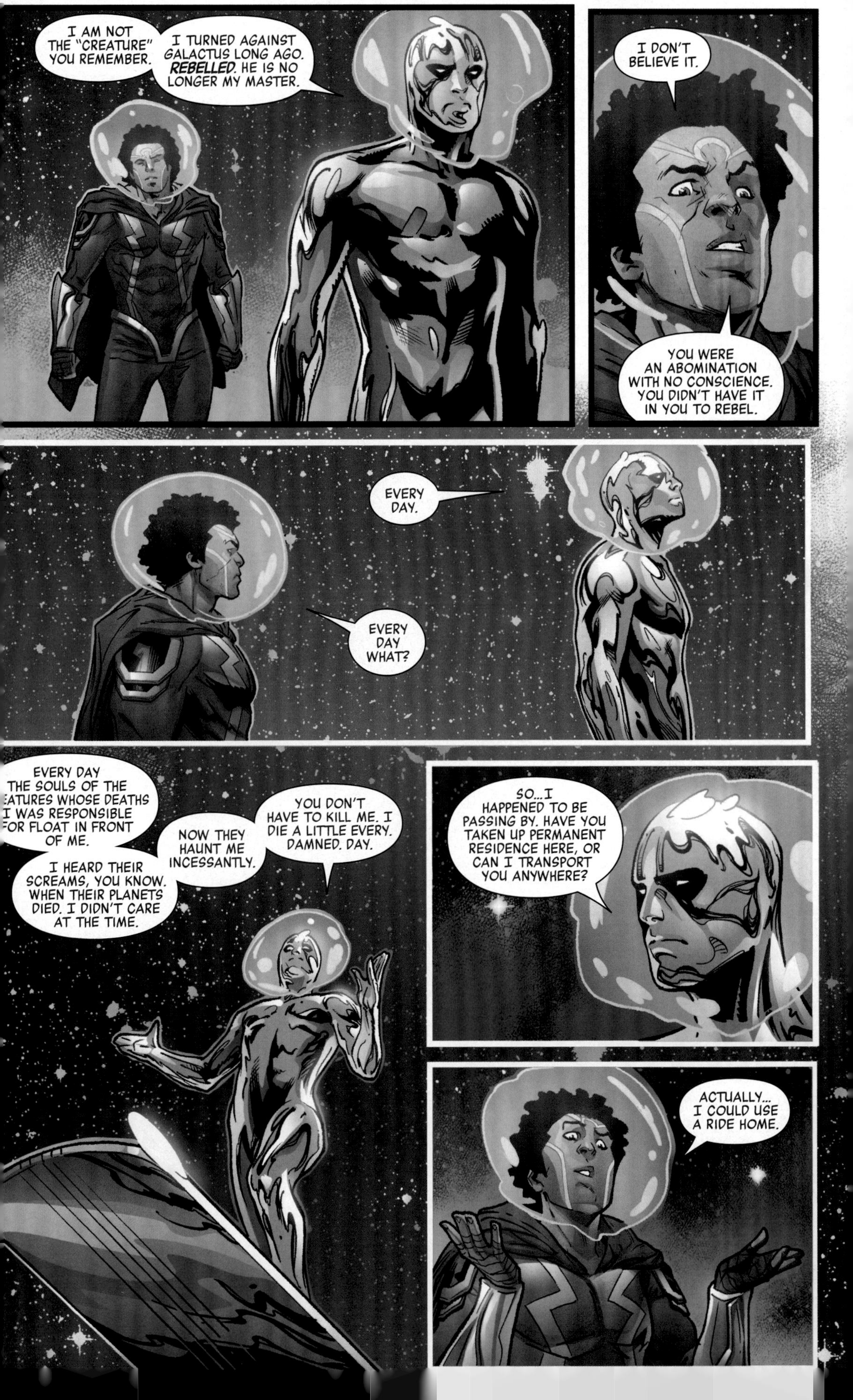

I AM NOT THE "CREATURE" YOU REMEMBER.
I TURNED AGAINST GALACTUS LONG AGO. REBELLED. HE IS NO LONGER MY MASTER.
I DON'T BELIEVE IT.
YOU WERE AN ABOMINATION WITH NO CONSCIENCE. YOU DIDN'T HAVE IT IN YOU TO REBEL.
EVERY DAY.
EVERY DAY WHAT?
EVERY DAY THE SOULS OF THE EATURES WHOSE DEATHS I WAS RESPONSIBLE FOR FLOAT IN FRONT OF ME.
I HEARD THEIR SCREAMS, YOU KNOW. WHEN THEIR PLANETS DIED. I DIDN'T CARE AT THE TIME.
NOW THEY HAUNT ME INCESSANTLY.
YOU DON'T HAVE TO KILL ME. I DIE A LITTLE EVERY. DAMNED. DAY.
SO...I HAPPENED TO BE PASSING BY. HAVE YOU TAKEN UP PERMANENT RESIDENCE HERE, OR CAN I TRANSPORT YOU ANYWHERE?
ACTUALLY... I COULD USE A RIDE HOME.

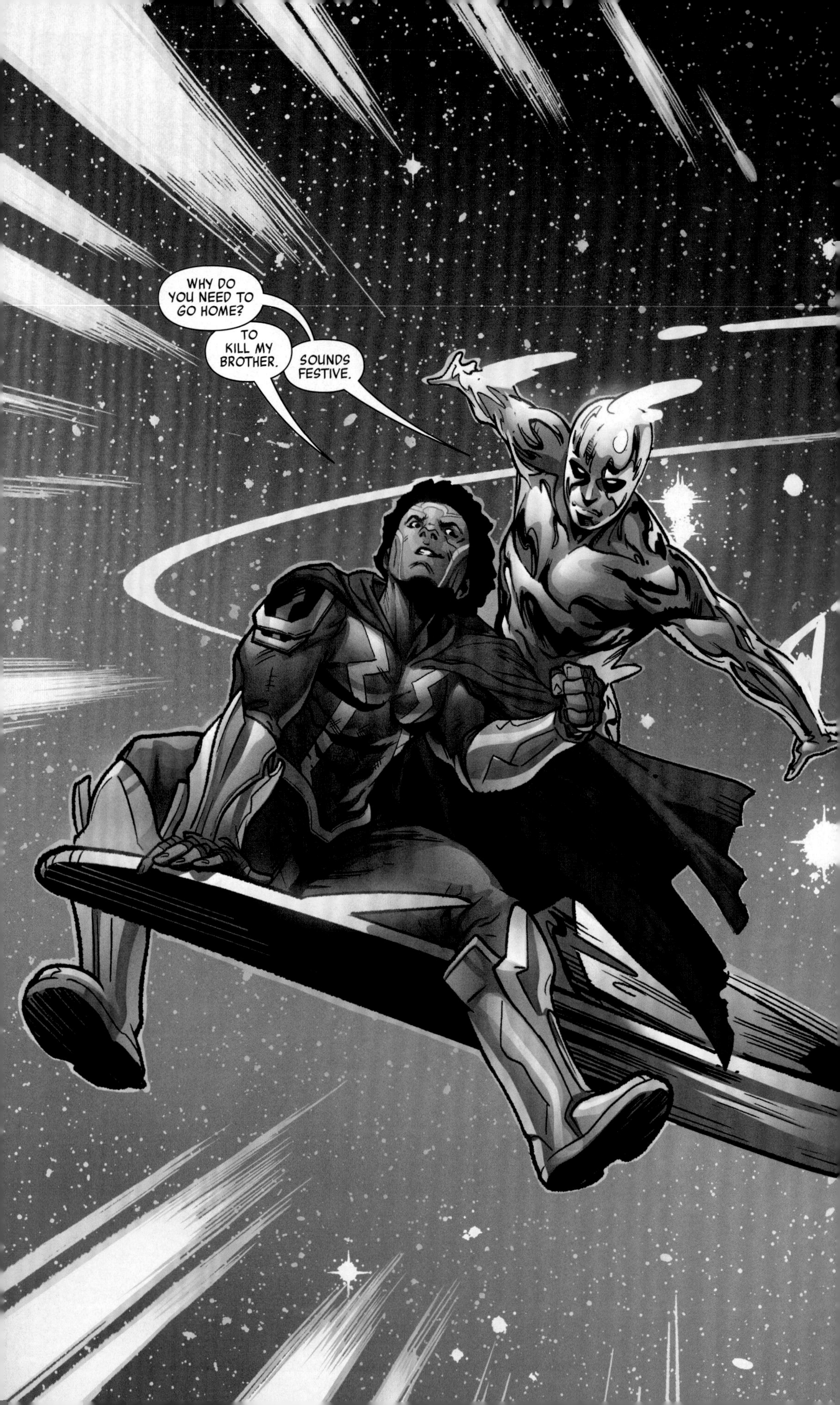
WHY DO YOU NEED TO GO HOME?
TO KILL MY BROTHER.
SOUNDS FESTIVE.

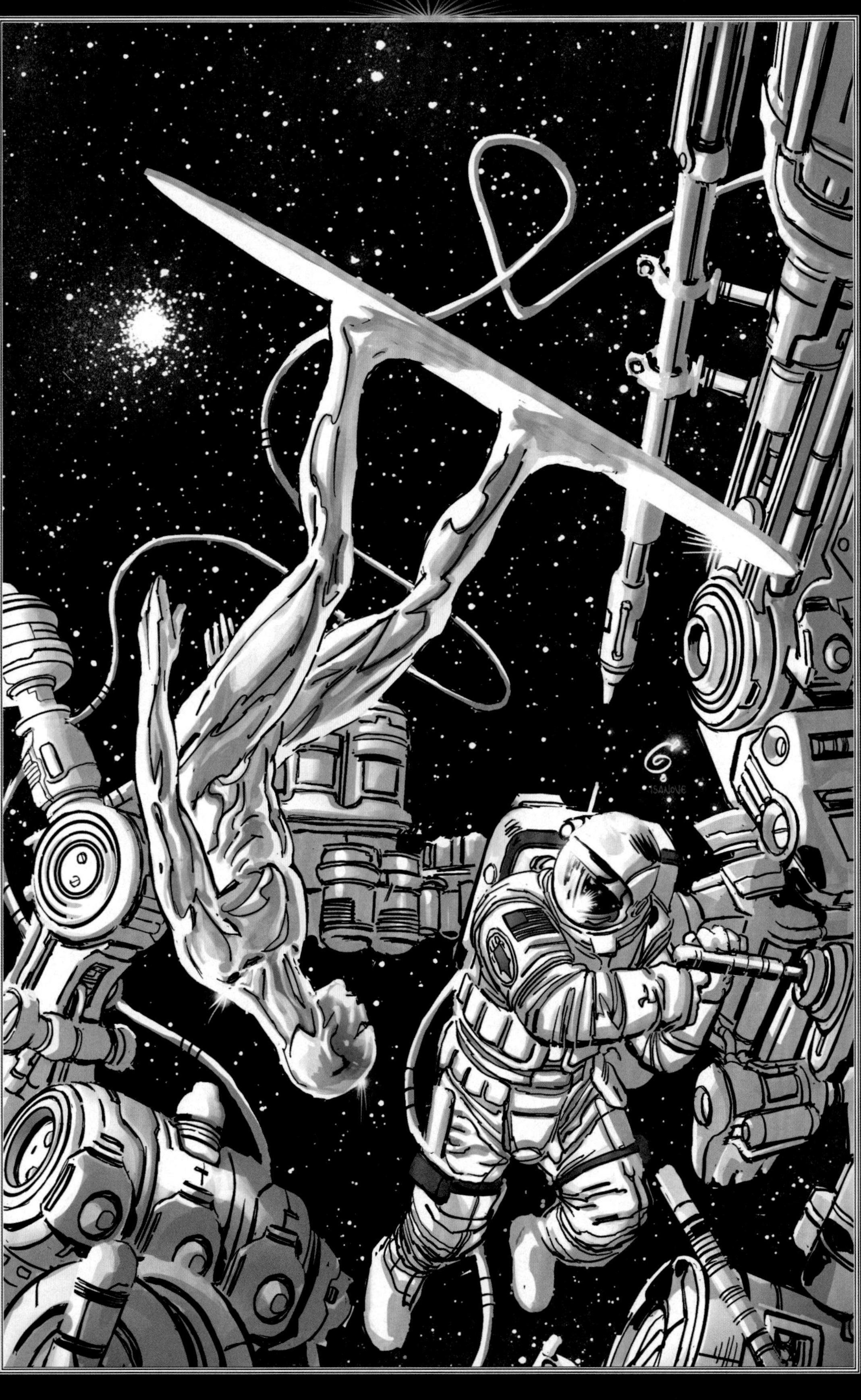
ISANOVE

SILVER SURFER: THE PRODIGAL SUN #1 VARIANT BY
RON GARNEY & RICHARD ISANOVE

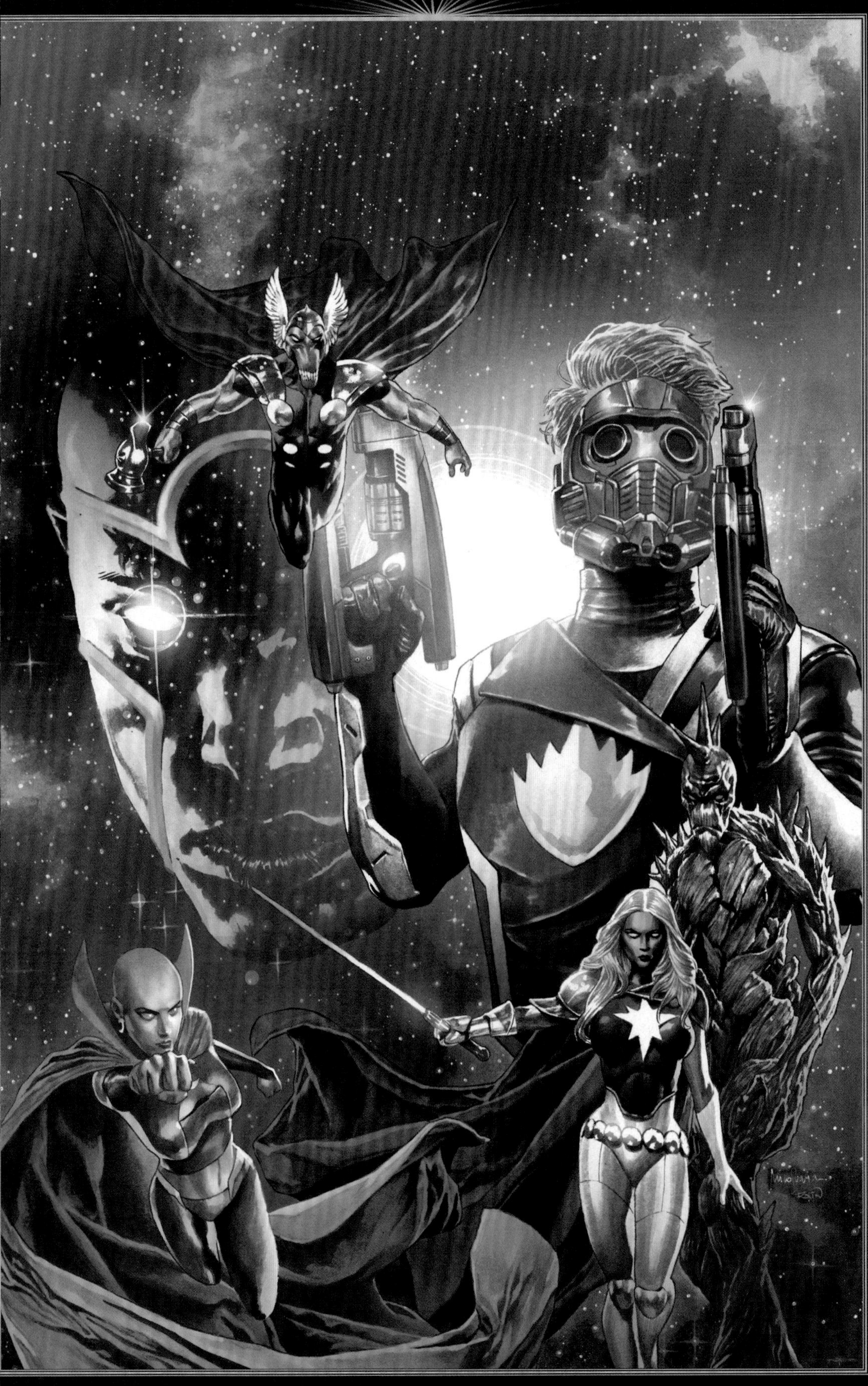

GUARDIANS OF THE GALAXY: THE PRODIGAL SUN #1

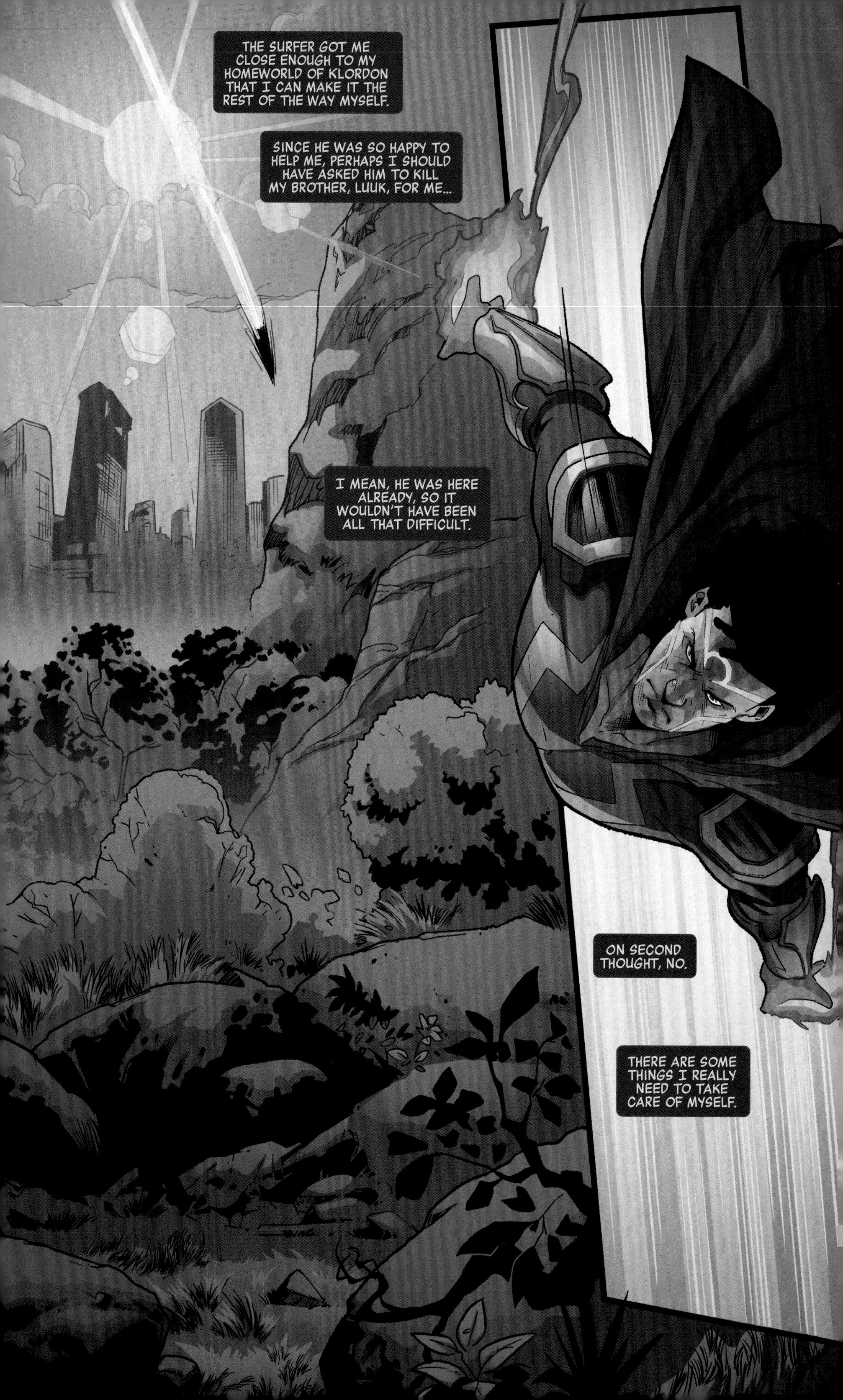
THE SURFER GOT ME CLOSE ENOUGH TO MY HOMEWORLD OF KLORDON THAT I CAN MAKE IT THE REST OF THE WAY MYSELF.
SINCE HE WAS SO HAPPY TO HELP ME, PERHAPS I SHOULD HAVE ASKED HIM TO KILL MY BROTHER, LUUK, FOR ME...
I MEAN, HE WAS HERE ALREADY, SO IT WOULDN'T HAVE BEEN ALL THAT DIFFICULT.
ON SECOND THOUGHT, NO.
THERE ARE SOME THINGS I REALLY NEED TO TAKE CARE OF MYSELF.

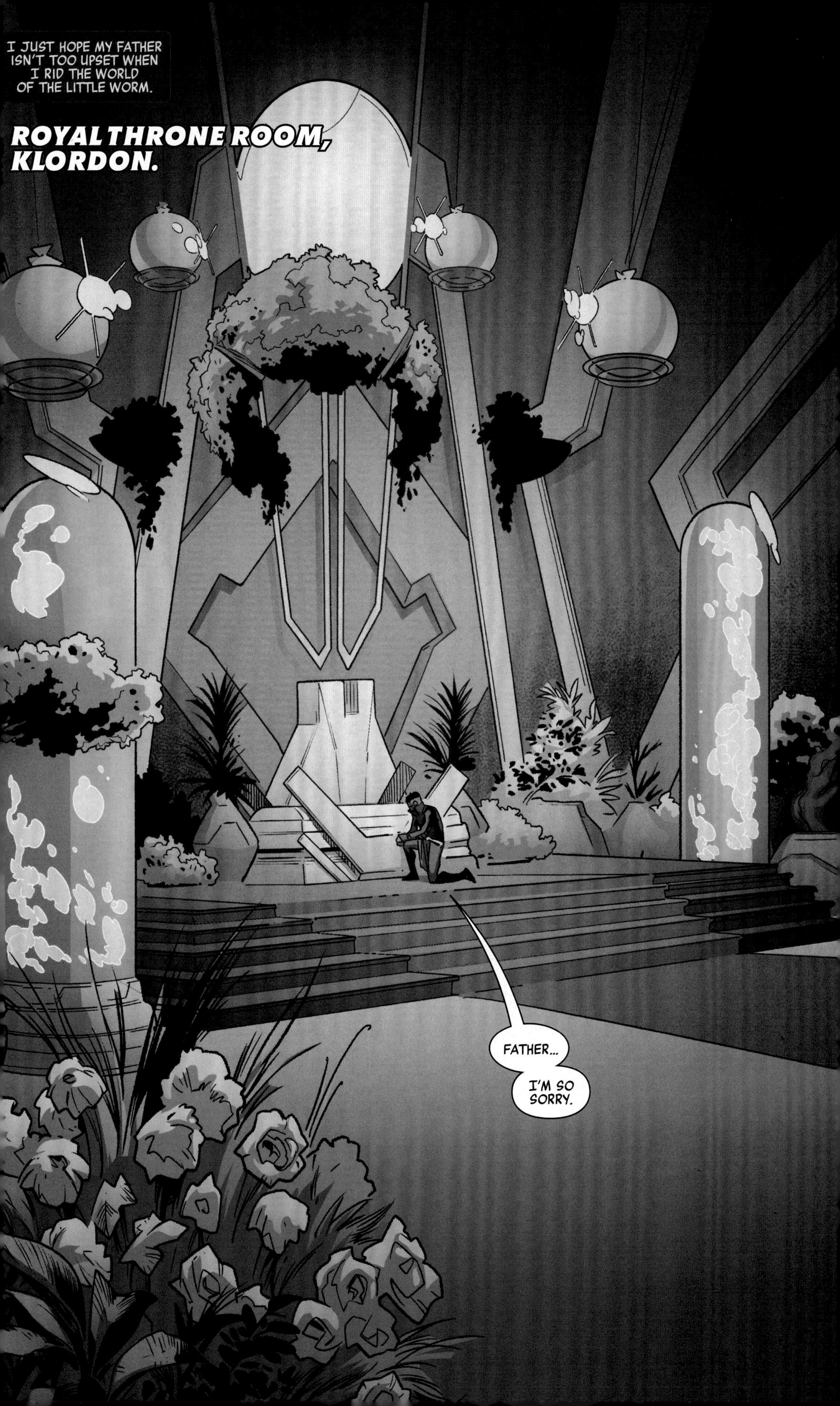
I JUST HOPE MY FATHER ISN'T TOO UPSET WHEN I RID THE WORLD OF THE LITTLE WORM.
ROYAL THRONE ROOM, KLORDON.
FATHER...
I'M SO SORRY.

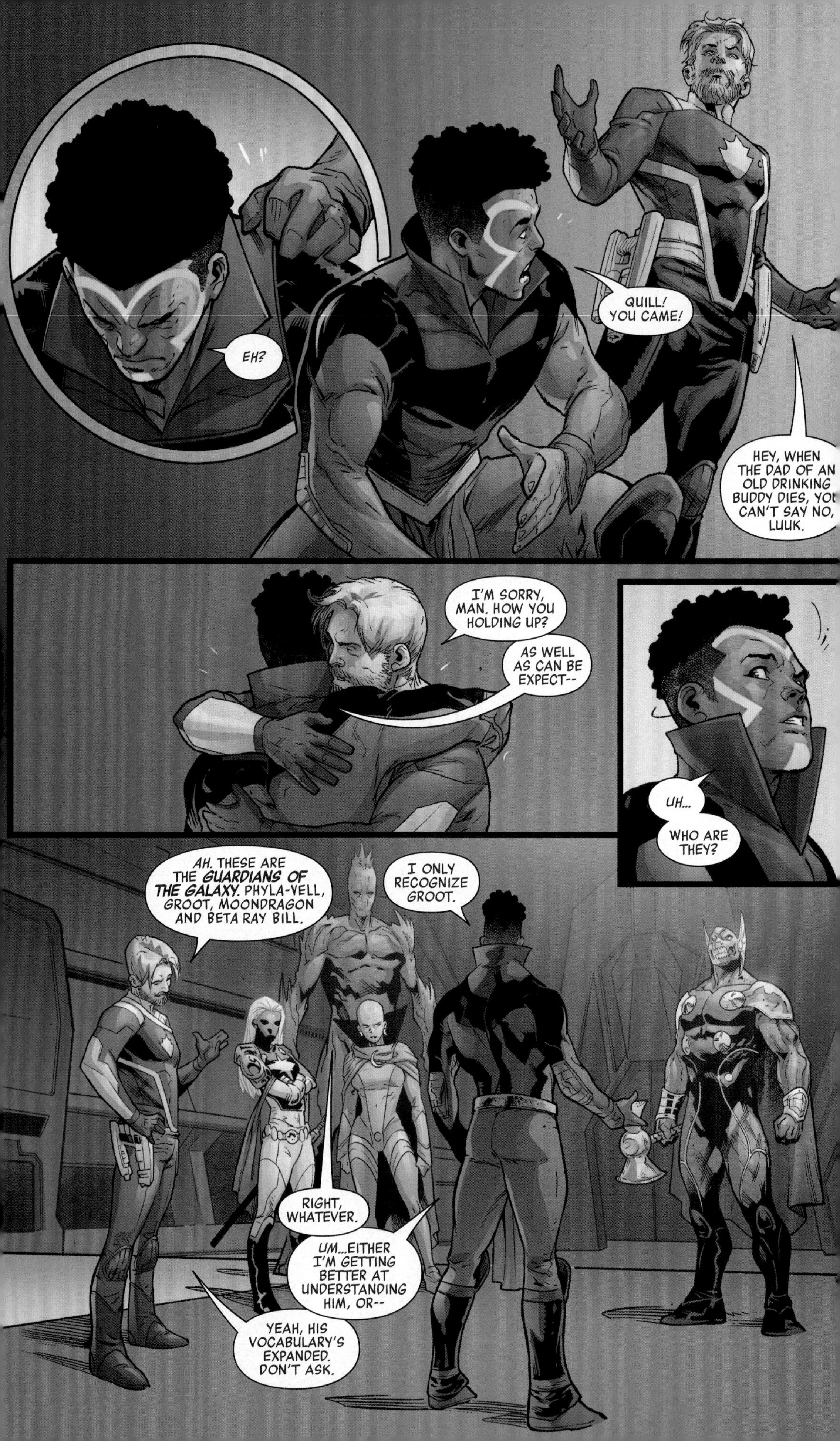
EH?
QUILL! YOU CAME!
HEY, WHEN THE DAD OF AN OLD DRINKING BUDDY DIES, YOU CAN'T SAY NO, LUUK.
I'M SORRY, MAN. HOW YOU HOLDING UP?
AS WELL AS CAN BE EXPECT--
UH...
WHO ARE THEY?
AH. THESE ARE THE GUARDIANS OF THE GALAXY. PHYLA-VELL, GROOT, MOONDRAGON AND BETA RAY BILL.
I ONLY RECOGNIZE GROOT.
RIGHT, WHATEVER.
UM...EITHER I'M GETTING BETTER AT UNDERSTANDING HIM, OR--
YEAH, HIS VOCABULARY'S EXPANDED. DON'T ASK.

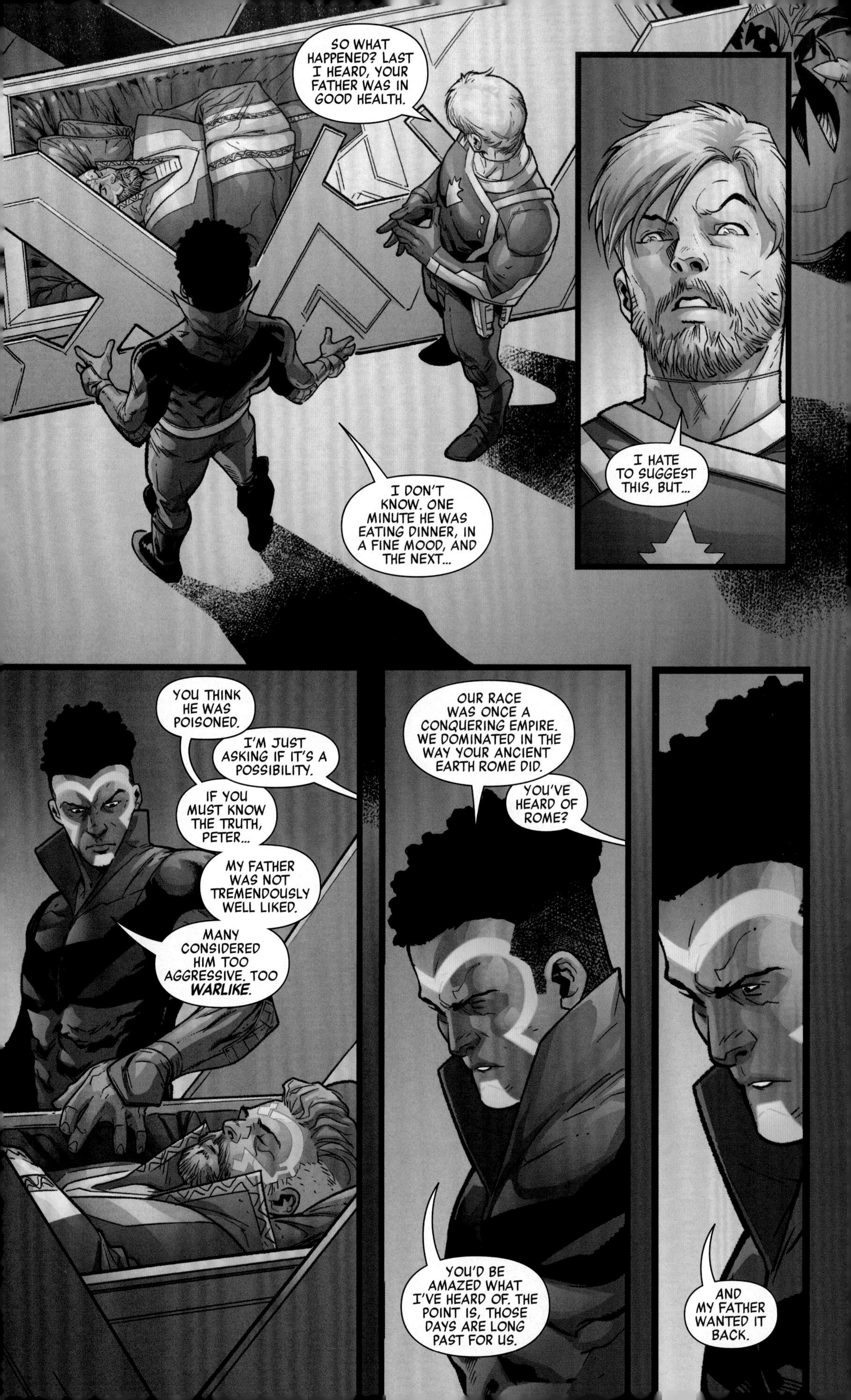
SO WHAT HAPPENED? LAST I HEARD, YOUR FATHER WAS IN GOOD HEALTH.
I DON'T KNOW. ONE MINUTE HE WAS EATING DINNER, IN A FINE MOOD, AND THE NEXT...
I HATE TO SUGGEST THIS, BUT...
YOU THINK HE WAS POISONED.
I'M JUST ASKING IF IT'S A POSSIBILITY.
IF YOU MUST KNOW THE TRUTH, PETER...
MY FATHER WAS NOT TREMENDOUSLY WELL LIKED.
MANY CONSIDERED HIM TOO AGGRESSIVE. TOO ***WARLIKE***.
OUR RACE WAS ONCE A CONQUERING EMPIRE. WE DOMINATED IN THE WAY YOUR ANCIENT EARTH ROME DID.
YOU'VE HEARD OF ROME?
YOU'D BE AMAZED WHAT I'VE HEARD OF. THE POINT IS, THOSE DAYS ARE LONG PAST FOR US.
AND MY FATHER WANTED IT BACK.

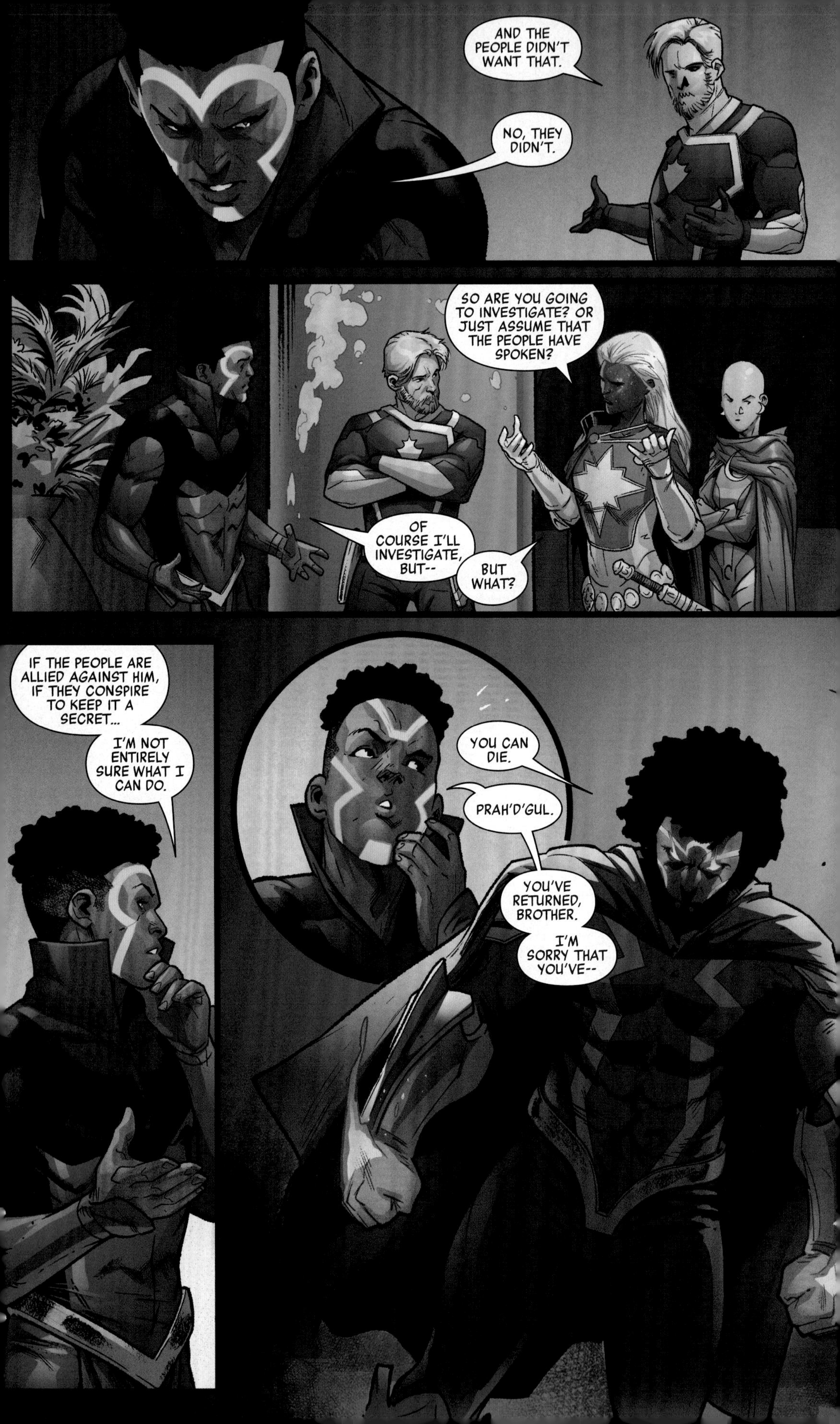
AND THE PEOPLE DIDN'T WANT THAT.
NO, THEY DIDN'T.
SO ARE YOU GOING TO INVESTIGATE? OR JUST ASSUME THAT THE PEOPLE HAVE SPOKEN?
OF COURSE I'LL INVESTIGATE, BUT--
BUT WHAT?
IF THE PEOPLE ARE ALLIED AGAINST HIM, IF THEY CONSPIRE TO KEEP IT A SECRET...
I'M NOT ENTIRELY SURE WHAT I CAN DO.
YOU CAN DIE.
PRAH'D'GUL.
YOU'VE RETURNED, BROTHER.
I'M SORRY THAT YOU'VE--

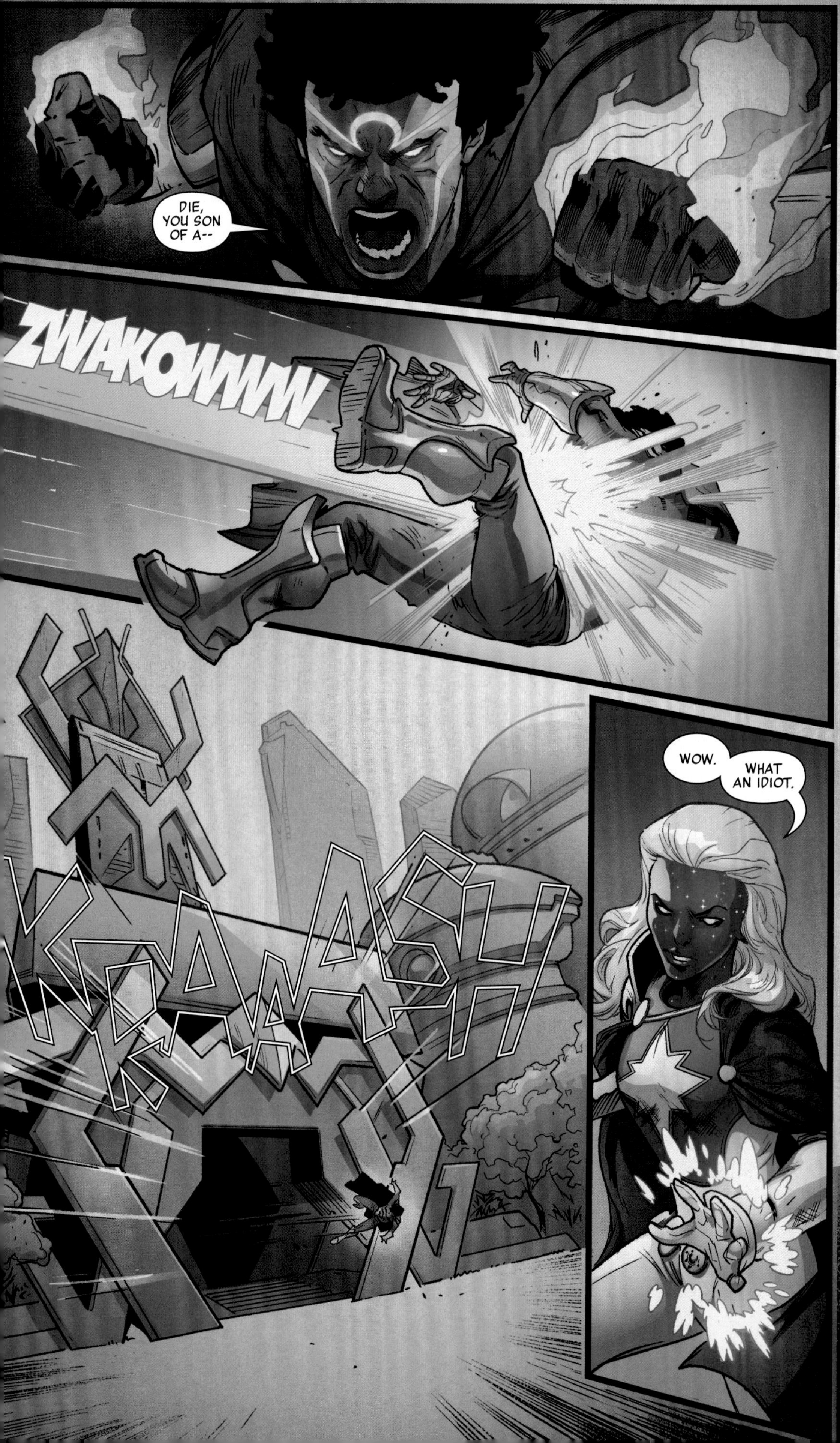
DIE, YOU SON OF A--
ZWAKOWWW
KRAAASH
WOW.
WHAT AN IDIOT.

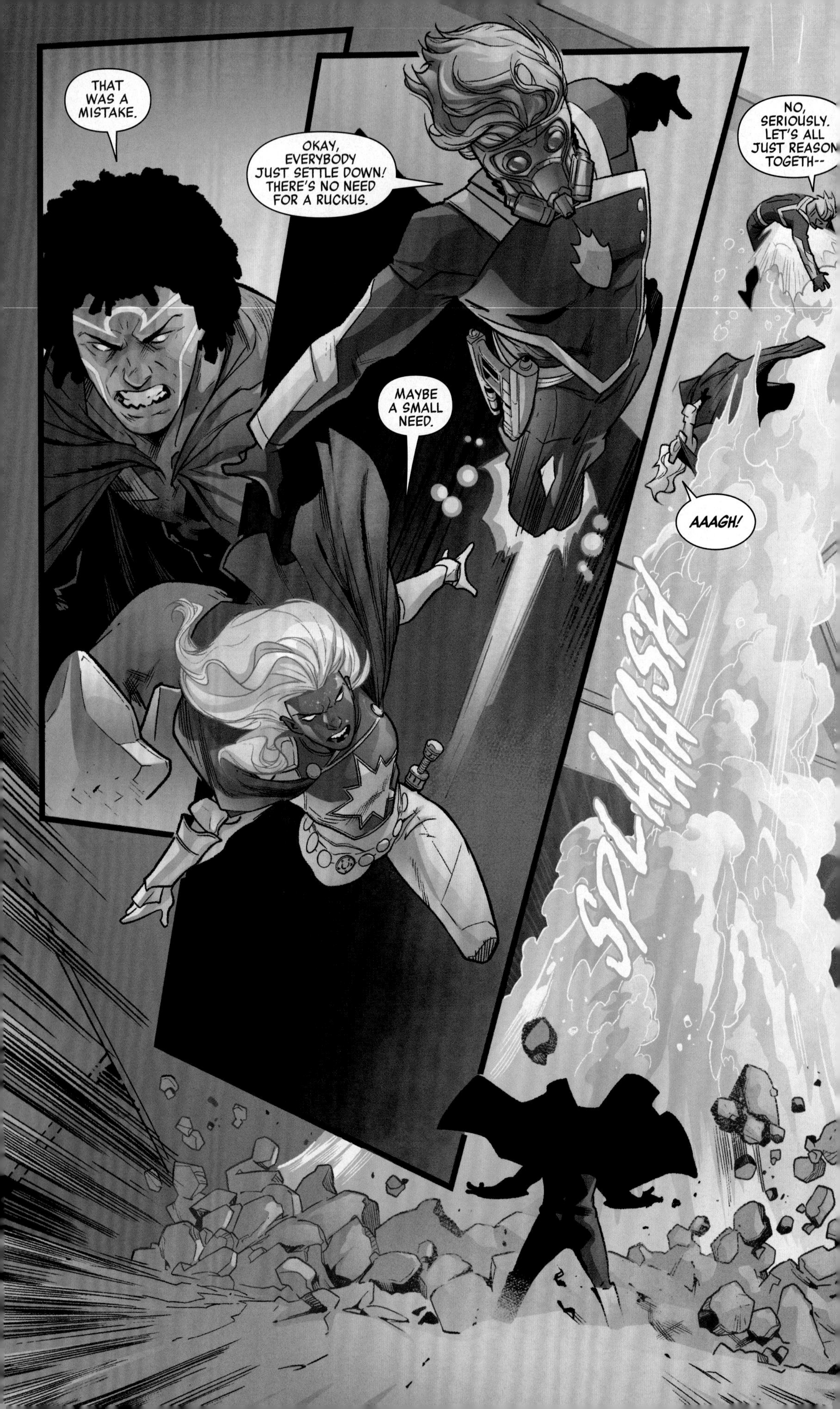
THAT WAS A MISTAKE.
OKAY, EVERYBODY JUST SETTLE DOWN! THERE'S NO NEED FOR A RUCKUS.
NO, SERIOUSLY. LET'S ALL JUST REASON TOGETH--
MAYBE A SMALL NEED.
AAAGH!
SPLAAASH

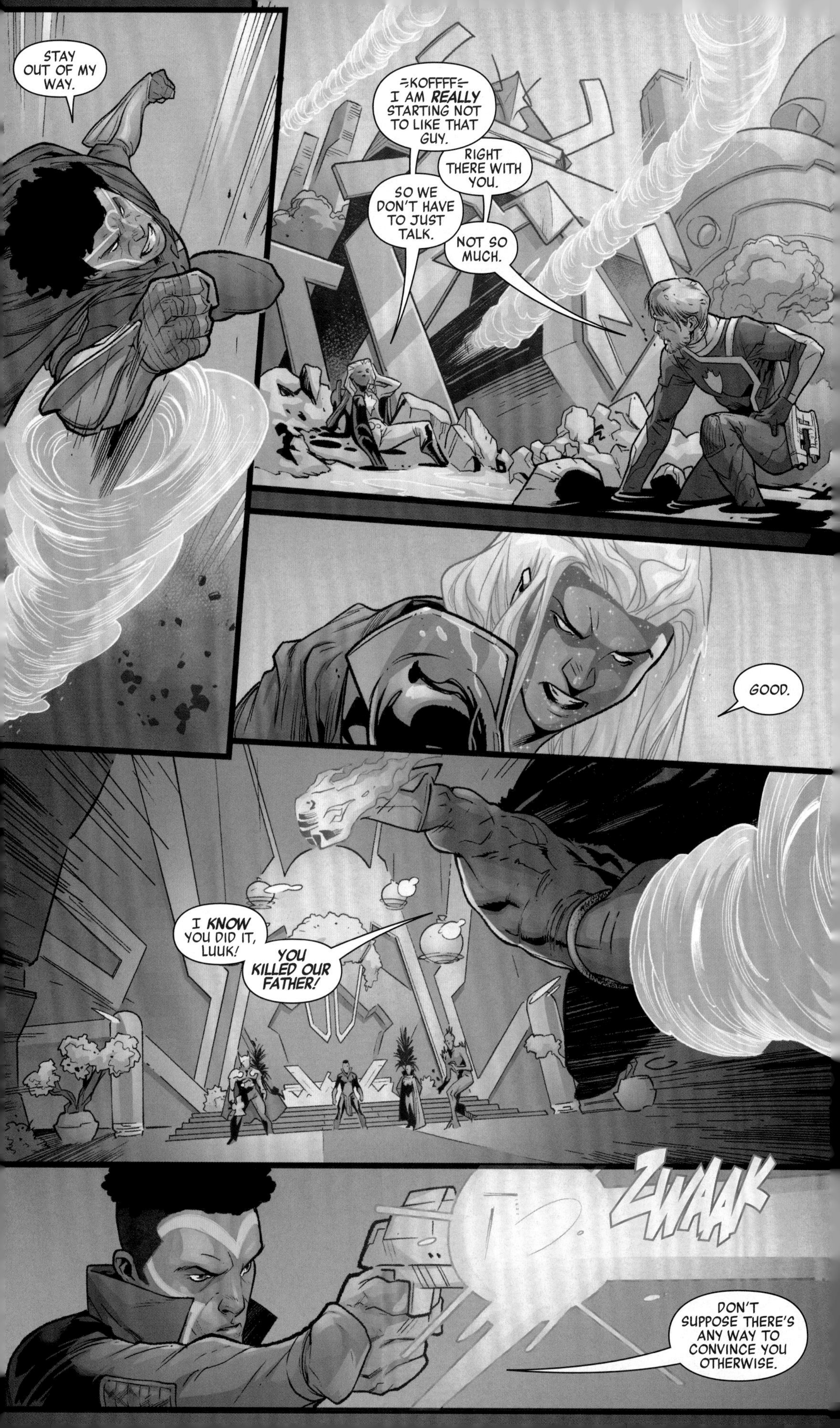
STAY OUT OF MY WAY.
=KOFFFF= I AM REALLY STARTING NOT TO LIKE THAT GUY.
SO WE DON'T HAVE TO JUST TALK.
RIGHT THERE WITH YOU.
NOT SO MUCH.
GOOD.
I KNOW YOU DID IT, LUUK!
YOU KILLED OUR FATHER!
ZWAAK
DON'T SUPPOSE THERE'S ANY WAY TO CONVINCE YOU OTHERWISE.

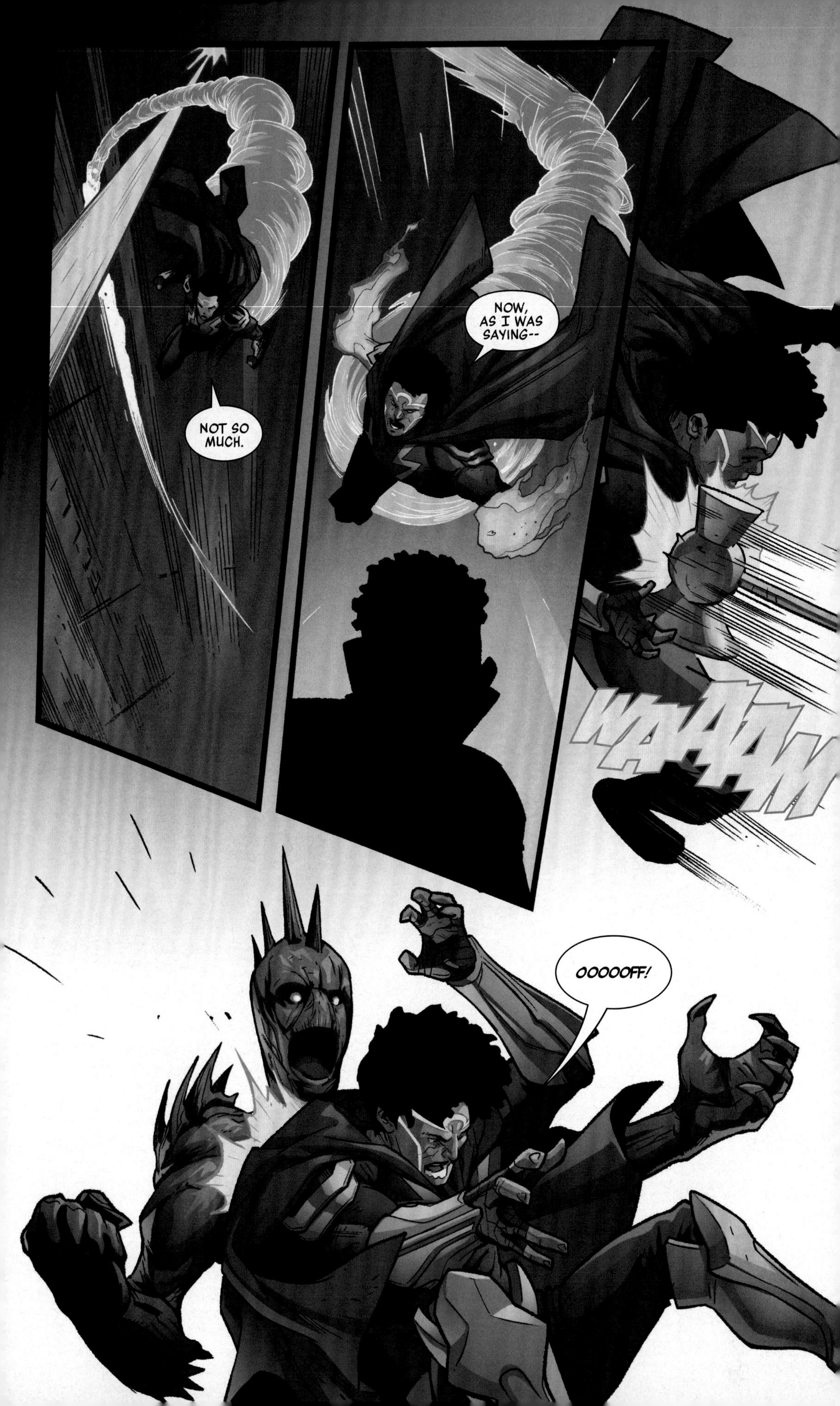
NOT SO MUCH.
NOW, AS I WAS SAYING--
WAAAM
OOOOOFF!

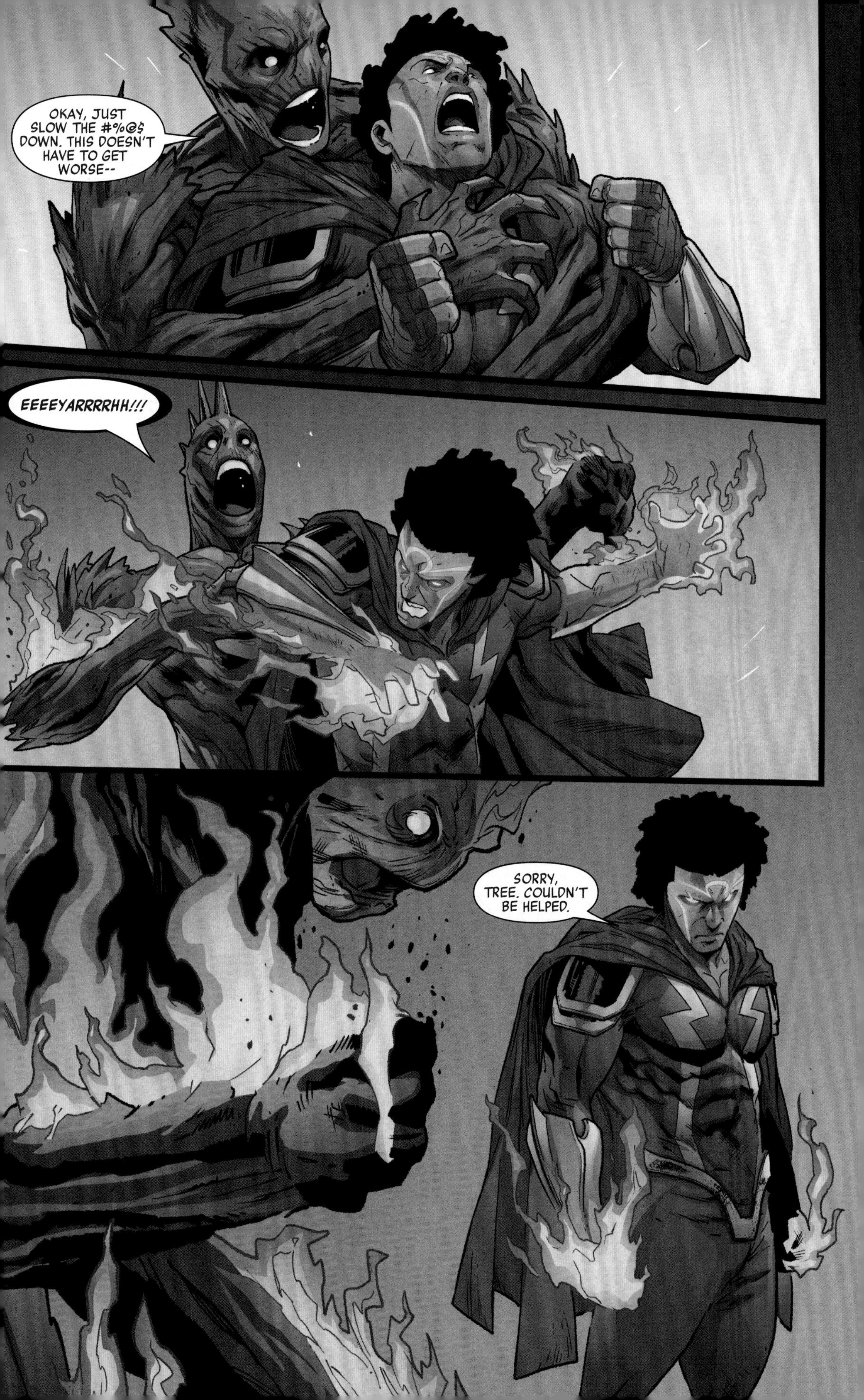
OKAY, JUST SLOW THE #%@$ DOWN. THIS DOESN'T HAVE TO GET WORSE--
EEEEYARRRRHH!!!
SORRY, TREE. COULDN'T BE HELPED.

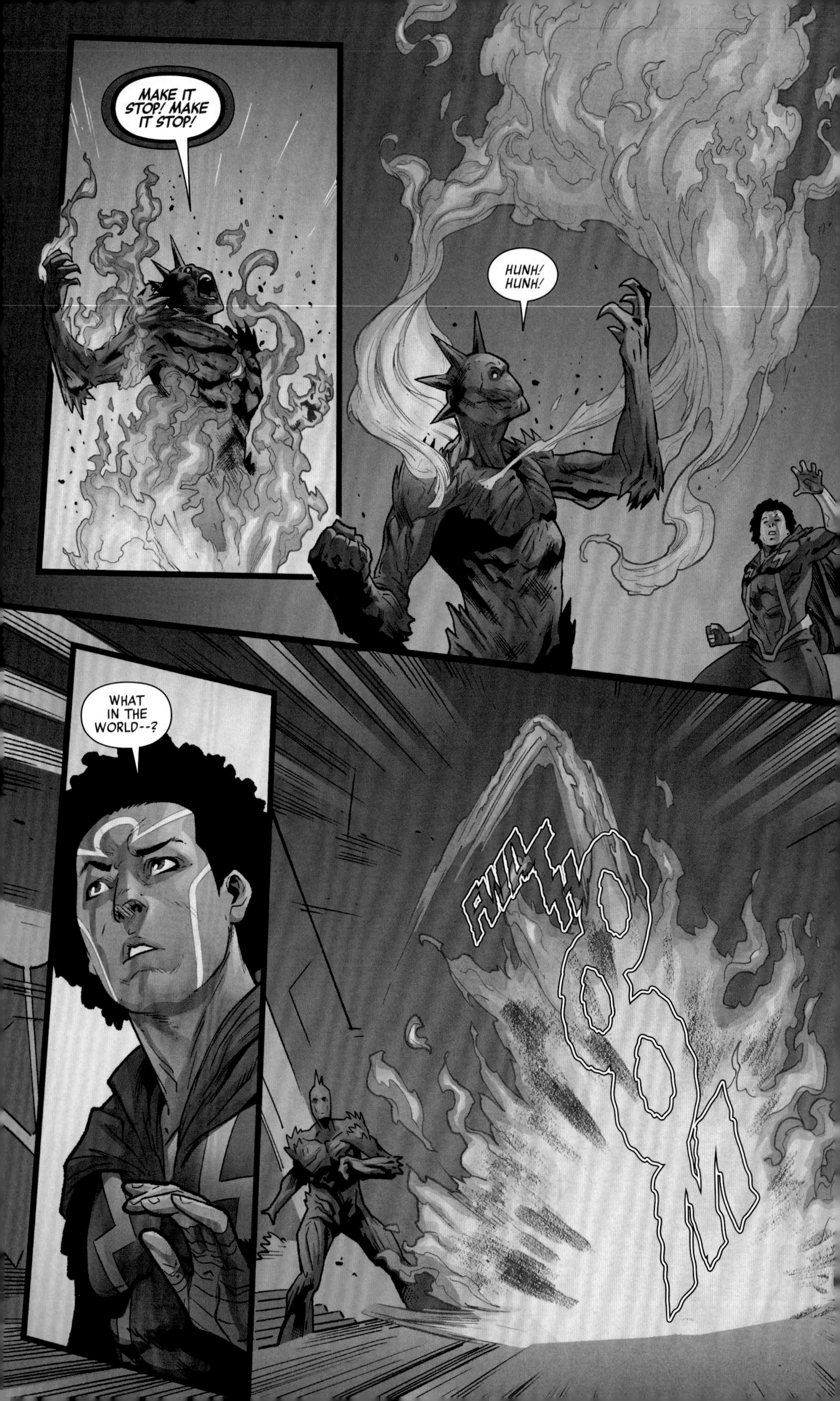
MAKE IT STOP! MAKE IT STOP!
HUNH! HUNH!
WHAT IN THE WORLD--?
FWUMPH
BOOM

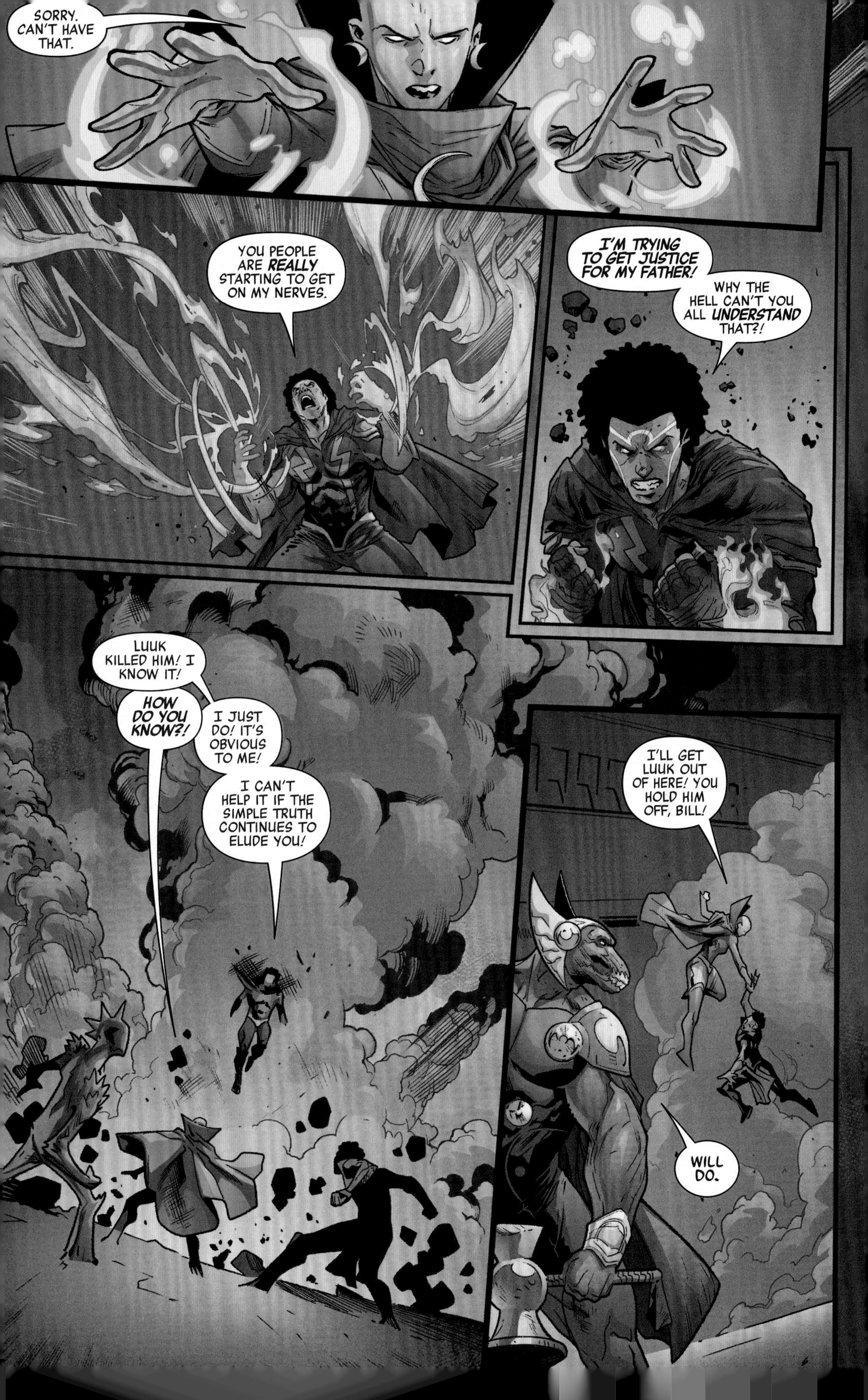
SORRY. CAN'T HAVE THAT.
YOU PEOPLE ARE **REALLY** STARTING TO GET ON MY NERVES.
***I'M TRYING TO GET JUSTICE FOR MY FATHER!***
WHY THE HELL CAN'T YOU ALL **UNDERSTAND** THAT?!
LUUK KILLED HIM! I KNOW IT!
***HOW DO YOU KNOW?!***
I JUST DO! IT'S OBVIOUS TO ME!
I CAN'T HELP IT IF THE SIMPLE TRUTH CONTINUES TO ELUDE YOU!
I'LL GET LUUK OUT OF HERE! YOU HOLD HIM OFF, BILL!
WILL DO.

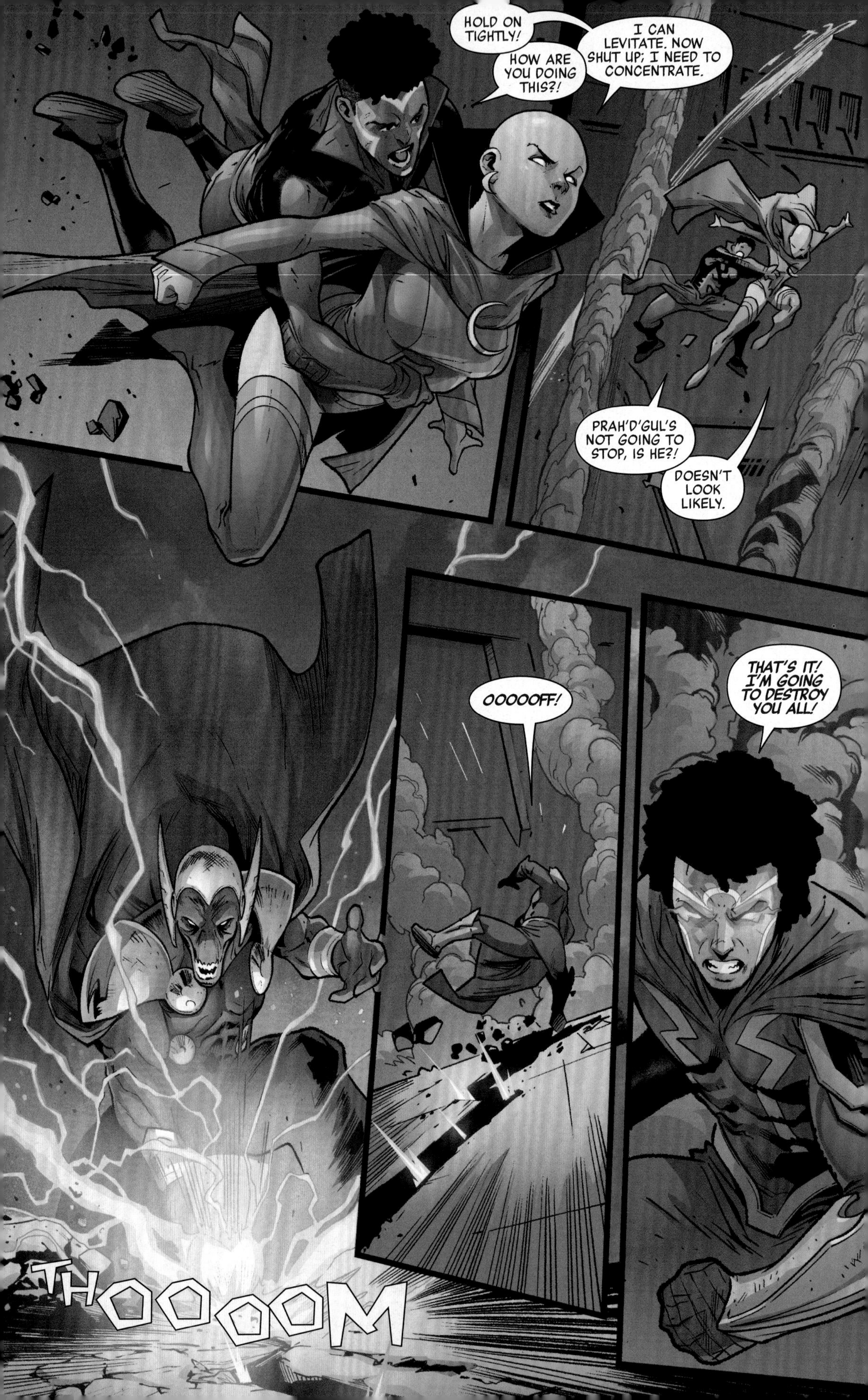
HOLD ON TIGHTLY!
HOW ARE YOU DOING THIS?!
I CAN LEVITATE. NOW SHUT UP; I NEED TO CONCENTRATE.
PRAH'D'GUL'S NOT GOING TO STOP, IS HE?!
DOESN'T LOOK LIKELY.
THOOOOM
OOOOOFF!
THAT'S IT! I'M GOING TO DESTROY YOU ALL!

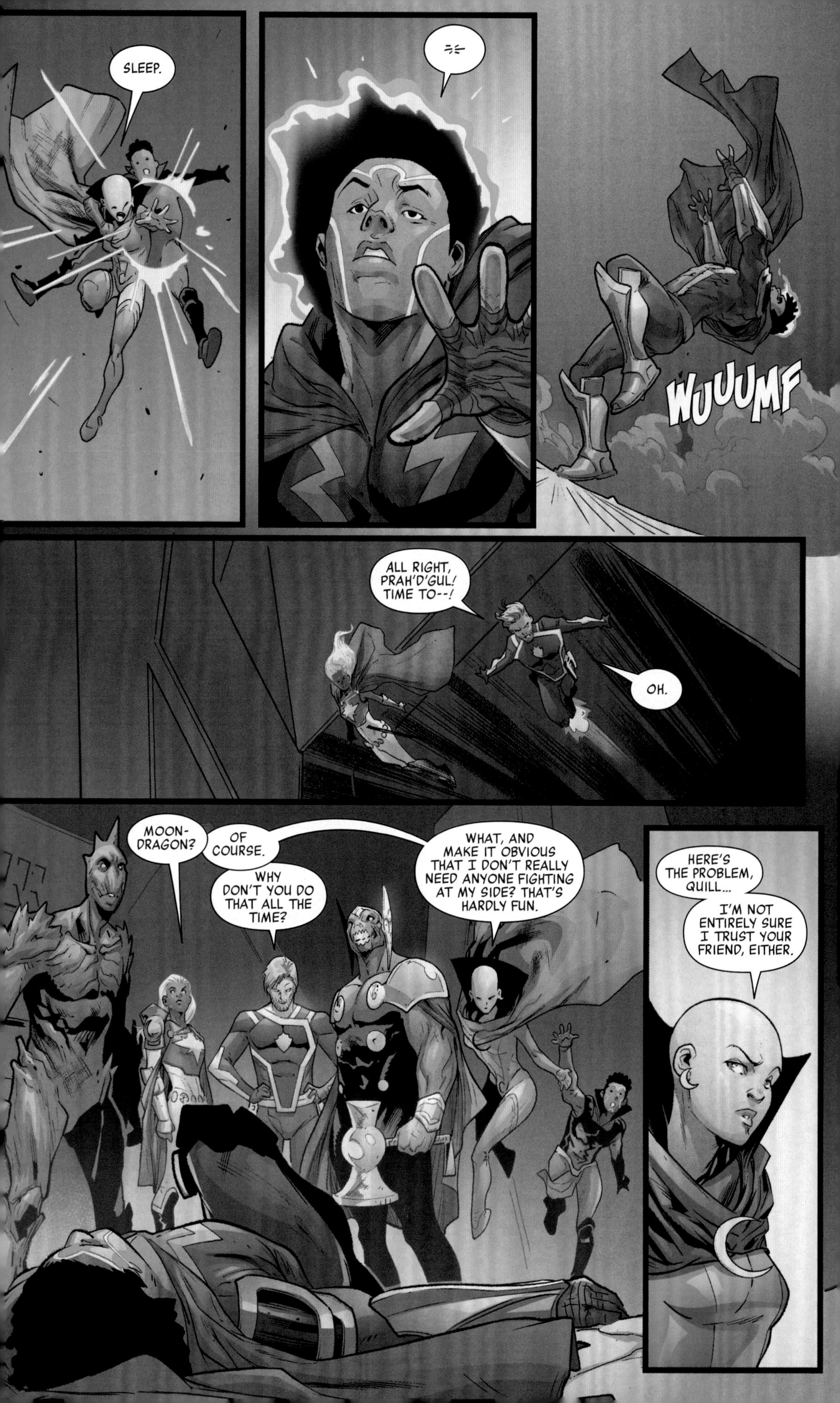
SLEEP.
=!=
WUUUMF
ALL RIGHT, PRAH'D'GUL! TIME TO--!
OH.
MOON-DRAGON?
OF COURSE.
WHY DON'T YOU DO THAT ALL THE TIME?
WHAT, AND MAKE IT OBVIOUS THAT I DON'T REALLY NEED ANYONE FIGHTING AT MY SIDE? THAT'S HARDLY FUN.
HERE'S THE PROBLEM, QUILL...
I'M NOT ENTIRELY SURE I TRUST YOUR FRIEND, EITHER.

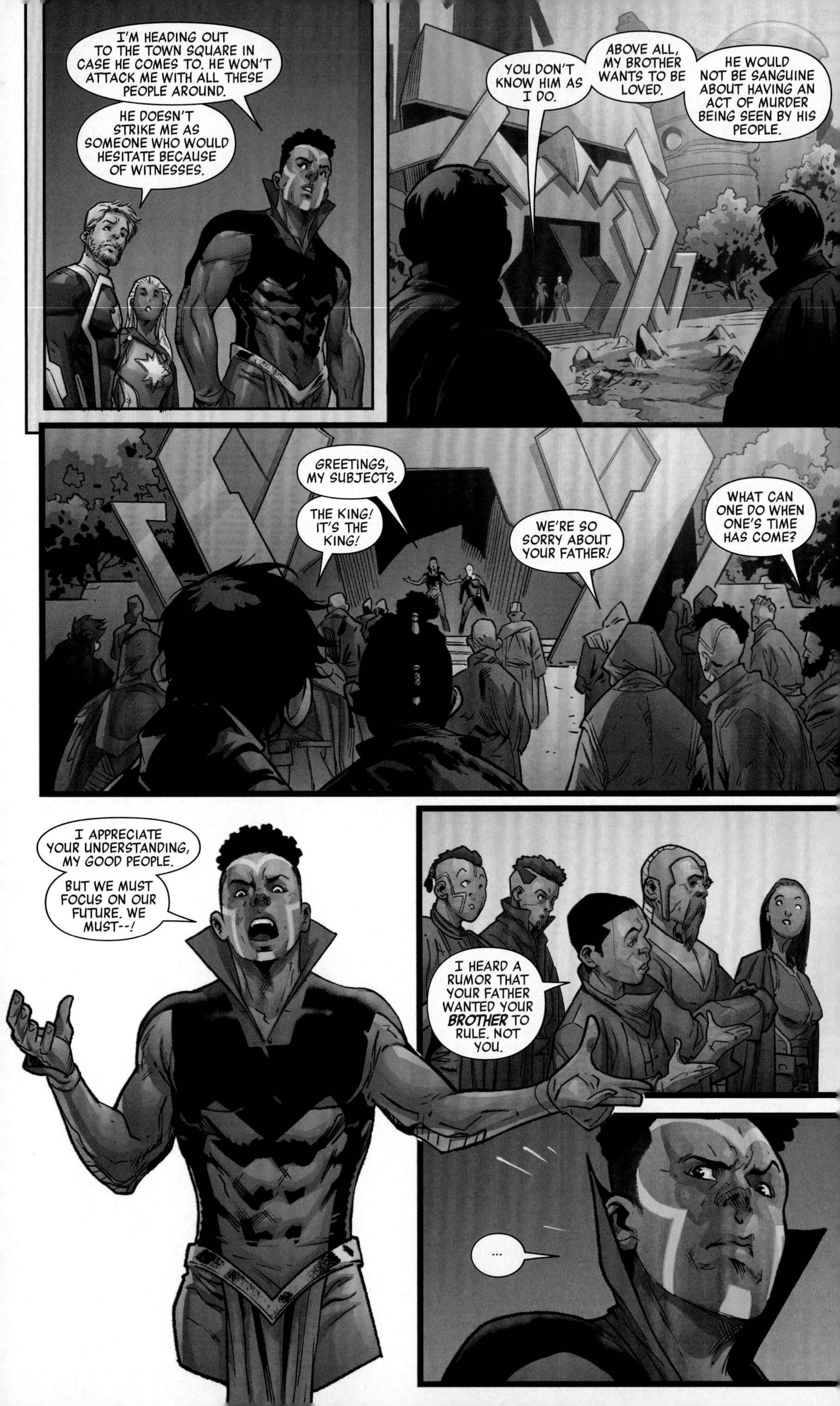

I'M HEADING OUT TO THE TOWN SQUARE IN CASE HE COMES TO. HE WON'T ATTACK ME WITH ALL THESE PEOPLE AROUND.
HE DOESN'T STRIKE ME AS SOMEONE WHO WOULD HESITATE BECAUSE OF WITNESSES.
YOU DON'T KNOW HIM AS I DO.
ABOVE ALL, MY BROTHER WANTS TO BE LOVED.
HE WOULD NOT BE SANGUINE ABOUT HAVING AN ACT OF MURDER BEING SEEN BY HIS PEOPLE.
GREETINGS, MY SUBJECTS.
THE KING! IT'S THE KING!
WE'RE SO SORRY ABOUT YOUR FATHER!
WHAT CAN ONE DO WHEN ONE'S TIME HAS COME?
I APPRECIATE YOUR UNDERSTANDING, MY GOOD PEOPLE.
BUT WE MUST FOCUS ON OUR FUTURE. WE MUST--!
I HEARD A RUMOR THAT YOUR FATHER WANTED YOUR BROTHER TO RULE. NOT YOU.
...

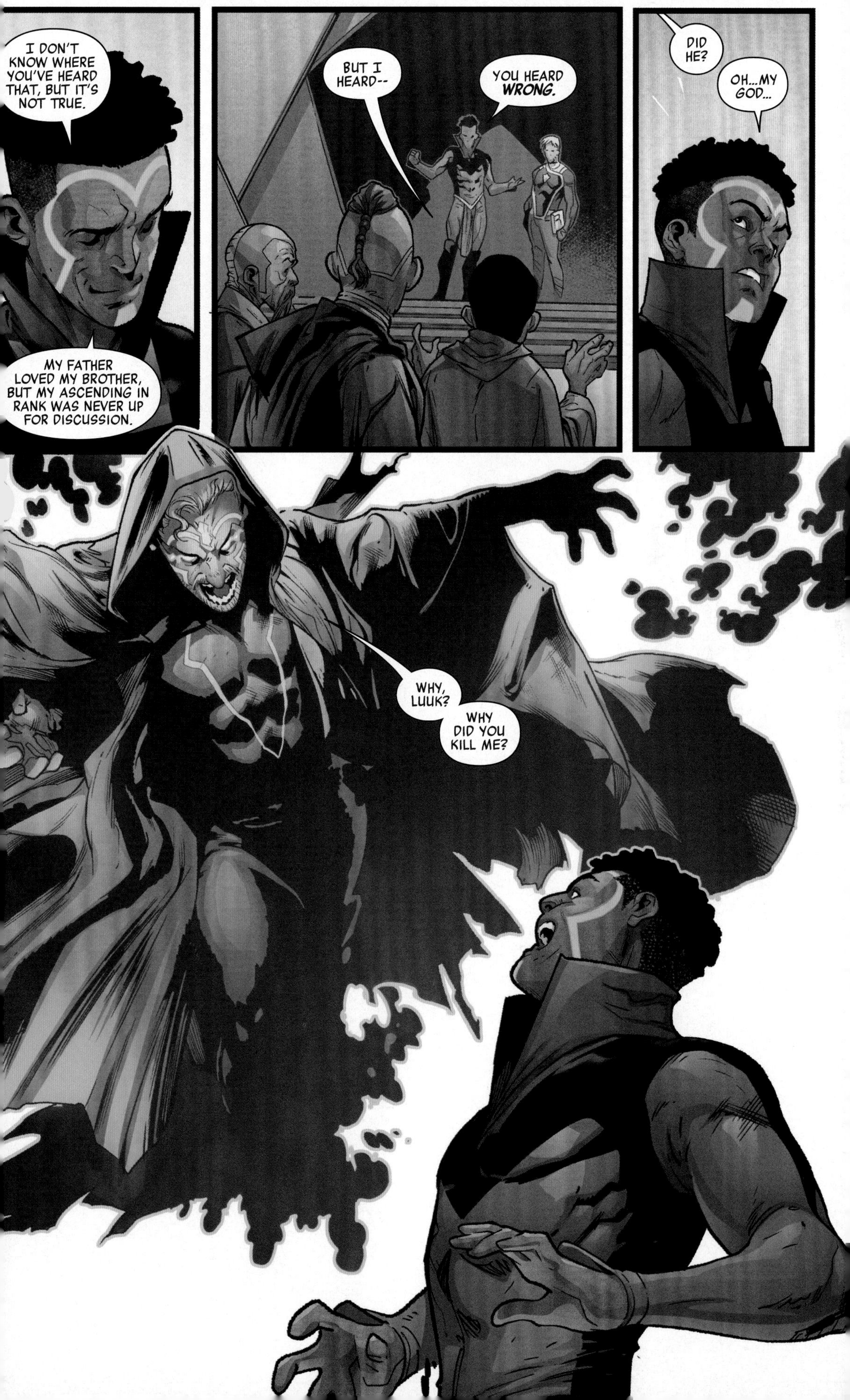
I DON'T KNOW WHERE YOU'VE HEARD THAT, BUT IT'S NOT TRUE.
MY FATHER LOVED MY BROTHER, BUT MY ASCENDING IN RANK WAS NEVER UP FOR DISCUSSION.
BUT I HEARD--
YOU HEARD WRONG.
DID HE?
OH...MY GOD...
WHY, LUUK?
WHY DID YOU KILL ME?

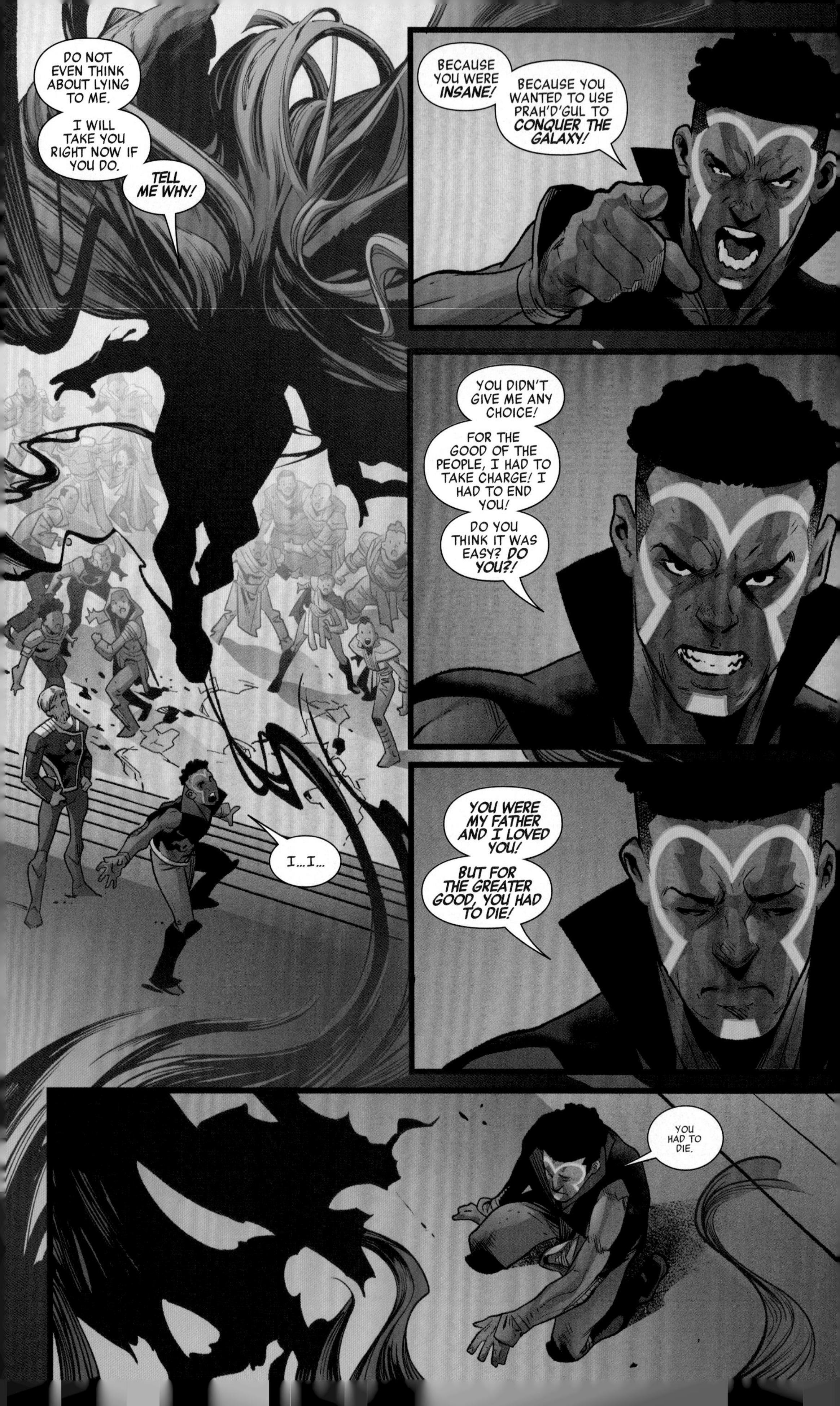
DO NOT EVEN THINK ABOUT LYING TO ME.
I WILL TAKE YOU RIGHT NOW IF YOU DO.
TELL ME WHY!
I...I...
BECAUSE YOU WERE INSANE!
BECAUSE YOU WANTED TO USE PRAH'D'GUL TO CONQUER THE GALAXY!
YOU DIDN'T GIVE ME ANY CHOICE!
FOR THE GOOD OF THE PEOPLE, I HAD TO TAKE CHARGE! I HAD TO END YOU!
DO YOU THINK IT WAS EASY? DO YOU?!
YOU WERE MY FATHER AND I LOVED YOU!
BUT FOR THE GREATER GOOD, YOU HAD TO DIE!
YOU HAD TO DIE.

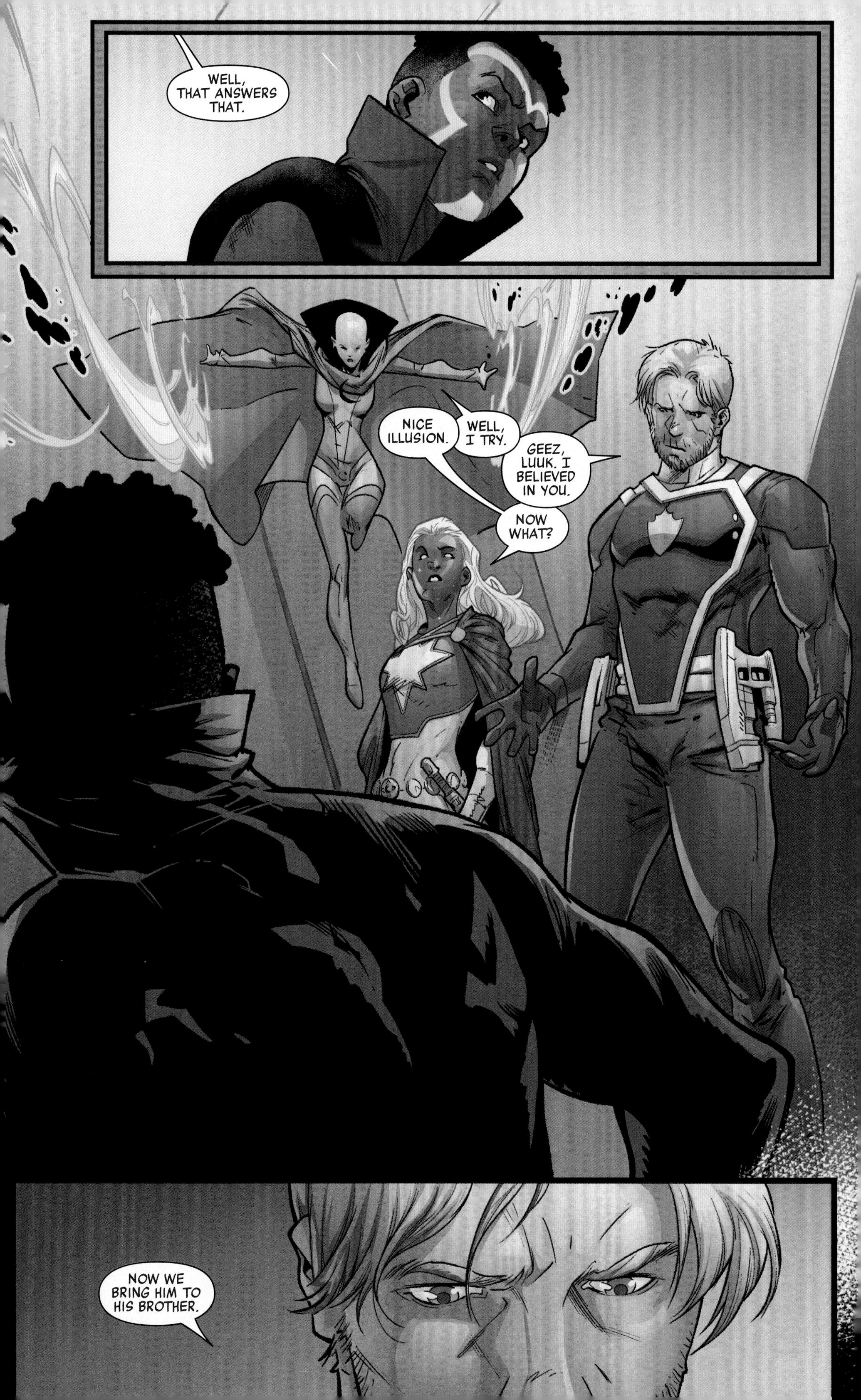
WELL, THAT ANSWERS THAT.
NICE ILLUSION.
WELL, I TRY.
GEEZ, LUUK. I BELIEVED IN YOU.
NOW WHAT?
NOW WE BRING HIM TO HIS BROTHER.

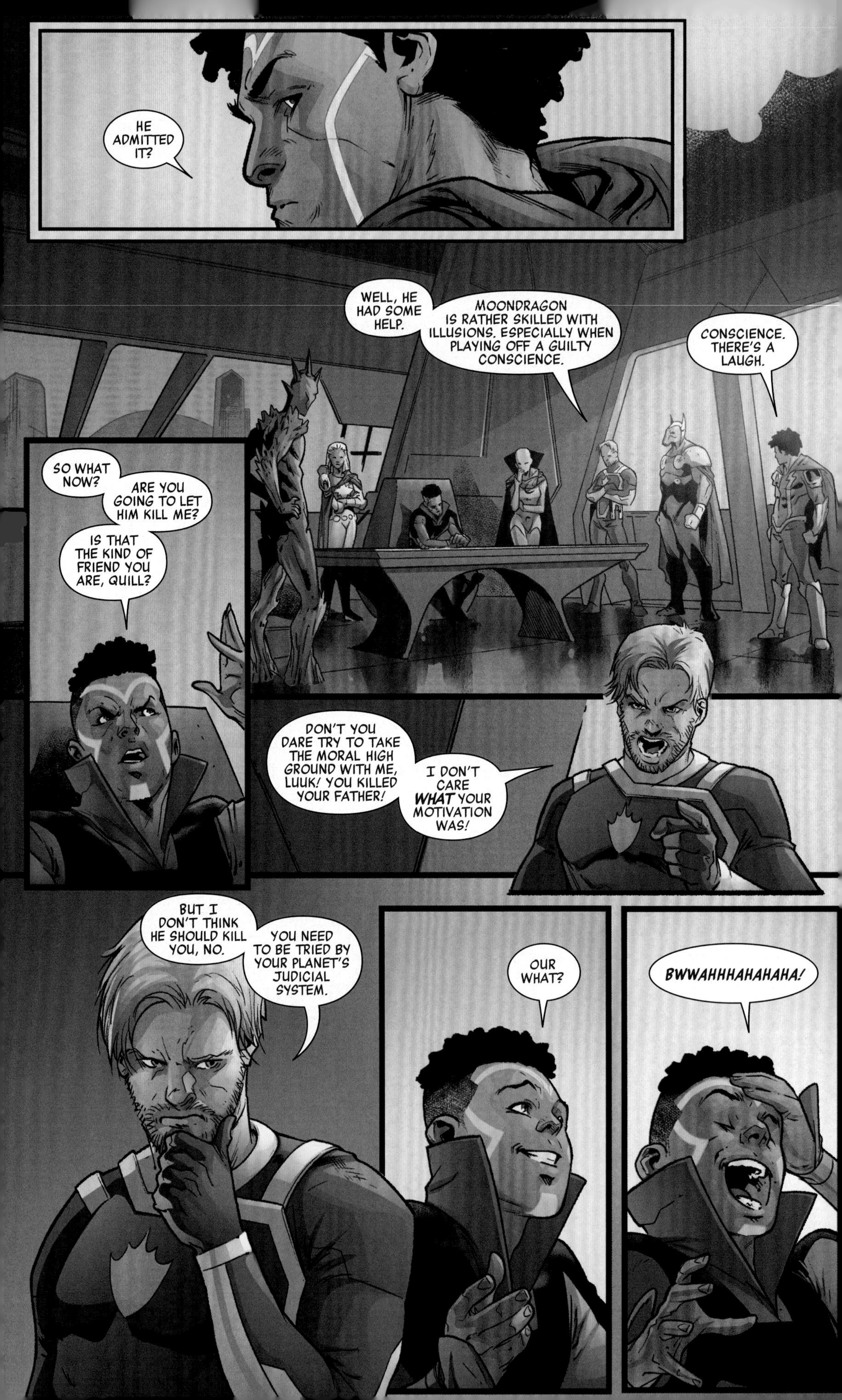
HE ADMITTED IT?
WELL, HE HAD SOME HELP.
MOONDRAGON IS RATHER SKILLED WITH ILLUSIONS. ESPECIALLY WHEN PLAYING OFF A GUILTY CONSCIENCE.
CONSCIENCE. THERE'S A LAUGH.
SO WHAT NOW?
ARE YOU GOING TO LET HIM KILL ME?
IS THAT THE KIND OF FRIEND YOU ARE, QUILL?
DON'T YOU DARE TRY TO TAKE THE MORAL HIGH GROUND WITH ME, LUUK! YOU KILLED YOUR FATHER!
I DON'T CARE WHAT YOUR MOTIVATION WAS!
BUT I DON'T THINK HE SHOULD KILL YOU, NO.
YOU NEED TO BE TRIED BY YOUR PLANET'S JUDICIAL SYSTEM.
OUR WHAT?
BWWAHHHAHAHAHA!

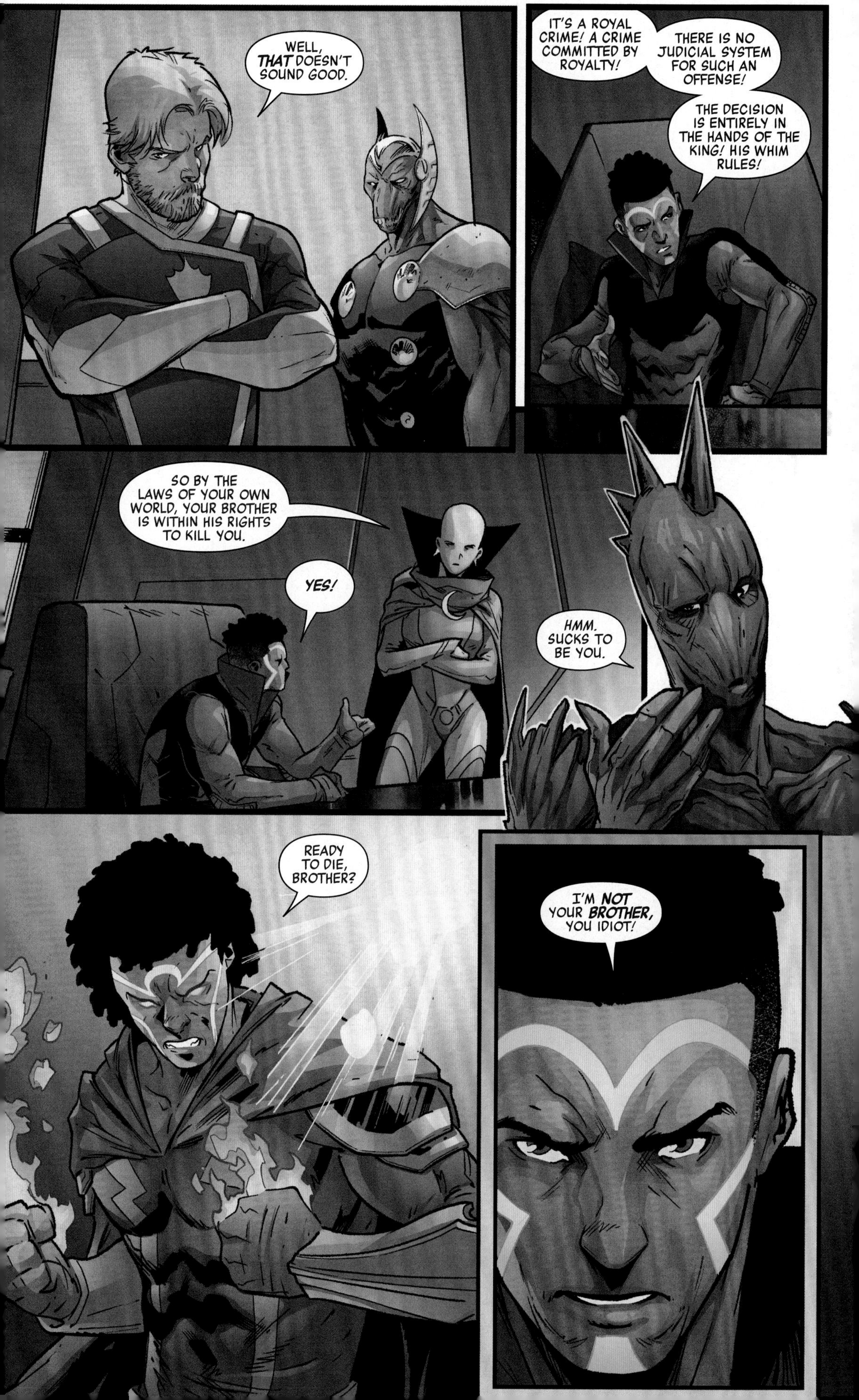
WELL, *THAT* DOESN'T SOUND GOOD.
IT'S A ROYAL CRIME! A CRIME COMMITTED BY ROYALTY!
THERE IS NO JUDICIAL SYSTEM FOR SUCH AN OFFENSE!
THE DECISION IS ENTIRELY IN THE HANDS OF THE KING! HIS WHIM RULES!
SO BY THE LAWS OF YOUR OWN WORLD, YOUR BROTHER IS WITHIN HIS RIGHTS TO KILL YOU.
*YES!*
HMM. SUCKS TO BE YOU.
READY TO DIE, BROTHER?
I'M *NOT* YOUR *BROTHER*, YOU IDIOT!

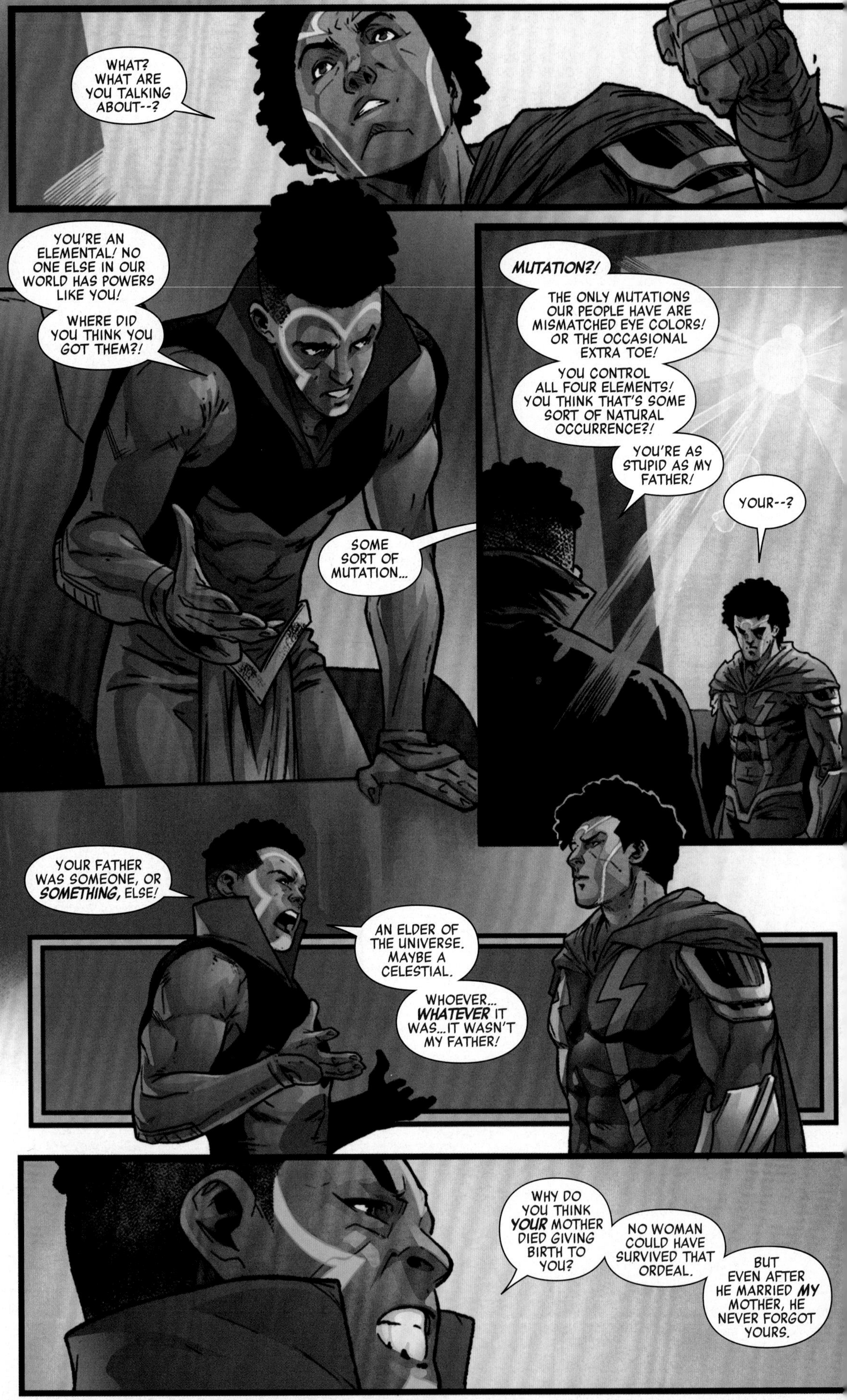
WHAT? WHAT ARE YOU TALKING ABOUT--?
YOU'RE AN ELEMENTAL! NO ONE ELSE IN OUR WORLD HAS POWERS LIKE YOU!
WHERE DID YOU THINK YOU GOT THEM?!
SOME SORT OF MUTATION...
MUTATION?!
THE ONLY MUTATIONS OUR PEOPLE HAVE ARE MISMATCHED EYE COLORS! OR THE OCCASIONAL EXTRA TOE!
YOU CONTROL ALL FOUR ELEMENTS! YOU THINK THAT'S SOME SORT OF NATURAL OCCURRENCE?!
YOU'RE AS STUPID AS MY FATHER!
YOUR--?
YOUR FATHER WAS SOMEONE, OR SOMETHING, ELSE!
AN ELDER OF THE UNIVERSE. MAYBE A CELESTIAL.
WHOEVER... WHATEVER IT WAS...IT WASN'T MY FATHER!
WHY DO YOU THINK YOUR MOTHER DIED GIVING BIRTH TO YOU?
NO WOMAN COULD HAVE SURVIVED THAT ORDEAL.
BUT EVEN AFTER HE MARRIED MY MOTHER, HE NEVER FORGOT YOURS.

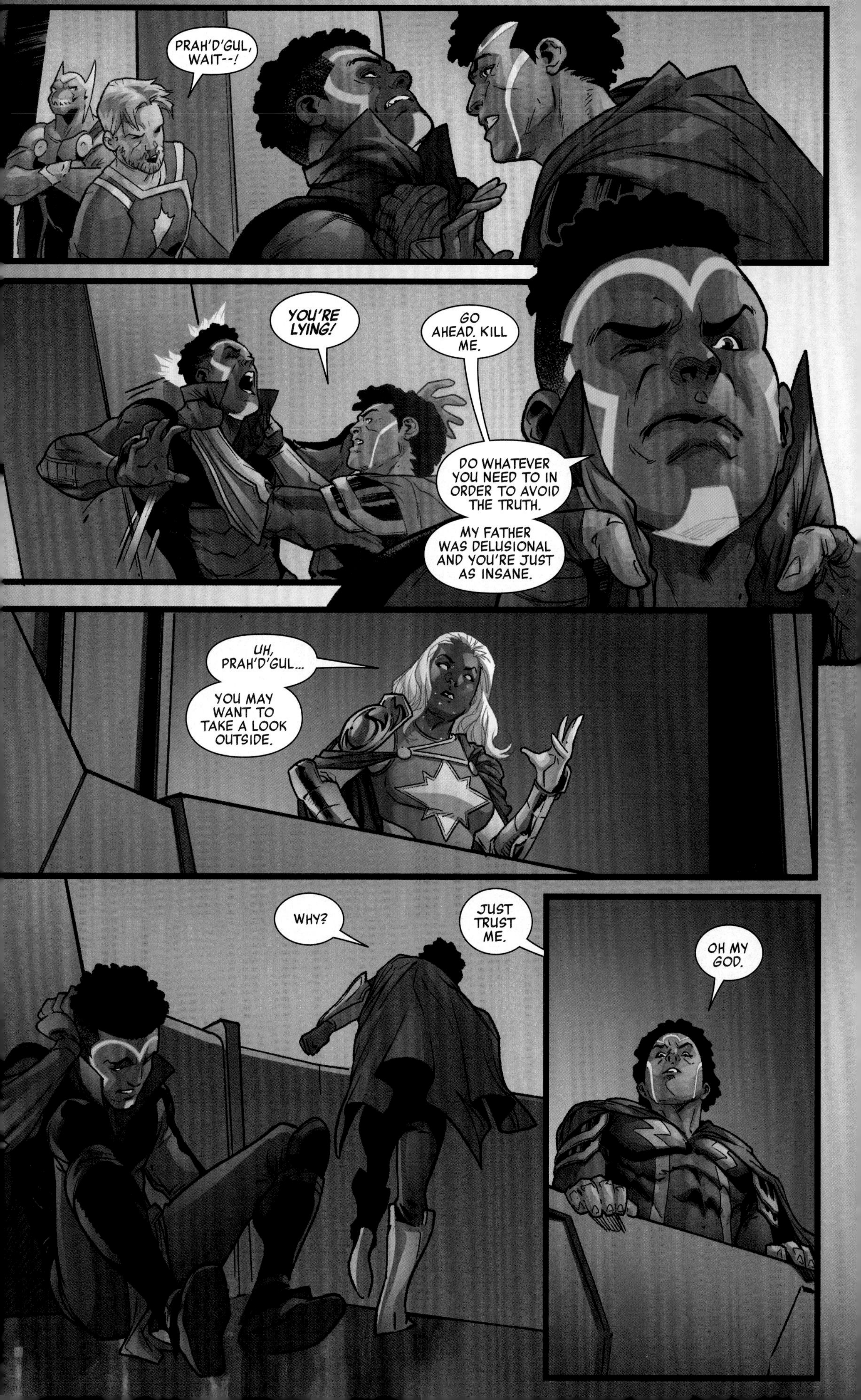
PRAH'D'GUL, WAIT--!
YOU'RE LYING!
GO AHEAD. KILL ME.
DO WHATEVER YOU NEED TO IN ORDER TO AVOID THE TRUTH.
MY FATHER WAS DELUSIONAL AND YOU'RE JUST AS INSANE.
UH, PRAH'D'GUL...
YOU MAY WANT TO TAKE A LOOK OUTSIDE.
WHY?
JUST TRUST ME.
OH MY GOD.

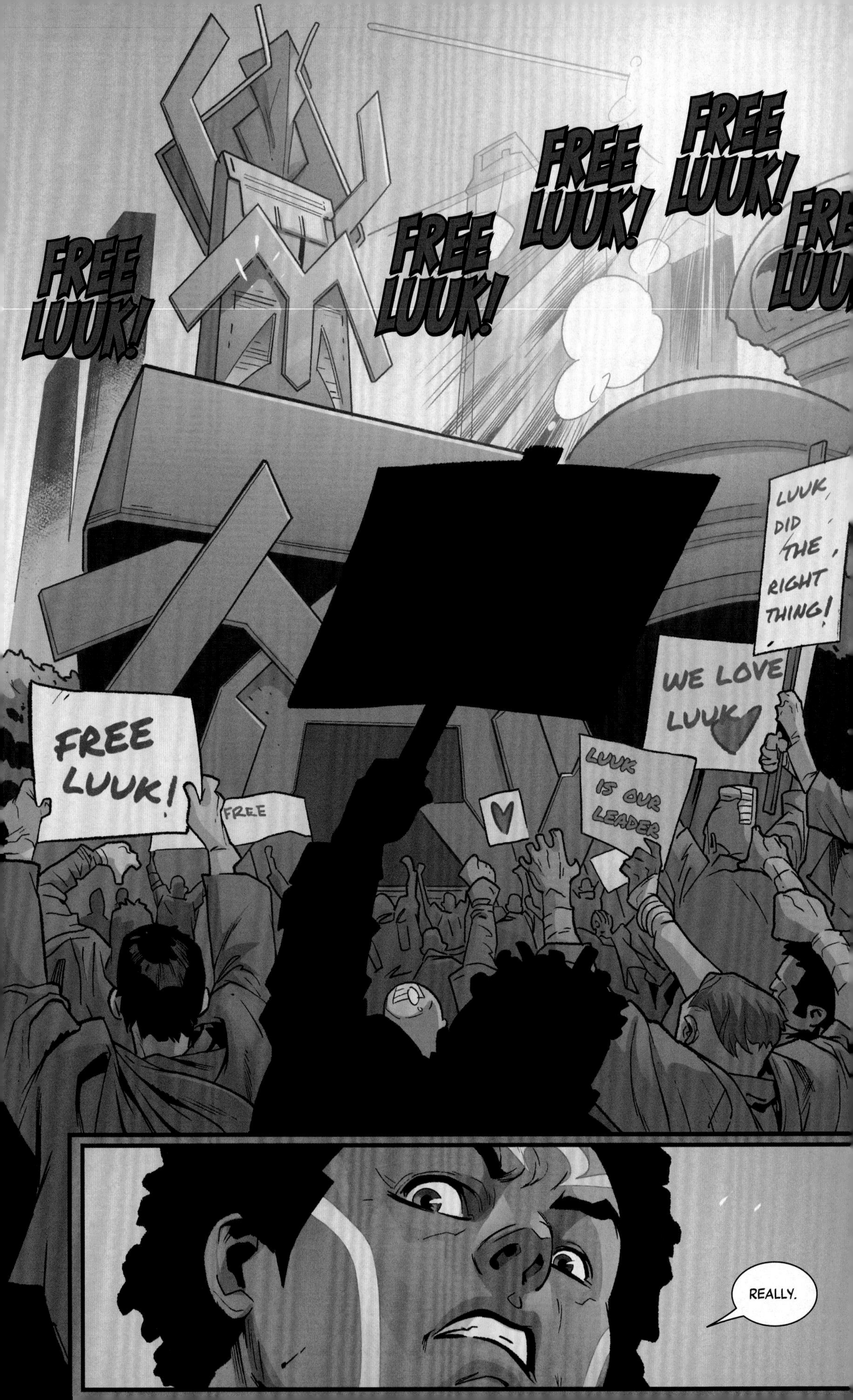

FREE LUUK!
FREE LUUK!
FREE LUUK!
FREE LUUK!
FREE LUUK!
FREE
LUUK DID THE RIGHT THING!
WE LOVE LUUK
LUUK IS OUR LEADER
REALLY.

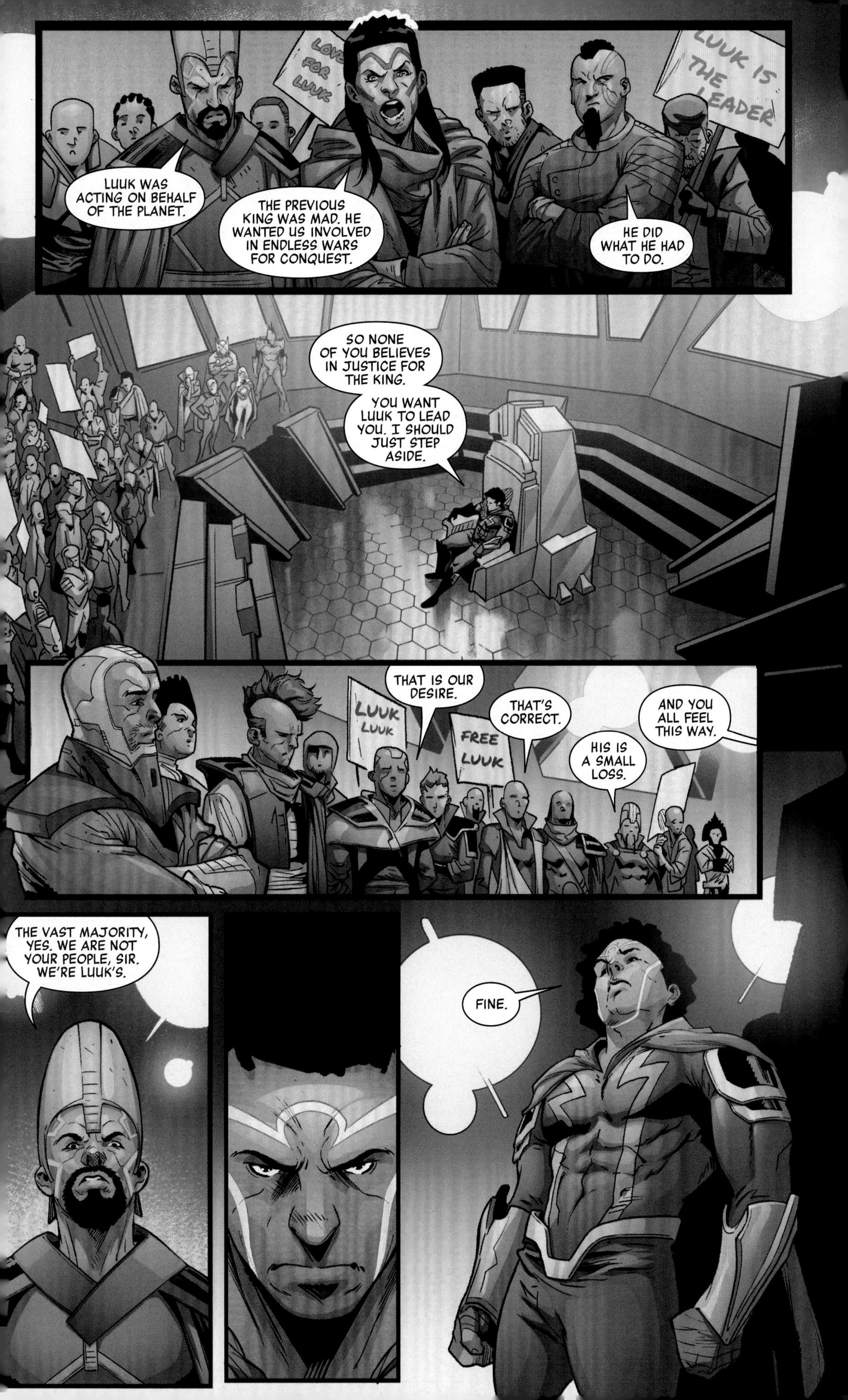
LOVE FOR LUUK
LUUK IS THE LEADER
LUUK WAS ACTING ON BEHALF OF THE PLANET.
THE PREVIOUS KING WAS MAD. HE WANTED US INVOLVED IN ENDLESS WARS FOR CONQUEST.
HE DID WHAT HE HAD TO DO.
SO NONE OF YOU BELIEVES IN JUSTICE FOR THE KING.
YOU WANT LUUK TO LEAD YOU. I SHOULD JUST STEP ASIDE.
LUUK LUUK
FREE LUUK
THAT IS OUR DESIRE.
THAT'S CORRECT.
HIS IS A SMALL LOSS.
AND YOU ALL FEEL THIS WAY.
THE VAST MAJORITY, YES. WE ARE NOT YOUR PEOPLE, SIR. WE'RE LUUK'S.
FINE.

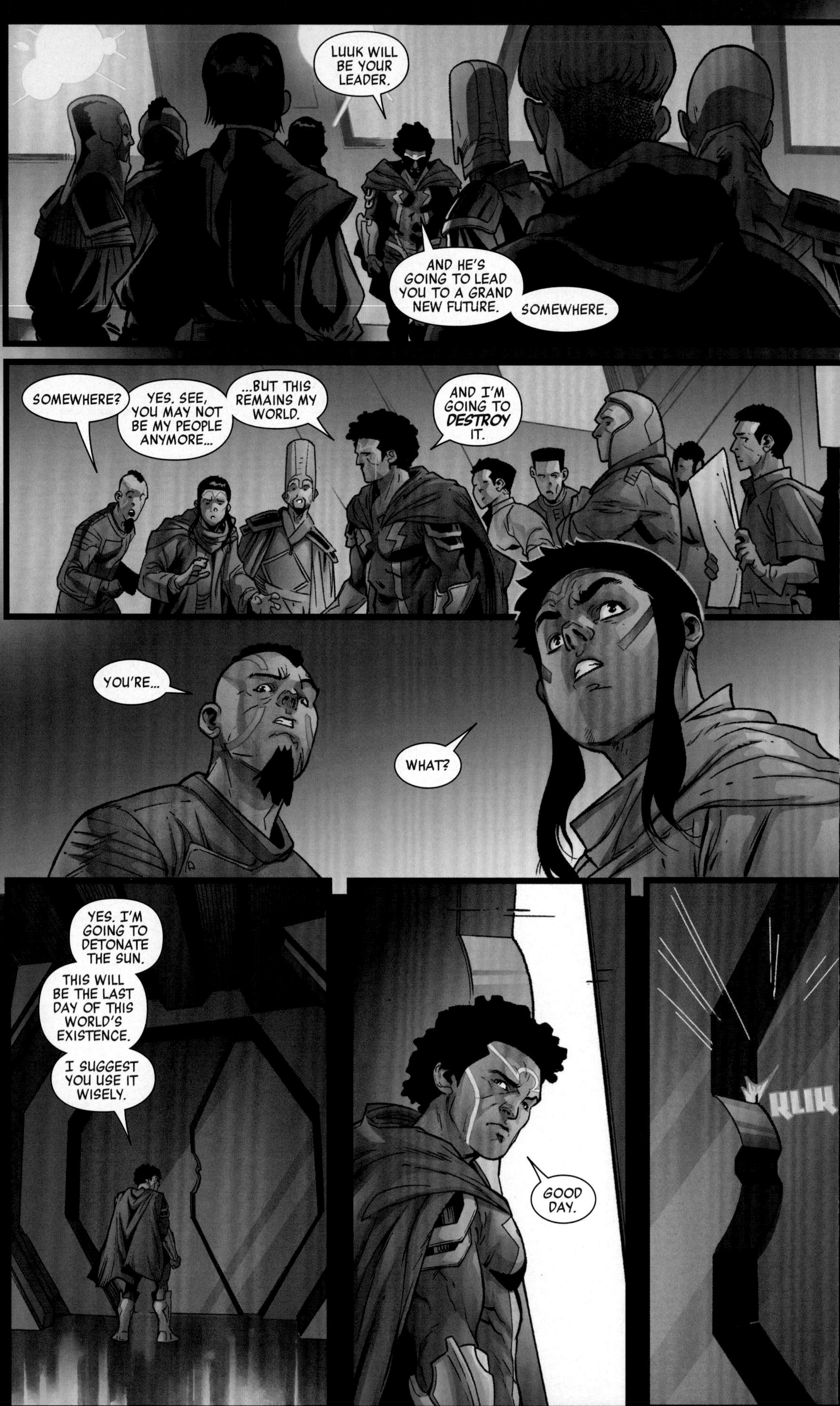
LUUK WILL BE YOUR LEADER.
AND HE'S GOING TO LEAD YOU TO A GRAND NEW FUTURE.
SOMEWHERE.
SOMEWHERE?
YES. SEE, YOU MAY NOT BE MY PEOPLE ANYMORE...
...BUT THIS REMAINS MY WORLD.
AND I'M GOING TO DESTROY IT.
YOU'RE...
WHAT?
YES. I'M GOING TO DETONATE THE SUN.
THIS WILL BE THE LAST DAY OF THIS WORLD'S EXISTENCE.
I SUGGEST YOU USE IT WISELY.
GOOD DAY.
KLIK

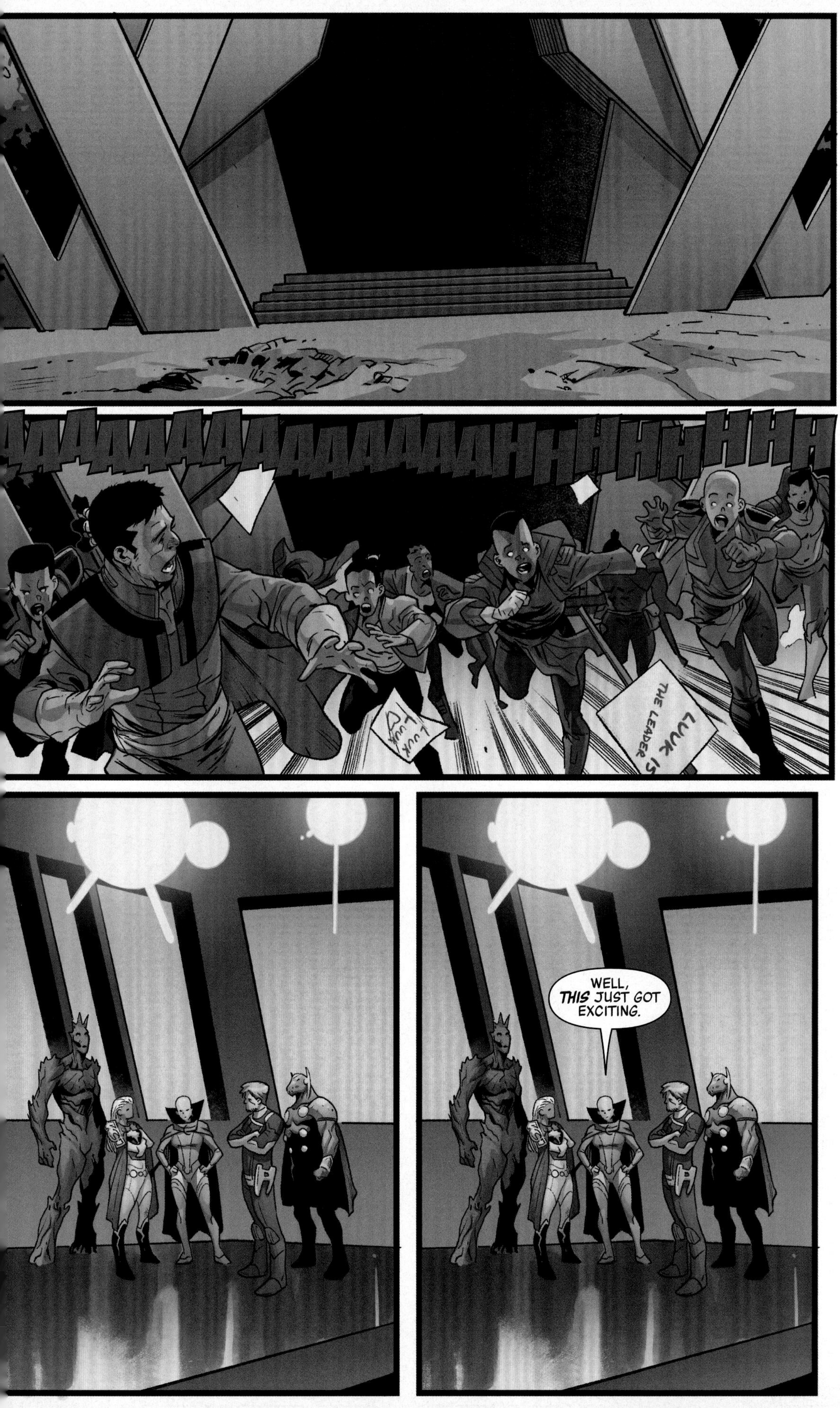
AAAAAAAAAAAAAAAAAHHHHHHH
LUUK
LUUK IS THE LEADER
WELL, *THIS* JUST GOT EXCITING.

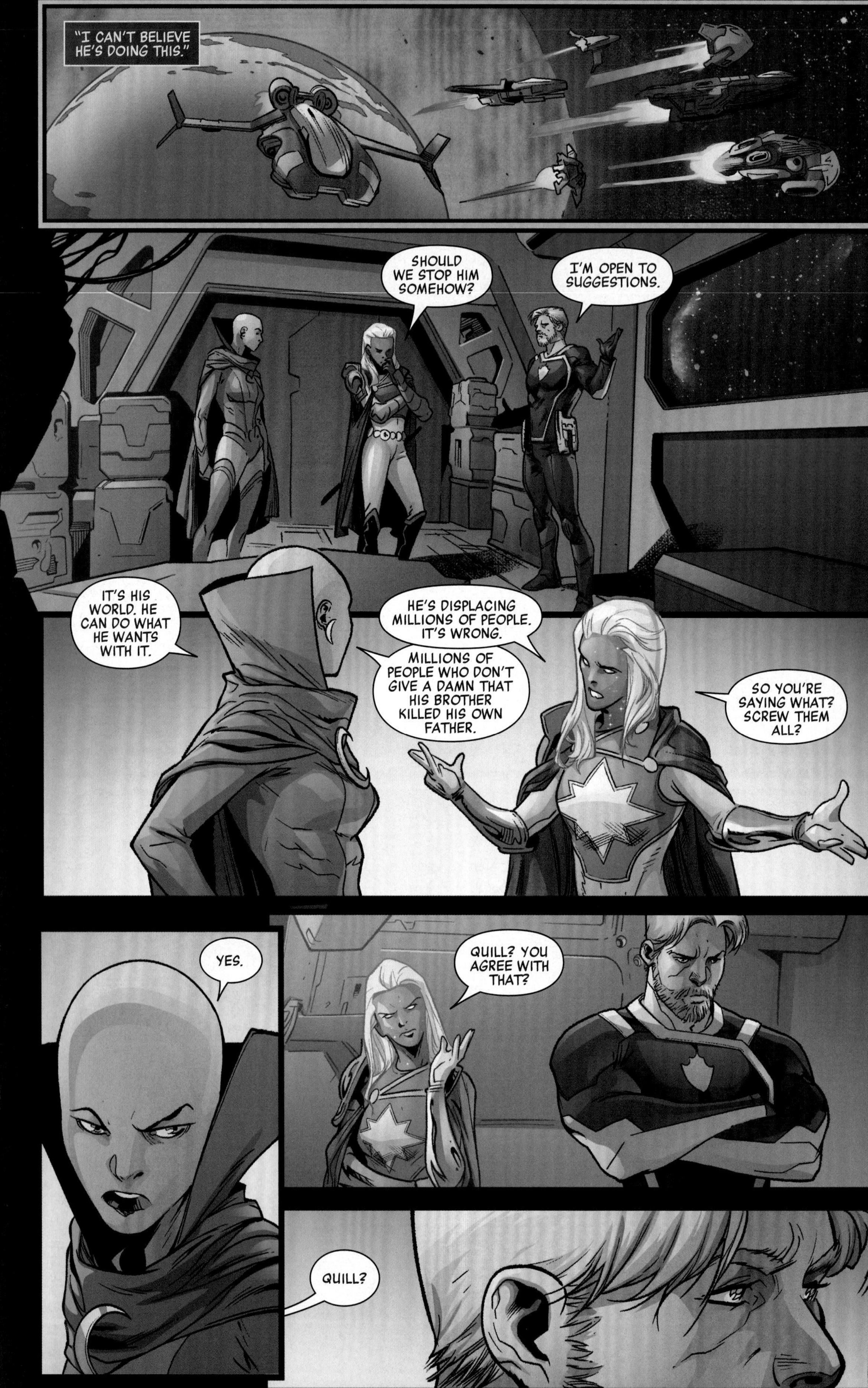
"I CAN'T BELIEVE HE'S DOING THIS."
SHOULD WE STOP HIM SOMEHOW?
I'M OPEN TO SUGGESTIONS.
IT'S HIS WORLD. HE CAN DO WHAT HE WANTS WITH IT.
HE'S DISPLACING MILLIONS OF PEOPLE. IT'S WRONG.
MILLIONS OF PEOPLE WHO DON'T GIVE A DAMN THAT HIS BROTHER KILLED HIS OWN FATHER.
SO YOU'RE SAYING WHAT? SCREW THEM ALL?
YES.
QUILL? YOU AGREE WITH THAT?
QUILL?

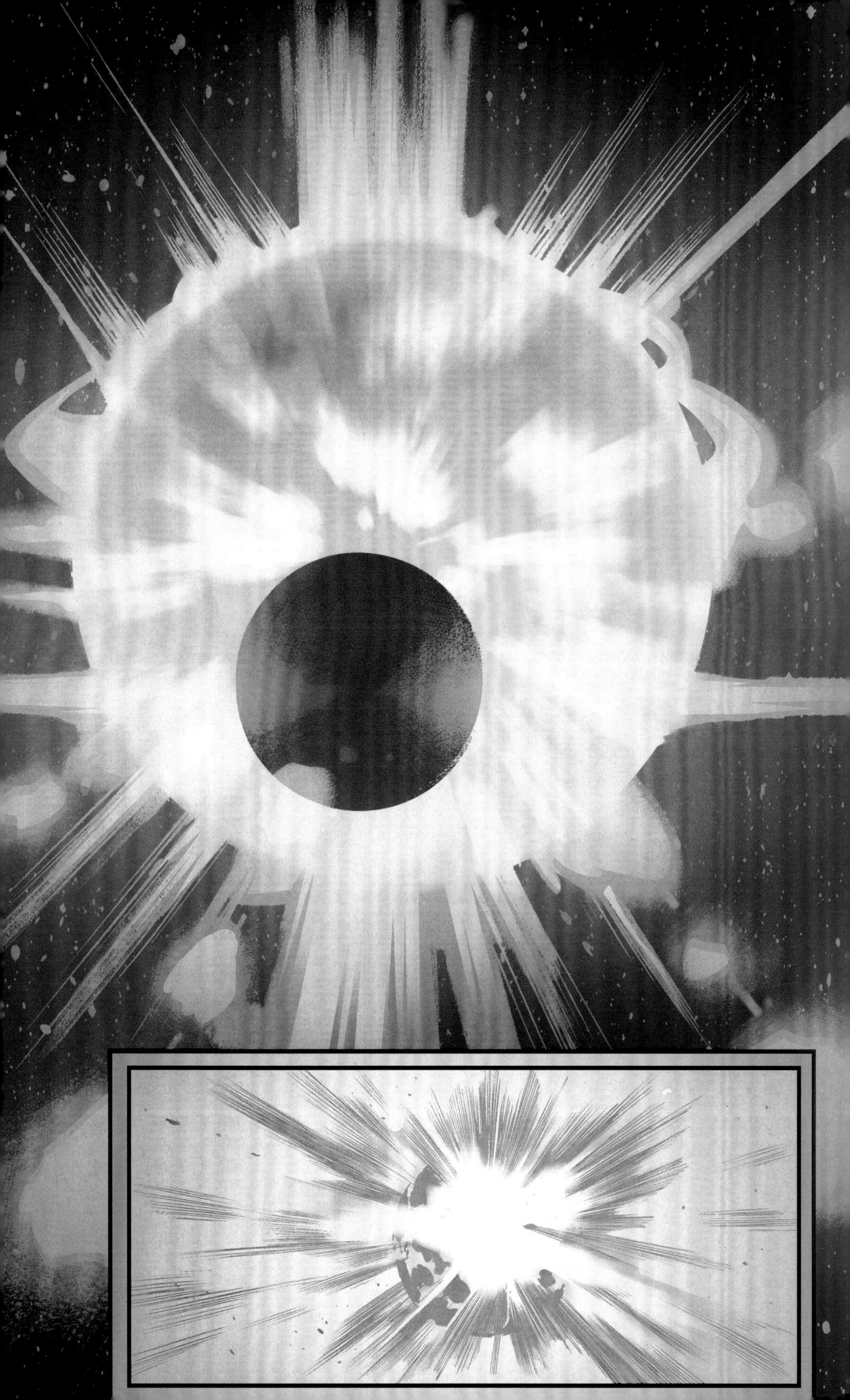

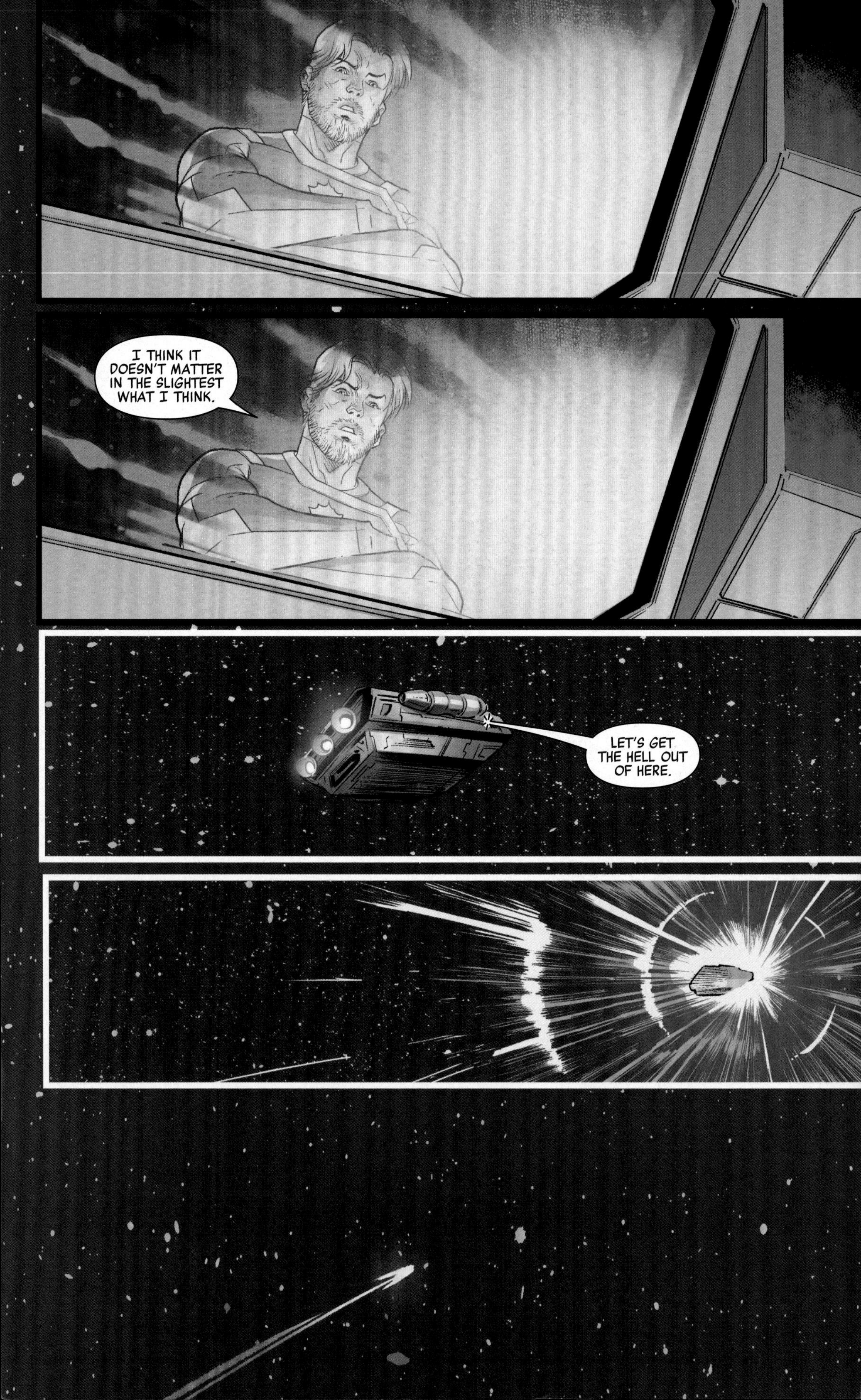
I THINK IT DOESN'T MATTER IN THE SLIGHTEST WHAT I THINK.
LET'S GET THE HELL OUT OF HERE.

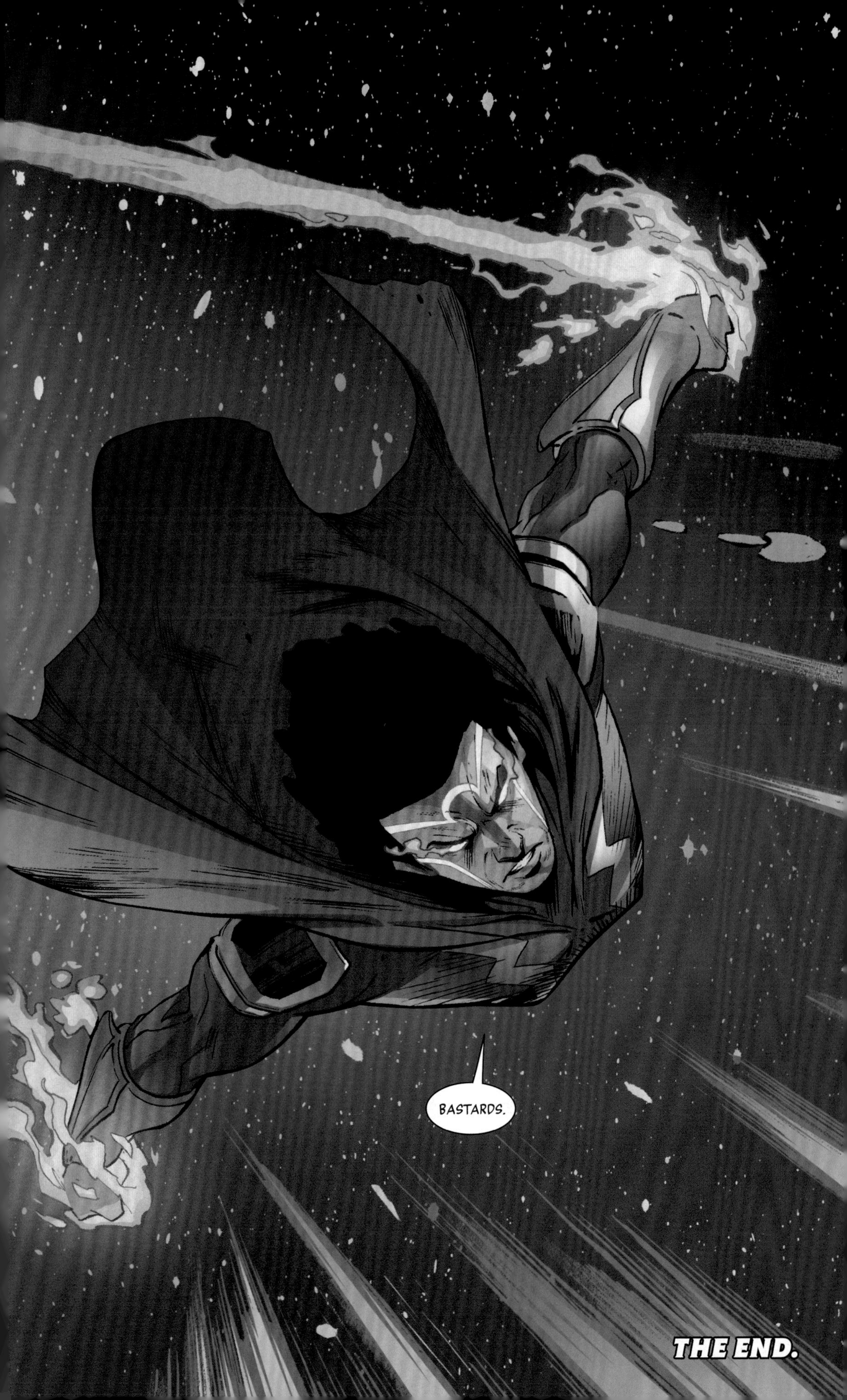
BASTARDS.
THE END.

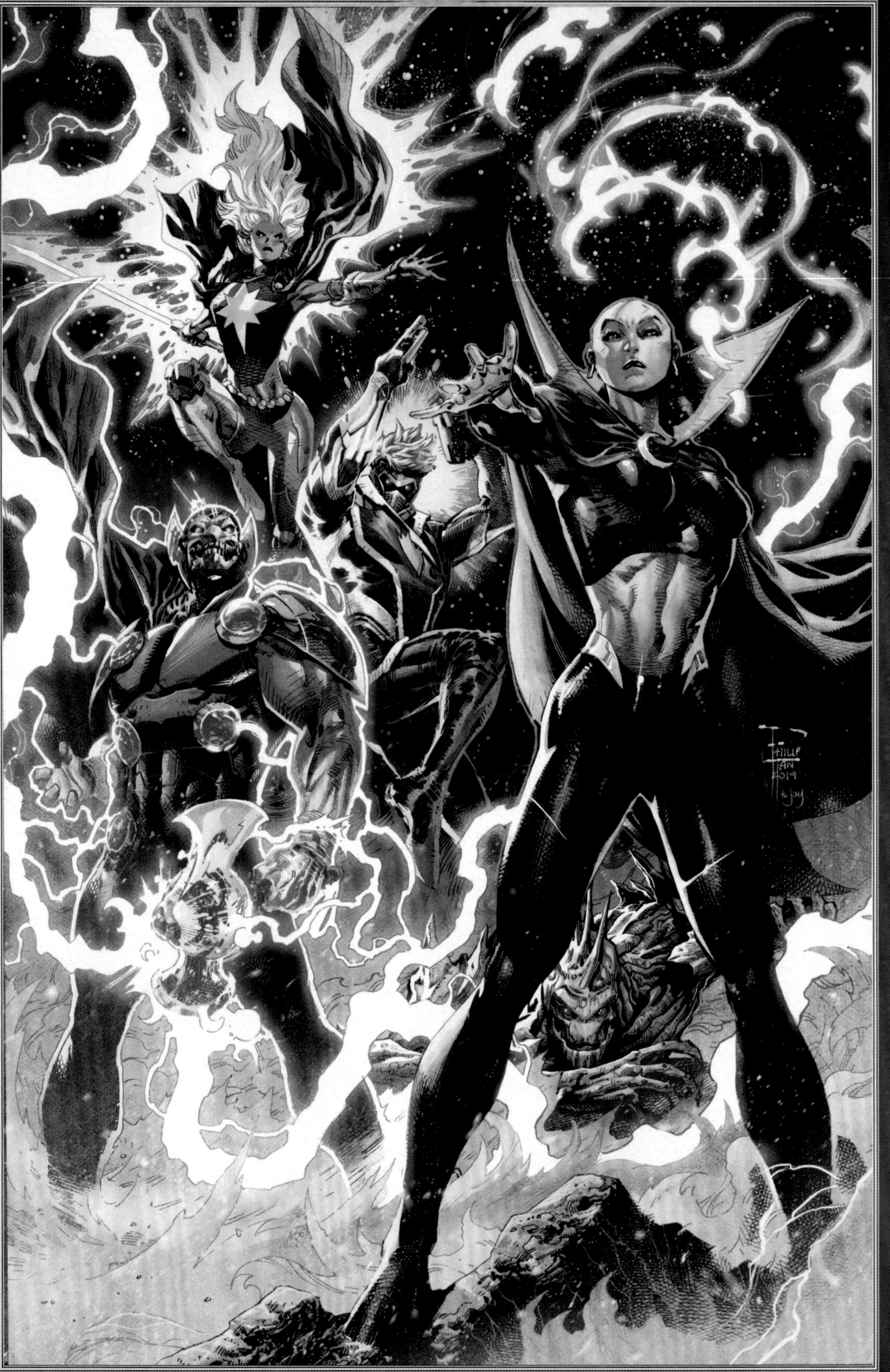

**GUARDIANS OF THE GALAXY: THE PRODIGAL SUN #1 VARIANT BY**
PHILIP TAN & JAY DAVID RAMOS

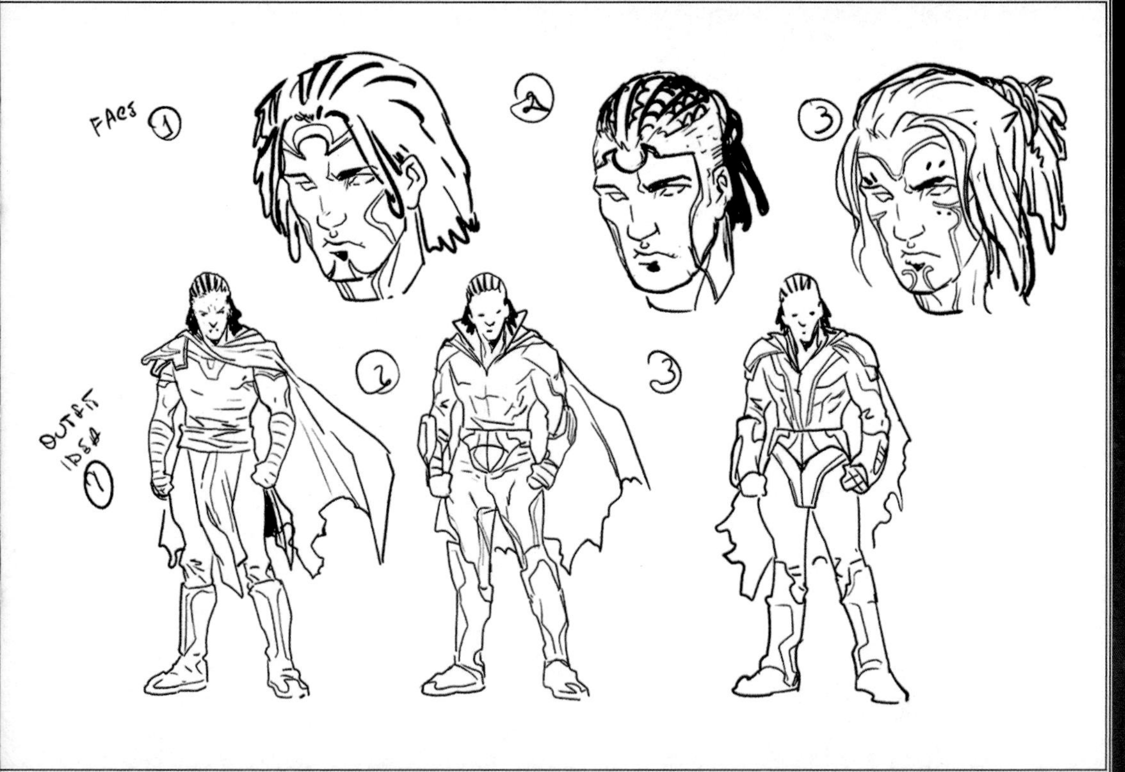
FACE 1
2
3
OUTFIT IDEA 1
2
3

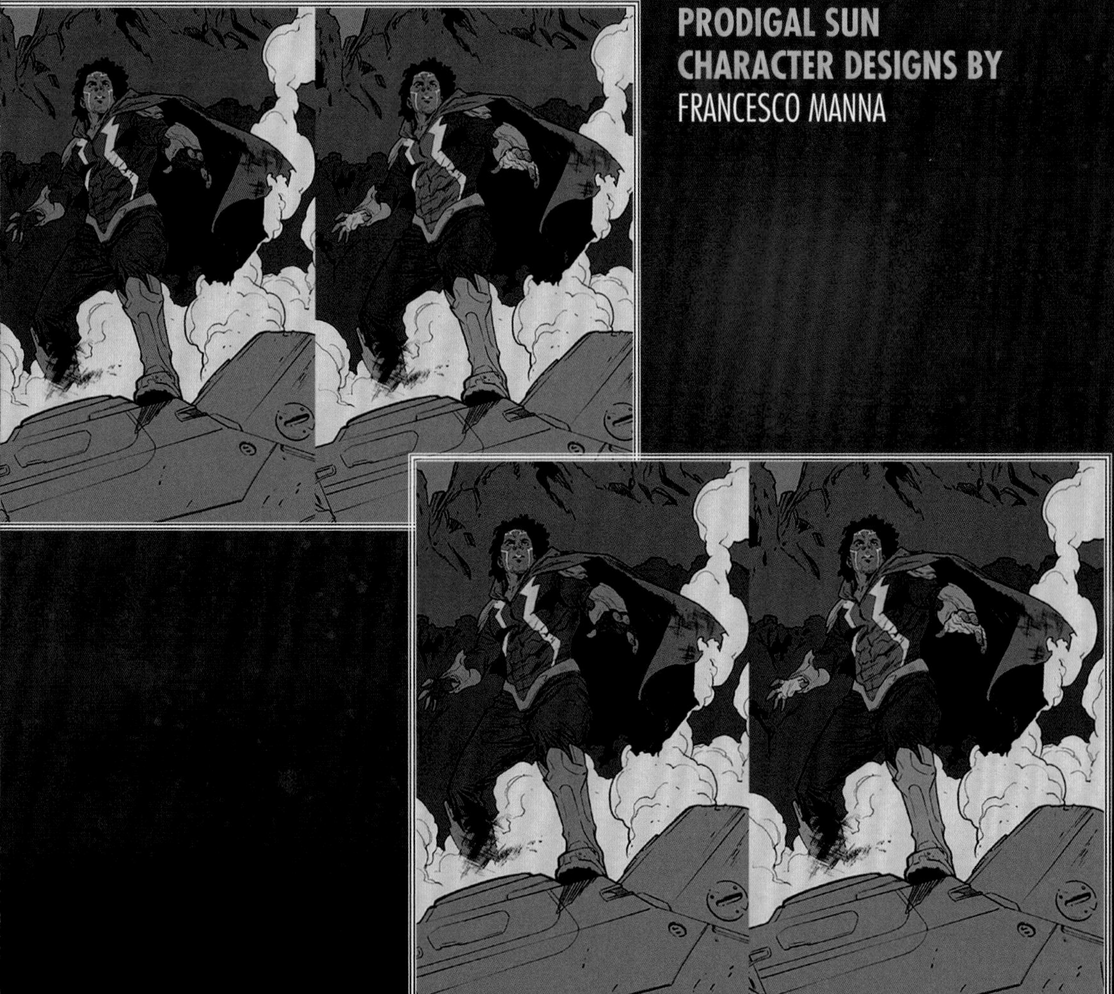

**PRODIGAL SUN**
**CHARACTER DESIGNS BY**
FRANCESCO MANNA

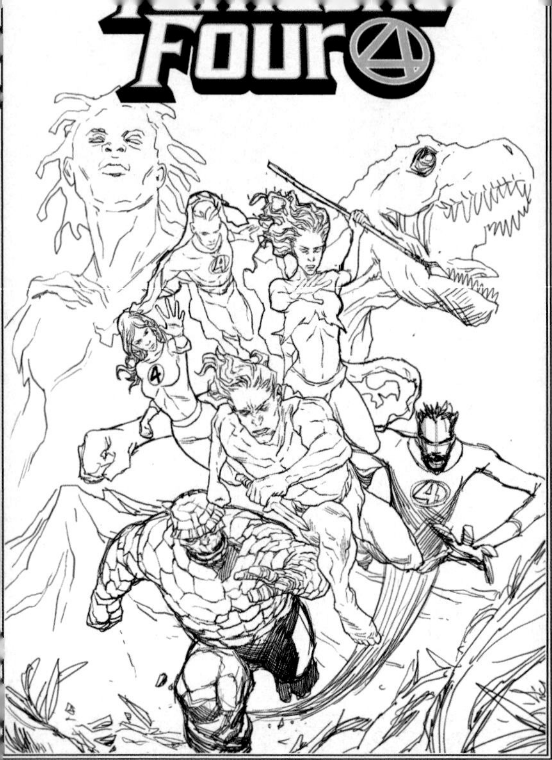
Four
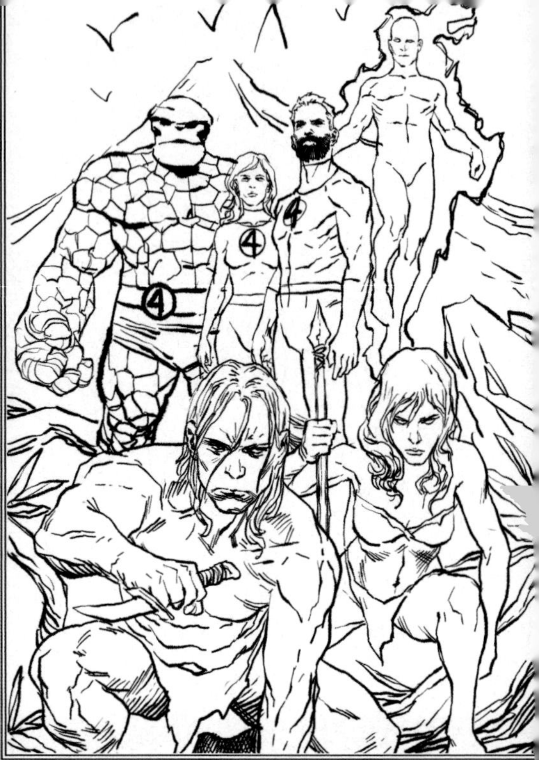
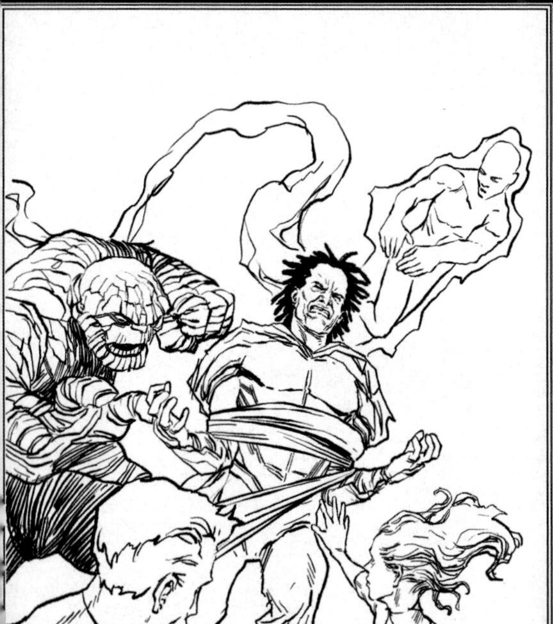
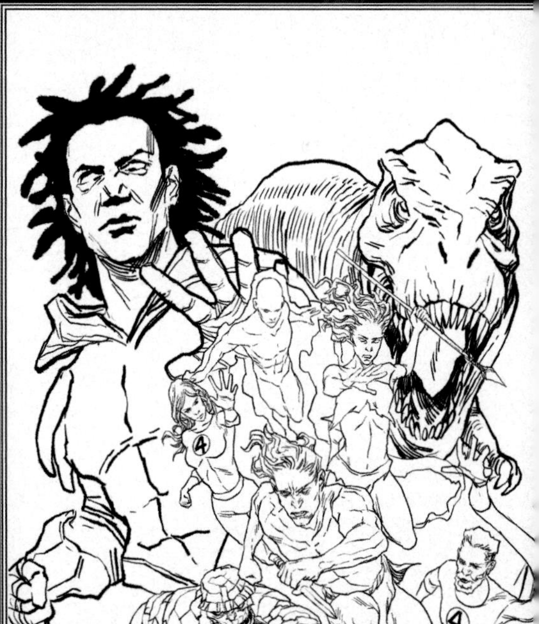

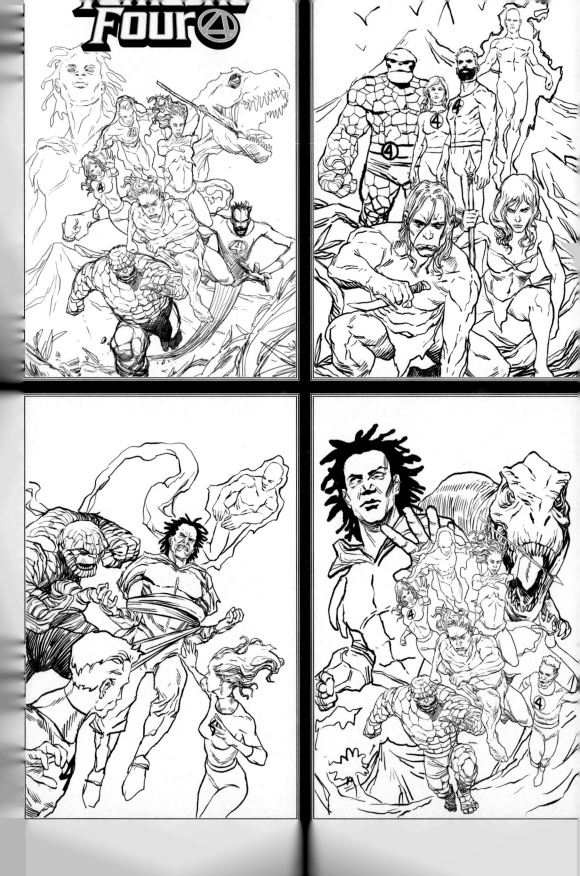

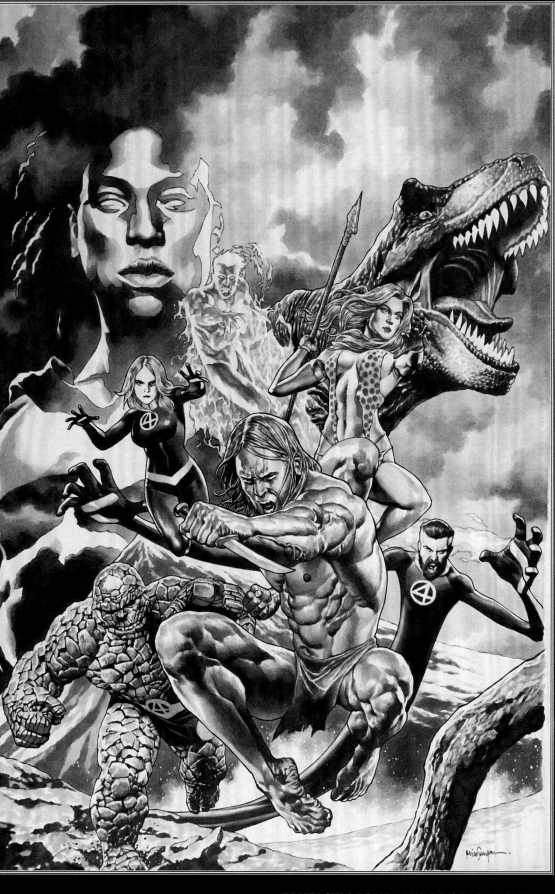

**FANTASTIC FOUR: THE PRODIGAL SUN #1**
COVER SKETCHES AND ART BY MICO SUAYAN

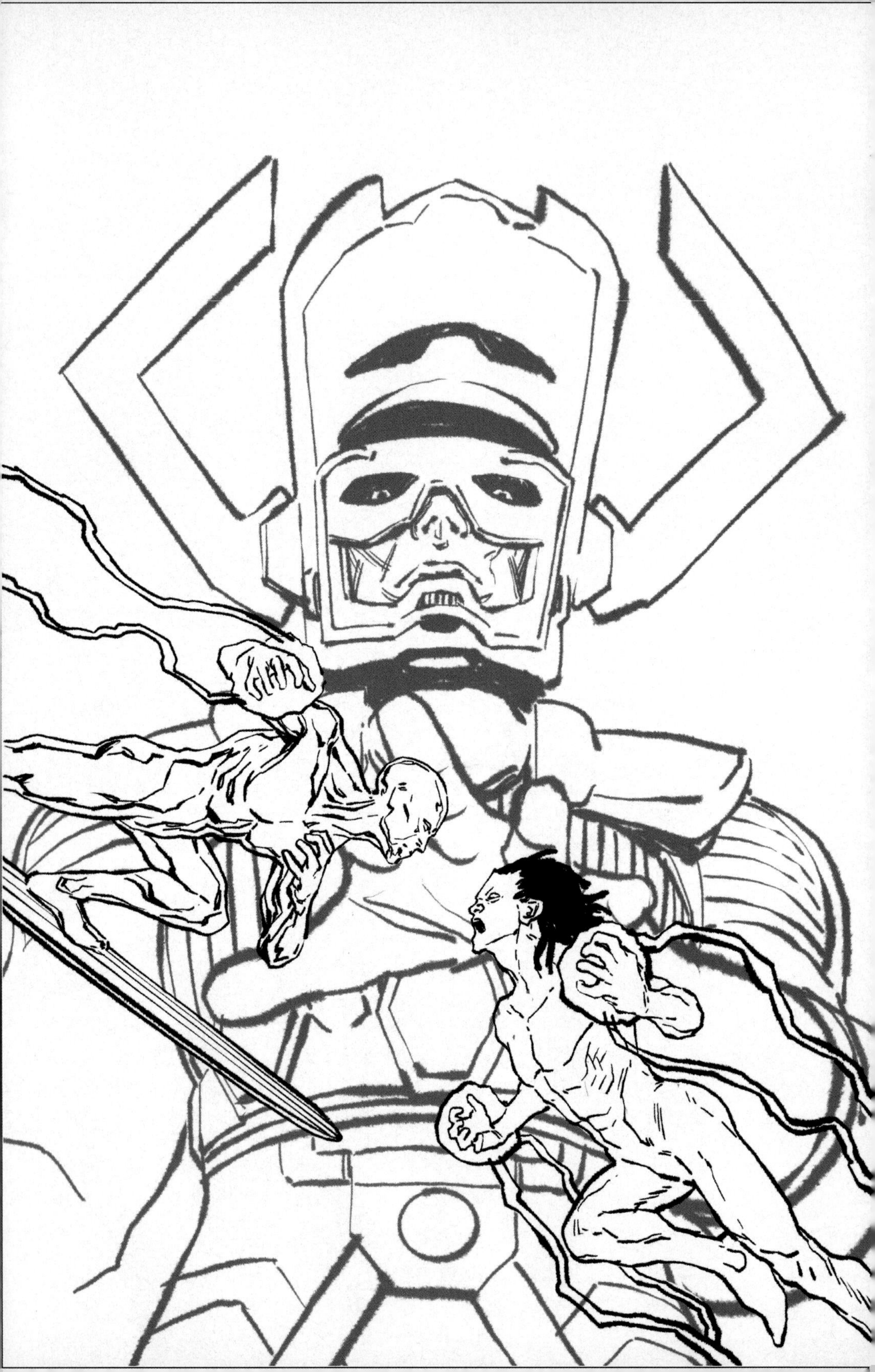

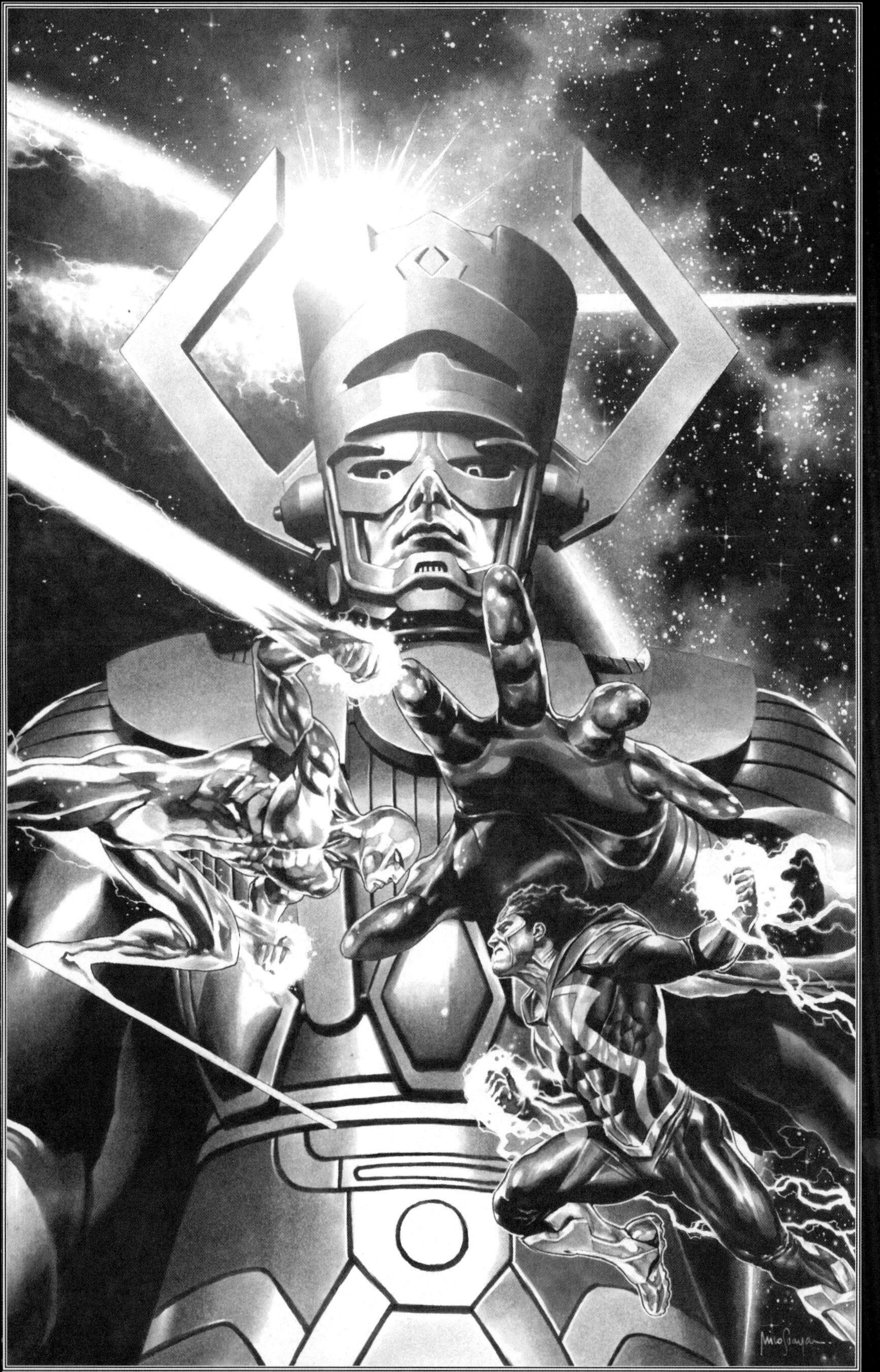

**SILVER SURFER: THE PRODIGAL SUN #1**
COVER SKETCHES AND ART BY MICO SUAYAN

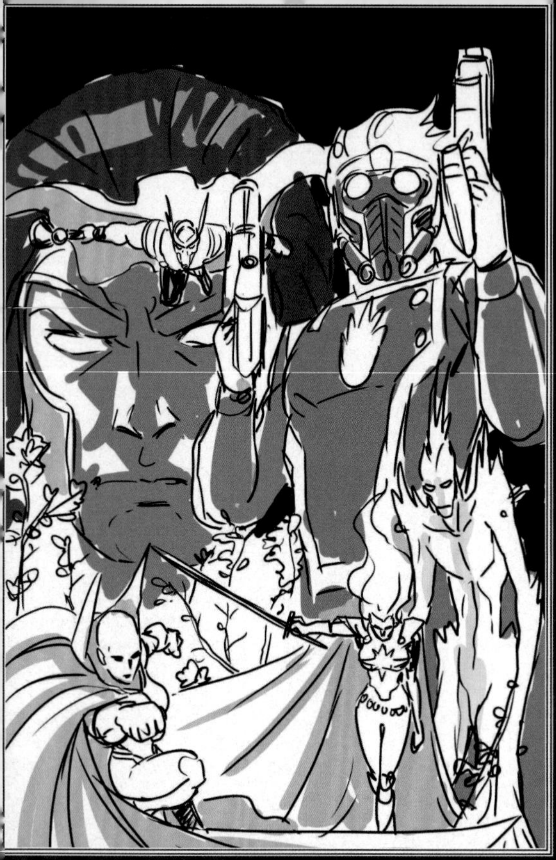
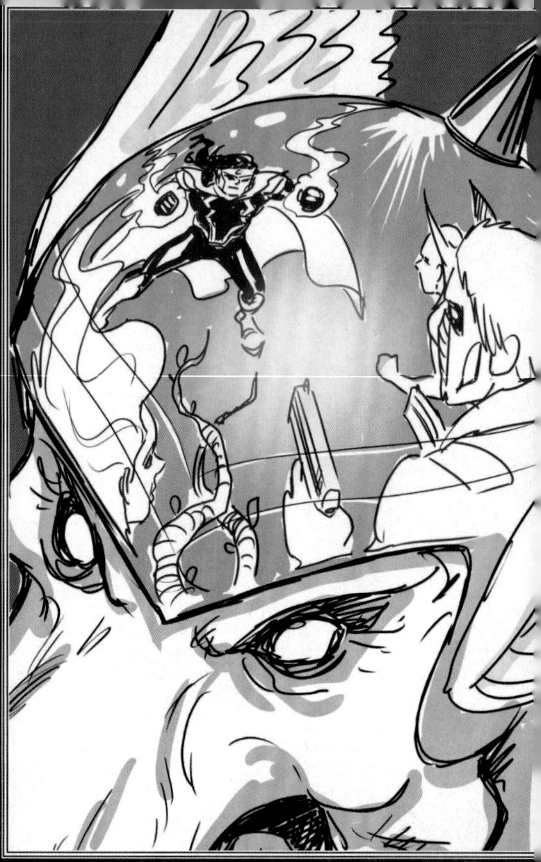
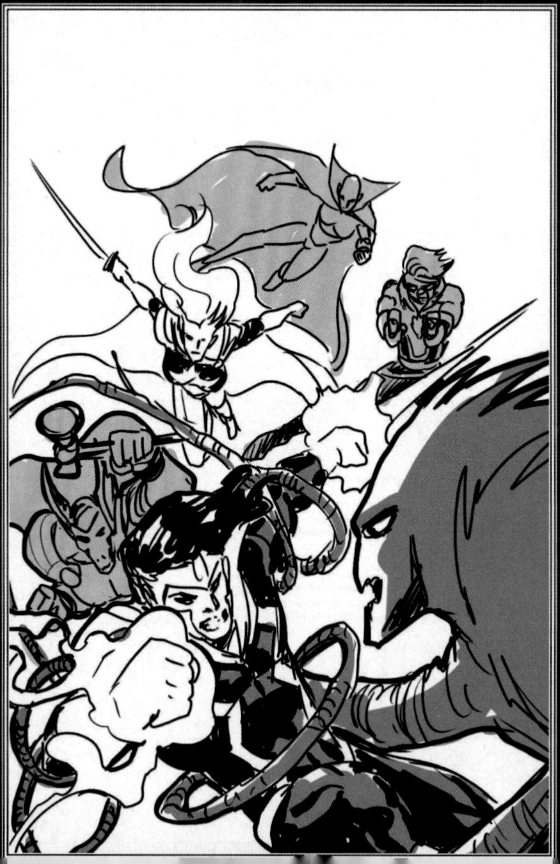

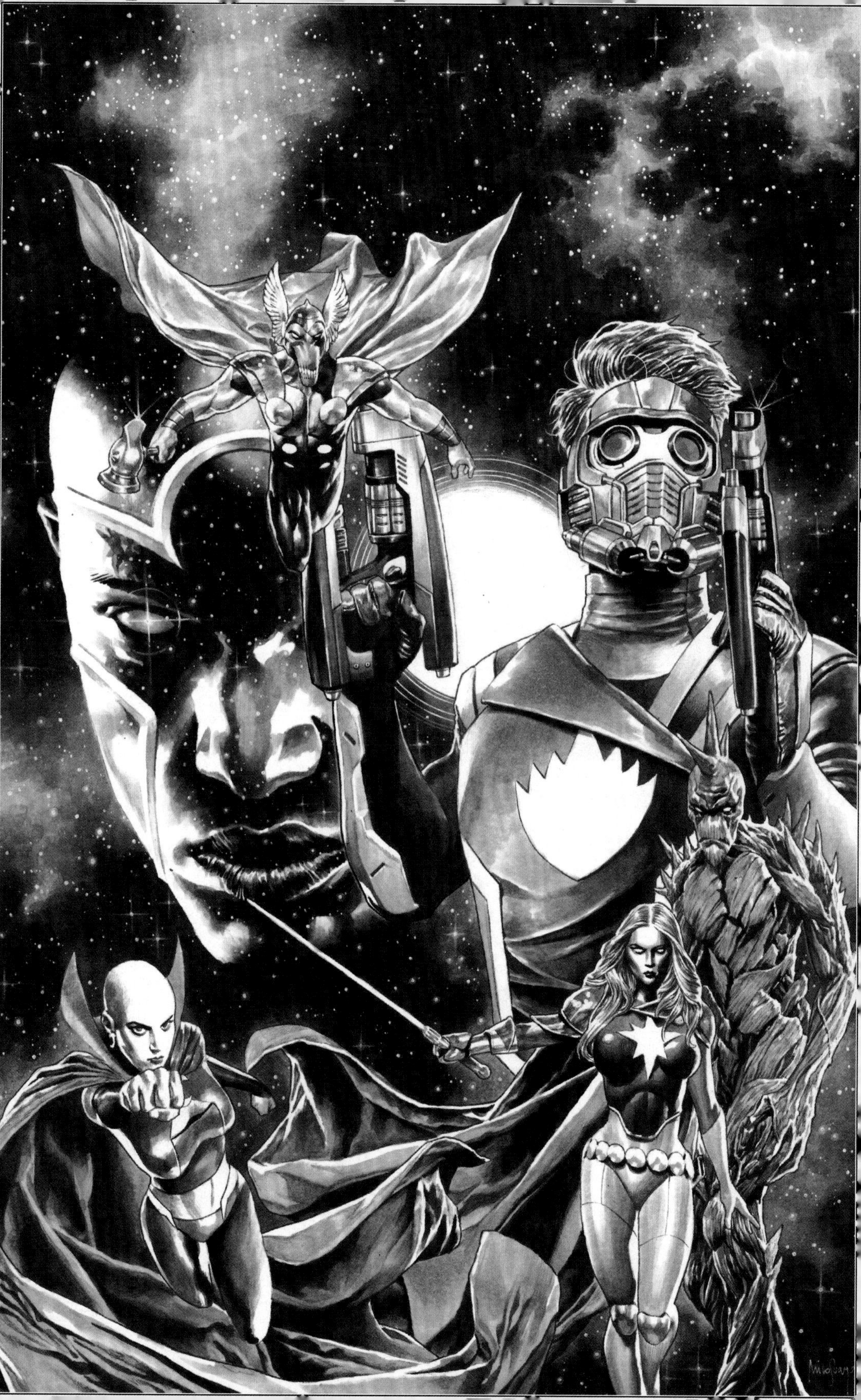

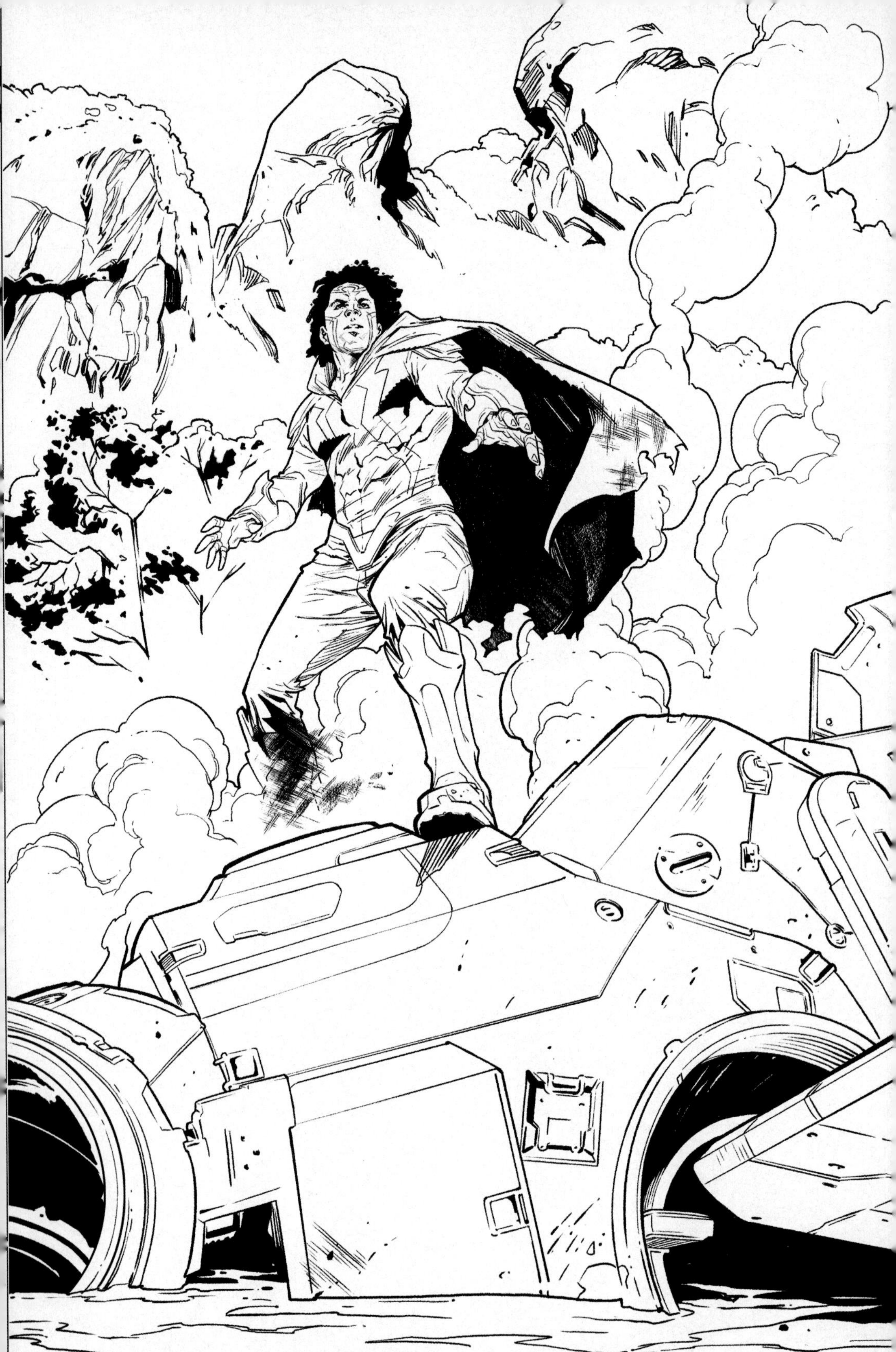

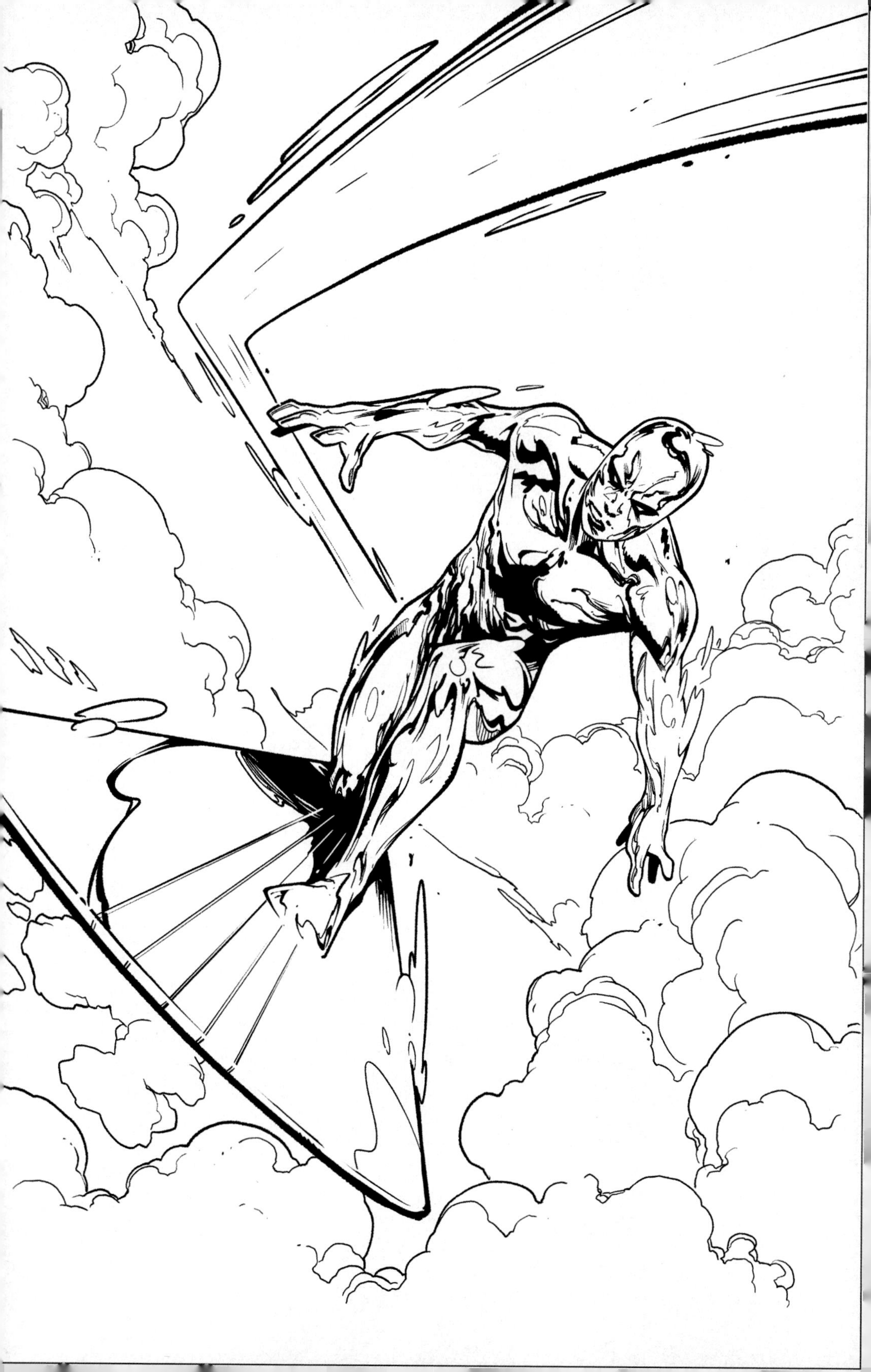

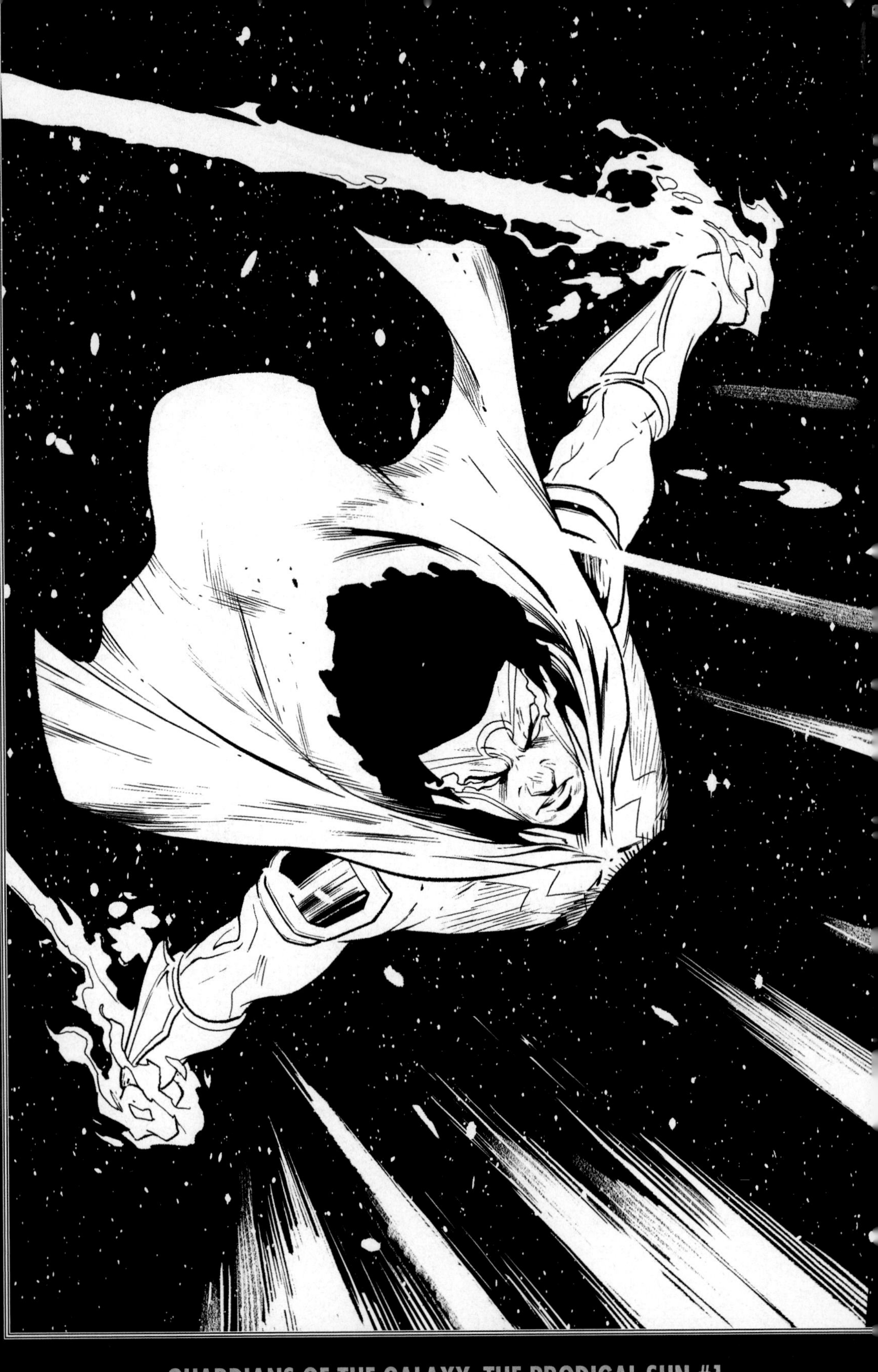

**GUARDIANS OF THE GALAXY: THE PRODIGAL SUN #1**
PAGE 30 ART BY FRANCESCO MANNA